One Half of
Robertson Davies

Books by Robertson Davies

FICTION

The Diary of Samuel Marchbanks
The Table Talk of Samuel Marchbanks
Samuel Marchbanks' Almanack
Tempest-Tost
Leaven of Malice
A Mixture of Frailties
Fifth Business
The Manticore
World of Wonders

PLAYS

Eros at Breakfast, and Other Plays
Fortune My Foe
At My Heart's Core
Hunting Stuart, and Other Plays
A Masque of Aesop
A Jig for the Gypsy
A Masque of Mr. Punch
Question Time

CRITICISM

Shakespeare's Boy Actors
A Voice from the Attic
Feast of Stephen: A Study of Stephen Leacock

(in collaboration with Sir Tyrone Guthrie)
Renown at Stratford
Twice Have the Trumpets Sounded
Thrice the Brinded Cat Hath Mew'd

One Half of Robertson Davies

by
Robertson Davies

THE VIKING PRESS   NEW YORK

Published in 1978 by The Viking Press
625 Madison Avenue, New York, N.Y. 10022

LIBRARY OF CONGRESS CATALOGING IN PUBLICATION DATA
Davies, William Robertson, 1913–
    One half of Robertson Davies.
    I. Title.
PR9199.3.D305   814'.5'4   78–2395
ISBN 0–670–52608–8

Printed in the United States of America
Set in Baskerville

Acknowledgment is made to Chatto and Windus Ltd.,
for permission to quote "Coureurs de Bois" from
The Wounded Prince by Douglas LePan.

Contents

One Half of
Robertson Davies

Preface

'THE TONGUE IS *one half of a man: but the other half is the heart.'* I *have always liked that proverb, because it does honour to the faculty of speech, and it is speech as much as anything that divides man from the lesser creation. Without it, we should have no abstract thought, probably little memory, and therefore nothing much in the way of foresight. Speech can be developed into a form of art, and thus puts some artistry within the grasp of every man. And, as the proverb makes clear, speech is a means of revealing what is in the heart. In offering this book to the public as one half of myself, I certainly mean to imply that the other half, of necessity, goes with it.*

All my life, it seems to me, I have been making speeches, or telling stories in public, and it has always been my desire to bring tongue and heart into an equal partnership. I cannot pretend that I have always succeeded, but I have done my best. Where I have failed, I hope that the heart was the senior partner, for I know what abysses of folly await those speakers who rely on the tongue for more than it can give.

This book is composed of pieces that were written to be spoken, and in all of them the qualities of speech are apparent. What is meant to be heard is necessarily more direct in expression, and perhaps more boldly coloured, than what is meant for the reader. The speaker must seize the attention of his audience, and take care not to tax it extremely, or be too sure of his welcome. So, when you read this book, will you

1

please try to hear *it, and to think of it as something* said *to you. A couple of centuries ago no such request would be necessary, for then everybody heard what they read, and at an even earlier time in history they spoke it aloud. We all know the story of the Renaissance cardinal who was compelled to suspend his studies because he had lost his voice. Nowadays we all have to read so much that we read very quickly, and teachers of reading condemn what they call 'verbalization', as if those who practised it were the kind of people who followed each line with a forefinger, and wetted a thumb when they turned the page. But there are great rewards for the verbalizers; they hear everything they read spoken plainly and expressively in the halls of the mind—those halls that can so readily become noble forums, splendid theatres, cathedrals or chapels, palaces or woodcutter's cottages. And they know that the ear—even when it is the mind's ear—is a surer judge of prose than the scampering, skipping eye.*

Because these pieces are, in the main, speeches, I decided not to cut out those passages at the beginning of each in which I have, so to speak, made my bow to the audience, paid it a few compliments, and thanked the Chairman. These are necessary decorums of public speaking, and to leave them out would be to do precisely what I am determined not to do—that is, to pretend that I am offering you something to read, rather than something to hear. And, to let you in on a speaker's secret, it is in such passages that he tries out his voice (because he is always fearful that it may have deserted him during the Chairman's introduction) and winds up his courage to a point which makes it possible for him to speak at all. Because, you see, the poor wretch is nervous.

Speakers' nerves affect them in various ways. Some tremble, some become frenzied. I lose all confidence, and suffer from a leaden oppression that makes me wonder why I ever agreed to speak at all; the Tomb and the Conqueror Worm seem preferable to delivering the stupid and piffling speech I have so carefully prepared. But there is no escape; speak I must, and I need a ritual paragraph in which to ease myself into the job.

The Chairman, of course, is as happy as a lark, and thinks the speaker must share his high spirits. Many public speakers have written peevishly about Chairmen; I tend to like them, and at the moment before they gesture me toward the reading-desk I envy them, because their task is done. But in nine cases out of ten the Chairman has, quite unwit-

tingly, dished me; he has said things that provoke such gloomy reflections that I can hardly force myself to answer his call.

He has, you see, approached me by what may be called the biographical path. He wants to tell the audience who I am, and he begins by telling them that I was born, and when, and where. As soon as he mentions the date of my birth I can see the audience doing a little sum in their heads, after which they look at me with renewed interest, to see how I am carrying the burden of my years. Most of them look at me with the unmistakable satisfaction of people who were born in bigger centres of population than I. I experience an unworthy wish that I had been born in Rome, or perhaps in Byzantium. This is low geographical snobbery. Does it matter where one was born? Yes, to an audience it does, and I see them looking for straw in my hair.

The Chairman next rehearses the details of my education, endured in a variety of hells. Because I am a professor, and a writer, and am about to make a speech, the Chairman suggests that my education partook of the character of a Roman triumph. But I know better. I was that most tedious of educational subjects, a Lop-sided Boy, capable of learning anything that interested me in record time, but cretinous in my failure to comprehend whatever I did not like. In the Puritan schools of my youth this was worse—much worse—than being thoroughly stupid. It was assumed that I could not master mathematics and science because I was shiftless. And so, as the Chairman tells of my educational obstacle race I see before me the angry faces of those who were so determined to teach what I simply could not learn, would not learn, and passionately loathed.

But the Chairman is determined to present me as a Child Marvel. 'At an unusually early age, he was appointed Literary Editor of Saturday Night,' *he carols. True, but at that time* Saturday Night *had a total staff of six, of whom one was the Editor's secretary. The Editor dealt with politics and the higher reaches of Art; two men dealt with Finance, which was a very big factor in that paper, itself a long-standing money-loser; there was a woman who did Women's Affairs; and then there was the Literary Editor, who did anything else that turned up, including books. The financial officers of the publishing company that produced the paper harried us unmercifully because* Saturday Night *did not attract enough advertising. I remember one time the advertising manager demanded, as we went to press, that I remove a six-inch book review because Pussyfoot Closet Tanks had come in late with a six-inch ad, and wanted the space. I hastened to comply, for priorities were well understood on that paper; Literary Editor I might be, but money was money, and Pussyfoot must be served.*

The Chairman is all kindness; as he romps through the public details of my life I am sadly aware of what lies behind them, but under the circumstances I cannot laugh or weep. I must keep my ears open for the moment when the Chairman looks indulgently in my direction and says, And now, ladies and gentlemen ...

Then I rise and trudge to the lectern and place myself behind it, knowing well what I look like. When I was a boy it was thought a great joke to hide in a dark room with a flashlight; when somebody— one's mother, for preference—came in, one put the flashlight inside one's mouth and turned it on. The effect was that of an eerily illuminated Floating Head. And that is what the speaker looks like; the light on the lectern shines up at him from below; the Floating Head opens its mouth. It utters.

The panic terror and the conviction of unworthiness and depression I have described are the speaker's own; the audience does not share them. They are, as a general thing, friendly and on the whole optimistic about what is to come. And that is as it should be, for the speaker must keep his personal miseries from them and give them equal measure of tongue and heart.

Is it all misery, then? No, no. I am reminded of the story (was there ever a speaker who was not reminded of a story?) about the great Sir Henry Irving, when he visited the American tragedian Richard Mansfield in his dressing-room after Mansfield had played Richard III. Mansfield complained bitterly about the strain on his nerves of public performance; sometimes, he said, he wondered if he could sustain his powers until the curtain fell. Irving, himself a great Richard, eyed his colleague sardonically and said: 'Well, Dick, m'boy, if you find it unwholesome, why do you do it?*' If I find public speaking distasteful, why have I done it so often over several decades?*

Because of the satisfactions of the tongue, when it is happily linked with heart, and for other reasons which are explained at greater length in the first piece in this book.

And now, ladies and gentlemen ...

ROBERTSON DAVIES
Massey College
University of Toronto
April 20, 1977

Ham and Tongue

THE FOLLOWING SPEECH *was given for The Cosmos Club of Washington, D.C., a distinguished group with a special interest in Literature, on April 6, 1977.*

WHEN I WAS ASKED to speak to you tonight I inquired, as speakers always do, what you wanted me to talk about. The first answer was the most daunting that can possibly be made to such a question: it was 'Feel at liberty to talk about anything you please.' Such an answer, so obviously intended as a courtesy, springing from a high-bred assumption that anything that came into my head would necessarily be welcome to such an audience as this, had the effect of driving every possible theme out of my mind. Or rather, to be more truthful, of driving out of my mind any theme upon which anyone could possibly wish to hear an after-dinner speech. Ponderous themes, depressing themes, themes so minatory as to partake of the character of prophecy suggested themselves to me, only to be dismissed with disgust and sinking spirits. But at last the idea came to me: 'Why not talk about making speeches? Why is it done, and how is it done?'

The more I thought about that subject, the more it

appealed to me. There are, I believe, something like three hundred millions of people on this continent at this moment. I have added a few additional millions, to include visitors from abroad who are here for the express purpose of making speeches. I estimate very roughly that of those three hundred millions, at least three hundred thousand are on their feet at this moment, talking to various groups drawn from the others. Speech-making is one of the principal pursuits of the Western World, but although everybody does it, nobody seems to talk about how it is done. We have keen critics of the techniques of all sports and pastimes, but who criticizes the technique of the speaker? Every art—drama, music, painting—comes under the reducing lens of the critic, except the art of making speeches. Literature, even on the lowest levels, is the fodder for thousands of critics, and the subject of countless graduate-school theses, but the body of a public speech is rarely examined as if it were a literary creation. The content of a speech is frequently chewed over, but the manner in which it is delivered and the circumstances of its delivery go undiscussed. One wonders why.

In part, I think, it is because there is a widespread belief that a public speaker is a more or less inspired creature, who is making up what he says as he goes along, and that he should not be held accountable for his grammatical muddles, his inaccurate facts, and his uncouth delivery. In my lifetime I have seen the growth of what might be called The North American Myth of Sincerity, a myth which suggests that anything that is done skilfully, or with accomplishment, is of less worth than what is botched. This Myth applies very strongly to the public speaker; the botcher is thought to be a worthy fellow, who is searching his soul for every word that falls maimed and bleeding from his lips. The reality is otherwise; sincerity can be as much a mannerism as anything else, and I am always suspicious of speakers who appear to be struggling for every sentence. They are frequently crooks, who have mastered their barbarous style just as, in an earlier day, they would have mastered the elements of rhetoric.

In my boyhood I heard many speakers of that earlier day, who prided themselves upon being spell-binders and silver-tongued orators. I have heard speakers of whom it was said—the remark was by no means original, but it never failed to give pleasure—that when they were infants the bees had clustered round their cradles, to sip the honey from their lips. In retrospect, I wonder if any bee ever came back for a second sip. They were very strong on manner, those spell-binders, but they were no better stocked with matter than their less gaudy contemporaries. At the time I heard them, their day was passing. The Age of Sincerity was dawning; I hope that I may live to see the sun set on the Sincere Speaker. There is only one way to make a speech, and that is to have something to say, and to say it as clearly as you can, in a fashion that does not insult or patronize your hearers. Easy to say: not in the least easy to do. Nor is the fault all with the speakers. The passion for public speaking that possesses us on this continent, the unquenchable thirst for everything from full-scale oratory to what is misleadingly called 'a few words', makes public speakers of thousands who would do better to remain silent, and drives those who have some knack for speaking to speak altogether too much.

Consider the situation in which we find ourselves. I am greatly complimented to have been asked to speak to you; I am delighted to be here. But common decency compels me to recognize that you would be far better off if you were being entertained by a first-rate conjuror, or a talented clown, or perhaps even by a ventriloquist. There was a time when this fact was given due consideration. When I was a boy I used often to go with my parents to political rallies, where candidates for Parliament appealed for votes. Those men were no fools. They included in their entourage an entertainer, who put the audience in a good mood. After the entertainer had delighted us with his comic songs and his imitation of a Red Indian reciting *The Charge of the Light Brigade*, we were softened up for the political address. As a boy, I had no vote; if I had been enfranchised, I should unhesitatingly have voted for the entertainer. I learned a lesson at those meetings, and it was this: if you haven't got a professional entertainer on your side, you should do your best to be entertaining in your own person.

I put this lesson into practice at an early age. At my school many prizes were offered, and two I regarded as my personal property; they were the prize for reading aloud, and the prize for public speaking. I sought them, not for glory, but for money. Each contest carried a prize of a finely bound book but, in addition, the right to buy twenty-five dollars' worth of books. Fifty dollars! It was the riches of Ali Baba in a day when a very good book could be bought for three dollars and fifty cents. The unappeasable lust for books which has been one of the glories and the nuisances of my life made it absolutely obligatory for me to get that money. How? Other boys had similar ambitions. But I had a degree of low cunning that was beyond my years, and I reduced the arts of reading and speaking to a formula drawn from the world of the sandwich-maker. It was, very simply, Ham and Tongue.

How well I remember those school contests! My rivals, who were fine boys and have since grown up to be fine men, went in very heavily for Sincerity. They knew where the wellspring of sincerity was; it resided in their fathers. They would admit, though of course not to the judges of the contest, that they had received some help from their fathers in preparing their speeches. In consequence the physician's son was apt to harass the audience with addresses on Man's Struggle Against the Common Cold, and the chartered accountant's son pontificated on Municipal Taxation—Whither? They shouted and waved their fists; the cords in their necks stood out with strain. But I was not a fine boy; looking back, I think I must have been rather a horrid boy, because I adopted a conversational manner, cracked a lot of jokes, and sometimes—I blush to recall—made fun of the other speakers. These were very probably the promptings of the Evil One, but the Evil One was a good friend to me, and I always got the fifty dollars.

I think that the Evil One must have whispered something to the Headmaster of the school as well, because during my time he changed the rules, and demanded that the speeches be extemporary, on subjects drawn from a list he prepared himself. The experts on the Common Cold and Municipal Taxation were flummoxed. But Ham and Tongue carried me through. My affectation of naturalness was precisely that—an affectation; my apparently conversational delivery was in fact quite a loud, carefully articulated yell; I could make myself heard over a brass band.

The Headmaster's purpose in changing the rules was to give us some experience of thinking on our feet. And so it did. It could not, however, do much for a boy who never by any chance thought in any other posture. Personally, I mistrust the notion of thinking on one's feet; I have known many speakers who prided themselves on that ability, and I am sorry to say that many of them were blatherers; they did not know when to stop. This took me some time to realize, because my father was a great admirer of these extemporary speakers; it was the fashion of his day to value length of oratory, and he exulted over political figures who could hold forth for two hours, without a note. My father particulàrly stressed this: 'Without a note!' he would cry, fixing me with a glowing eye. So when my turn came, I naturally tried to speak without notes, but I soon found that it was not for me. Not merely notes, but a prepared script was what I liked. Of course I did not know it, but I was part of a movement toward the prepared speech, with a type-script for the assistance of reporters who cannot write shorthand.

The prepared script also has its dangers. Politicians were probably the first to discover that the script might as well be prepared by somebody else. But no—I wrong them; credit for that discovery belongs to the clergy. Politicians—slapdash fellows with a boundless faith in the gullibility of mankind—all too often gave speeches which were as new to them as to the audience, and not infrequently they came upon words that were unfamiliar to them and ideas that surprised them.

I know all about that. My own political career was a very quiet one: I was a back-room literary hack. I recall writing a series of broadcast speeches for a political aspirant whose fame had been gained as a professional hockey-player. Nothing could persuade him to look at his speech before going on the air, and although I did my level best to write in his own style and vocabulary, such as it was, every now and then he would gag over something—a subordinate clause, or a crumb of unfamiliar punctuation—and reveal himself in all his pitiable insufficiency. Once I gave him a joke, and that was a very great miscalculation, because the cast of his mind was not jocular. Having uttered the joke, and being dimly aware that some-thing untoward had happened, he tried—if I may so express it—to suck the joke back out of the microphone. His commit-tee were displeased with me, but as they were not paying me anything and I was writing simply out of political loyalty, I could afford to ignore their huffing and puffing.

Another experience as a political ghost-writer found me preparing speeches for a man who had been, thirty years earlier, a modest success as a baseball player. He was convinced that his small fame was still resounding in the minds of the youth of the day, and he kept urging me to get it into the speeches. 'Tell them I'm a straight shooter,' he would say. So I did, but without conviction, for he was so plainly not a shooter at all; he was a magazine of blanks, and he lost the election. He seemed to think that I was a contributing cause. You cannot make a Demosthenes out of an old ball-player; you cannot even cloak him in the grey mantle of Phoney Sincerity. If he has no conception of Ham and Tongue, you are beaten, and so is he.

When I speak of Ham, I hope that you do not think I recommend a grossly histrionic style of delivery. That used to be popular. There were speakers who wept, speakers who were immense in their indignation, speakers who were hugely sarcastic. At the very bottom of the list came the speakers who told funny stories.

A funny story is, in itself, a good thing, but we have not the appetite for them that existed in our grandfathers. Their taste now seems to us to be gross; their delight in stories involving dialect or racial characteristics is out of fashion. But there was a day when a speaker who rose to his feet and declared that the situation in which he found himself re-minded him of the Scotchman, the Irishman, and the Jew who went to a funeral could hold an audience in the palm of his hand. Scotchmen, Irishmen, and Jews were all, by definition, funny, but the real gold of the story lay in the funeral. In Canada forty years ago funerals were surefire.

Let me recall one of these rib-binders. A Scotchman was attending the funeral of his wife, and when the ceremony was concluded, and everyone had left the graveyard, he was to be seen standing by the grave, looking into it with a counte-nance set in what might have been taken for deep grief. A friend approached him, and said, gently: 'Well, Jock, so Margaret's gone.' 'Aye,' said the bereaved husband. 'She was always a good wife to you,' said the friend. 'Aye, so she was for fifty years and more,' said the widower, and then, after a moment's reflection, 'but ye ken I never really likit the wumman.'

I have seen that joke throw an audience into paroxysms. Scotchmen and their wives nudged one another in ecstasy and slapped one another's thighs as they laughed at it. Irishmen and Jews laughed, at the same time wondering how they could adapt the story to their own races. But of course that was out of the question; there was something resolutely Scotch about it, and you could no more change it than you could hope to bleach a piece of tartan.

All of these modes of oratory depended heavily on Ham, that quality of histrionism without which a public speech is as piffle before the wind. Ham is out of favour in our age of sincerity, except for the assumption of fake modesty of which I have already spoken. When I left the world of journalism to become a university professor I quickly discovered that Ham was nowhere so deplored as in the academic world. The professor who calls upon the arts of rhetoric and oratory to make his students pay attention quickly wins a name as a charlatan. I have always been glad of my twenty years in the newspaper world, because it taught me many useful things, and one of them is that the public has no particular objection to a charlatan if he does not overstep the bounds of modesty and artistic restraint. Better the charlatan you can hear than the sincere scholar who lulls you to sleep with a sound like the moan of doves in immemorial elms. My own education was prolonged and various, and my best professors were all hams.

I recall with particular affection a Scotsman who was lecturing about the Romantic Poets; he was trying to give us some understanding of the stress of soul and intolerable pressure of imagination that made those men great, and I suppose we looked uncomprehending. He paused, and walked to the window, and looked out at the snowy landscape for perhaps a full minute, and then he said, in a sorrowful voice: 'I don't suppose there is one of you mutts who has the slightest idea what I'm talking about.' What happened? Did we rise in indignation? Did we rush to his office and burn his library, and demand that he apologize on his knees before we would consent to hear another word? No; we sat up straight and listened very hard and loved him forever after. About two weeks ago I sent a contribution to a fund to create a scholarship in his name. Greater love hath no student than this: that he lay out hard cash to memorialize a dead professor.

That was Ham. What about Tongue?

To me, it is almost wholly a matter of vocabulary. We have all met those excitable, exuberant people who assure us that they just love words. People who just love words too often delight in the showy siftings of the dictionary. I would rather listen to somebody who loved meanings better than words themselves, a speaker who would remain silent rather than use a word he did not truly know. People who just love words are all too often the people who talk about 'meaningful interface', and spend a lot of time on 'marginal variables' whenever they set out upon an 'in-depth overview'. Doubtless these expressions have some original meaning, but as the people who just love words use them they are gaudy toys, bearing the same relationship to a perceptible meaning that a Christmas tree ornament bears to a fine jewel.

The true word-lover must be constantly on the alert to changes in language. When I was a young man at Oxford I took heed of the fate that befell an American friend of mine, who was reprimanded on his oral examination because he dearly loved the word 'motivate' and used it often. The examiner who rebuked him was an old man, who explained courteously and patiently—but oh, the courtesy and patience of Oxford can burn like a refiner's fire!—that the word had no respectable ancestry, that it could not be derived from Latin and had sneaked into the language from France and Germany; it was a low word which my friend would do well to scrub from his tongue with acid. I took warning by my friend's experience, and I shrink from 'motivate' still. But much time has passed; 'motivate' is now in the *Oxford English Dictionary* and I have become a fossil, in this respect at least. My recollection of this incident makes me cautious about rebuking my own pupils when they say 'prestigious' when they mean 'distinguished'. To me 'prestigious' means, and always will mean, juggling tricks, because it derives from *praestigiae*, and when it is used in the modern way I feel as though a rusty sword had been thrust into my—well,not perhaps into my heart, but into some sensitive part of my body. But I do not want to parade as a conservator of endangered species in the world of words. Let the unlettered yahoos ravish the language; what do I care? But I refuse to join in the gang-bang.

I refuse for what I consider a good reason. I am not one of those tedious people who writes to the papers correcting other correspondents about English usage. No, my concern is that of a writer, and on occasion a formal speaker, who wants to be as careful and even pernickety about meanings as he can. Without precision of meaning we damage not simply language, but thought. The language we share is beautiful and alarmingly complex. Try as we may, we are all likely to make mistakes, and very few among us can claim to know the English language in perfection. But we can try.

A humbling lesson for me came about a few years ago when I had an Oriental student of great promise who was terribly worried about English idiom. Blithely I undertook to help him, and we set to work to go right through Fowler's *Modern English Usage*, I to explain and he to learn. It was not long before I was over my head in difficulties and my Japanese friend was in gales of laughter. I was embarrassed because of my ignorance and he was embarrassed because it was wholly against his code to laugh at a professor. What do you say when someone asks: 'Why do they say "Let's drink toast," when they are drinking wine? What does it mean, "By hook or by crook?"' But we managed to laugh our way through from A to Z with great benefit to us both; the difference is that he has remembered most of what we learned, whereas I have lapsed into my old bad habits. To this day I cannot be sure when I should use 'that' and when I should use 'which', but my secretary knows, and between us we keep up some sort of pretence.

It is the idioms that ensnare us, and never so fatally as when we have learned them by ear rather than by the eye. Some years ago I was being introduced at a dinner where I was to make a speech, and the man who had undertaken this dangerous work had the easy fluency of a politician. Having told his hearers my age—which is something about which all audiences feel an unseemly curiosity—and all the jobs I had held, he announced solemnly: 'Mr. Davies is a man of many faucets.' There was a little coarse laughter, but most of the audience looked at me with new respect.

Ham and Tongue are the essentials of public speaking, and ideally they should be balanced in roughly equal quantity. Shakespeare supplied a splendid object lesson in the Forum Scene in *Julius Caesar*. The first speaker is Marcus Brutus, and he is a skilled rhetorician; schoolmasters and professors delight in demonstrating how finely balanced is his address to the mob. But Brutus was wholly a patrician; he was too much a gentleman to stoop to emotional appeals. The second speaker of the day, as you recall, was Mark Antony. He was no mean rhetorician, but in addition to Tongue he had a splendid endowment of Ham, and we all know what happened. Brutus won respect, but Antony started a riot.

Now I must make a confession. It is many months since I was invited to speak to you, and in the interval several letters have passed between your club and myself. It was in one of the earliest of these that the suggestion was made that I speak about any subject that took my fancy, and a few weeks ago I fished that letter out of my files and set to work. Not until I was well launched did another letter work its way up through the debris on my desk, asking me to speak about my books. What was I to do? Should I discard Ham and Tongue, and prepare a new speech? That would have been the proper course of action, but for some time I have hankered to talk in a public speech about public speaking, and I could not quite persuade myself to give up the chance. So I decided to do both, and now I am going to talk for a while about my books, and then, I understand, we are to have a period of questions.

It is a queer business, being an author, and I do not fit into any of the well-known categories. To begin with, I never meant to be one. I did not, as a child, write stories; I greatly preferred to read them. Later, in my schooldays, I wrote verses—I do not regard them as poetry—because my school had a prize for the best poem written every year. I wanted that money, because it was awarded not in cash, but in a credit on a bookshop. Other boys wrote from the heart; very frequently they wrote about girls. The girls I knew were not very good subjects for poetry, because they laughed a lot, and poetry addressed to themselves would have put them into fits. So I wrote about my school, and instead of writing with the kind of poetic freedom that was popular at the time, I wrote in heroic couplets. I knew that I had only the slightest lyric feeling, but I was a demon on technique, and I could mint a couple of dozen couplets, given time and hot chocolate, which was the favourite tipple of my Muse. I always won, and I know now that it was morally wrong that I should have won. A boy who had bled a bad lyric was a poet, even if a bad poet, and I was just a deft cabinet-maker, a technician. Here again the Evil One stood at my elbow, but in my defence I must add that he seems to have been at the elbow of the judges, as well, and made them prefer technique to passion.

What I really wanted to do was to write plays. And I did. And most of them have been acted, and some of them have been acted several times. But until quite recently, being a playwright in Canada was uphill work, and there was no money in it whatever. Like most persistent playwrights, I eventually achieved some productions abroad, and even joined the gray, inglorious army of those who have failed on Broadway, but I knew that there must be some other, more effective way of grabbing the public by the windpipe and making it listen to what I had to say. So I tried my hand at writing a novel, and lo! it worked. Of course all the critics of novels said that I wrote like a playwright; now that my novels are reasonably well-known, and because I still write plays, the critics are apt to say that I write plays like a novelist. Critics, of course, have no such problems; they all write a peevish, falsely jocose prose which, like all literary styles, is a mirror of their souls.

The novels of mine which have been most warmly received are the three last to appear; they are called *Fifth Business, The Manticore,* and *World of Wonders.* They are usually referred to as a trilogy, and I am quite in agreement with that, but honesty demands that I say that I never meant to write a trilogy. I wrote one book about three men, and it was well liked, especially by a large and generous group of readers in the United States. But I still had things to say about another of the men who was essential to the story, so I wrote a second book. It was never my intention to follow it with a third, but at last I did so, because the matter of the third book was still troubling me, and there was only one way to get it out of my mind. But there was no planned trilogy, I assure you.

Why did people like it? I think it is because I have discovered, over the course of the years, what I am. I have already told you that as a boy I was without the fervour that inspired my rivals in the public-speaking contests. I have confessed without a blush that I am no poet. But I seem to have emerged as a moralist; my novels are a moralist's novels.

It sounds dreadful, does it not? But if we are faithful to that careful use of words that I was talking about earlier, we quickly set aside the notion that a moralist is a sad creature who points to the right as the rest of mankind rush blindly to the left. A moralist is one who looks at human conduct with as clear an eye as he can manage, and says what he sees, drawing, now and then, a few tentative conclusions. He is not necessarily someone who beats the drum for a particular code of conduct, someone who rebukes what he believes to be sin, someone who looks down on people who are driven by passion, craving, or fear. But if passion, craving, or fear are what ail them, he will not pretend that it is otherwise. He is compassionate but he strives not to be deluded.

Of course he will be driven now and then to come to a few conclusions, but he will be cautious about giving them a too general application. He will observe that quite often people reap what they have sown. If he is honest he will admit that it is sometimes very difficult to know what they have sown, or to be certain about what the harvest is.

That is the principal theme of my trilogy. I began it because for many years I had been troubled by a question: to what extent is a man responsible for the outcome of his actions, and how early in life does the responsibility begin? I concluded, not without long debate, that it began with life itself, and that a child was as responsible as anyone else if it chose a course of action knowingly. In *Fifth Business,* in the first few lines, a boy makes a choice: he wants to hurt his companion, so he throws a snowball at him, and in the snowball is a stone. The snowball hits somebody else—a woman who is brought to bed prematurely of a child whose struggle for life is long and heroic. The consequences of the snowball with the stone in it continue for sixty years, and do much to shape the lives of three men, and in a lesser way to influence the lives of many people whom they encounter. One man becomes a speculative scholar with a touch of the saint about him: one man lives a sensual, self-serving life and dies, at the age of seventy, because he is suddenly faced with the reality—or one of the realities—of what he is: the third man lives heroically, in the sense that his life is a struggle against severe odds, and achieves a queer kind of fame. Any of the three is a man whom we might like, or detest, if we met him casually. All three are, in various ways, liars. All three do some good in the world and some evil. But it is in the inner life that one is almost a saint, one a failure, and one a hero.

Because I do not think it part of a novelist's task to bamboozle and puzzle his readers, the novels are written in a fashion that makes them seem to be simpler than in fact they are. I strive to write as clearly as I can. Because of this limpid quality in the prose some readers think they have understood what in fact they have missed. Teachers ask young people to read the books who are not really ready for them, and the results are sometimes amusing. A couple of weeks ago a very nice young man of seventeen came to see me because he had to write an essay about this trilogy, and when he appeared he was equipped with a list of questions. He fired the first one at me as soon as he sat down. 'What do you consider the chief structural weakness in your trilogy?' he said. I looked him in the eye and said: 'I don't think it has any structural weakness; I think it's just great.' He was not prepared for that; his teacher was training him for criticism, and of the monstrous vanity of the artist he knew nothing. But he was a nice boy and he said: 'Well, you see, there's no unifying theme that runs through all three books.' 'Is that so?' said I, and suggested that the theme of the single action that bore results for sixty years might meet his need. He had not noticed that, but he was very severe with me about my unhappy proneness to coincidence, which was, he said, not like life. But, I countered, 'This is a novel; if you want life, you can find it on the street, and an incoherent mess it will be; a novel is a work of art, not *cinéma vérité*. And I am an artist, not a child with a Kodak and a tape-recorder.' We parted on very good terms, and I was so bold as to suggest that his teacher might not be doing him a favour by making him take novels apart with a critical apparatus of the approximate delicacy of a wrecking-iron.

These teachers are a queer lot. A few years ago a whole class of high school students came to see me to talk about my work. I explained to them that I wrote first of all to entertain my readers, but that I did not think that entertainment was necessarily trivial, and that I had been lucky in finding readers who wanted to be entertained just as deeply and seriously as lay in my power. But the teacher who was with the class would have none of that; he knew where my weakness lay. He demanded if my books were not sometimes funny. I admitted that I certainly hoped that was so. Then he moved in for the kill. He demanded, sternly, 'Don't you think your use of humour will keep your books from living?'

It was hard to reply because the question opened up so many unexpected realms of speculation. For one thing, it had never occurred to me to wonder whether my books would live or not; I was simply pleased to get them born and before the public. But then—'your use of humour'. What did he mean? It was spoken as if he suspected me of injecting myself with humour, as with some vile drug, and then sitting down with peals of maniac laughter to write so long as the fix lasted, without a prudent regard for my claim on immortality, which notoriously wants no truck with humour. I don't know what I said. He stopped me cold.

It was because I have never consciously 'used' humour in my life. Such humour as I may have is one of the elements in which I live. I cannot recall a time when I was not conscious of the deep, heaving, rolling ocean of hilarity that lies so very near the surface of life in most of its aspects. If I am a moralist—and I suppose I am—I am certainly not a gloomy moralist, and if humour finds its way into my work it is because I cannot help it, and am not strongly conscious of it. Certainly I do not 'use' humour, but there are times—several times every day—when I am conscious that I am possessed by it, and a man possessed is a poor commentator on his possession.

One:
Garlands and
Nosegays

Edward Johnson

BEFORE TELEVISION, *and indeed before radio became widely popular, public performers had magic of a kind rather different from what we associate with them now. This tribute to Edward Johnson, given in Guelph, Ontario, at a concert by Jon Vickers, in 1973, to raise money for a scholarship fund to commemorate Johnson, tries to recapture something of the excitement of a concert in a Canada now fifty years in the past.*

WHEN I WAS ASKED to say something to you this evening in praise of Edward Johnson I did all the usual things—read what was to be found in books of reference, culled opinions about him from books of reminiscence, and talked to people who had some knowledge of the man and his career. Nothing that I heard or found out in this way carried full conviction to me. Nothing added to or illuminated the impression of the man I already had. Because I have an impression, you see, that has lasted since 1927, when I heard him give a recital in the town where I lived—it was the city of Kingston—and it has not dimmed with the passing of time. Indeed, it has gained in clarity, for what I had seen and remembered as a boy has in the meantime been augmented by what I have heard and understood as a man.

Perhaps you are not impressed by the powers of recollection and appreciation of a boy of fourteen? I can only suggest, with whatever modesty I can muster, that it depends a good deal on the boy. I was the kind of boy who liked concerts, and brought a retentive memory and keen observation to them. I was fourteen; Edward Johnson, therefore, must have been forty-six. I heard him at the height of his powers as a tenor. What was it like?

There was an excitement about it that cannot all be attributed to my youth. Concerts were not so common then as they are now, and concerts by artists of international celebrity were rarities in Kingston, though it was a university city. Therefore we—and when I say we, I mean the musical people in Kingston, of whom I was proud to consider myself one—looked forward to the occasion for several weeks beforehand, and when the night came, there was great brushing-up and personal adornment, I can tell you, for in those far-off days people thought it the proper thing to put on their best in order to hear music. It was not snobbery; it was a way of honouring the art, and the artist. It was our contribution to the unique quality of the occasion, and it put us in a receptive mood. We understood the spirit of Haydn, who put on his Court dress when he was about to compose.

The concert took place in the largest of the university halls, which was Grant Hall. Some of you will know it. It is a large hall, and its style of architecture is what is called Romanesque; it is impressive rather than light-hearted, but it is acoustically excellent. And if the surroundings were solemn, the audience was not; we were excited, and I think I may claim to have been as excited as anyone, for we expected something fine. And that is exactly what we got.

I do not know whether you would have considered it fine. The singing, of course, was unique, for every artist of the first rank is unique. No great singer is exactly like another. But the program might have seemed to you to be not quite the sort of thing to which you have grown accustomed. We have so many concerts nowadays, and the technique of recording has become so refined, that all music-lovers have a wider acquaintance with the literature of music than was possible then. There were audiences for recitals of *lieder*, and for the works of a single composer, but they were not to be found very often in Canada, and certainly not in Kingston—though I assure you that it was, and still is, no mean city. We hoped, modestly, to hear a little of everything. We looked forward to eager discussion afterward about what we had liked best, and why. We had, I think, perfect faith that we were going to hear a fine concert and—this was what gave a special edge to the occasion—we were going to hear a Canadian, one of our own, who had beyond all question achieved world celebrity. There was a spice of chauvinism in our enthusiasm, and who would say that we were unjustified, or wrong?

We knew how right we were the moment Edward Johnson stepped on the stage. He had that air of splendid confidence that marks the man who is sure of his welcome. He knew how glad we were to see him. But—and this was the element that set the tone of the evening—he made it amply clear that he was glad to see us. He smiled, but it was not the impersonal smile of the artist on tour, whose smile does not vary by one millimetre of tooth from city to city. And this, I think was one of the things that made Edward Johnson a great concert performer; he gave a personal quality to everything he did. If you wish to be cynical you may put this down to an accomplished platform technique. But—I wonder. I was only fourteen and I fell under his spell immediately, but when I look back now I do not think I was deceived. I have seen and heard several hundred singers since then, and very few of them have had that quality. I think it was the ability of the great artist to make each evening of artistic creation a unique act of evocation.

It taught me something, though I did not understand what the lesson was until many years afterward. The lesson was this: there is only one time that matters for an audience and the musician whom they have come to hear, and that time is now—this very instant. The precise technique and creative power which served last week, or last year, or the extra creative energy the artist hopes to put into his performance next week for some other audience, will not do. Art, if it is to be great art, must be created afresh every time for the special group that has gathered to experience it. That was what Edward Johnson did: he made a concert specially for us.

Of course there were printed programs, but he did not stick to the program. There were changes and surprises, and we felt that they were made because something in us, and something in the artist that evening, made the changes happy and inevitable.

What did he sing? All sorts of things. As I have said it was not one of those concerts which is designed to be an illumination of a particular school of music, or a special composer. He began with two Italian songs from the eighteenth century, liquid and caressing, which we very well knew were to warm up his voice. We were pleased to hear him warming up, but there were perhaps too many people of Scottish descent in that audience to respond fully to songs of that sort. Then he sang an English folksong, and we knew we were getting down to business. Then he sang what the program called Rodolph's Narrative from *La Bohème*; you know it; it was 'Che gelida manina'. We knew it, too, because it was one of Edward Johnson's most popular Victor Red Seal Records, and every note was familiar to us. But it was not just like the record, the nuances of which were impressed on us from many listenings; it was slightly different; it was for us. And it brought down the house.

I said that the program contained a bit of everything. We proceeded to songs in French, and German, and more Italian, and as we continued, the recital, without ceasing to be a notable concert, became a party as well. Mr. Johnson, having perhaps had time to look at the faces and physical characteristics of his audience, asked our permission to sing a Scots song. We gave it, with a roar, and he sang 'Leezie Lindsay' in a manner which I recall as being quite extraordinary. For, without in the least patronizing or belabouring the song, or stressing its Scots elements unduly, he sang it so that to this day, when I read the word 'chivalry', I hear the voice of Edward Johnson declaring

My name is Lord Ranald Macdonald

Many men have lived and died without exerting as much influence on a single life as that lovely old song made on me, in about two minutes.

He sang a great many encores, for he was generous and we were, perhaps, demanding as audiences used to be. He finished the formal part of his concert with 'Vesti la giubba' from *Pagliacci* and he acted it splendidly, in a fashion suitable to a concert—not too much, nothing in excess, but giving us a whiff of the great opera houses of the world without in any way affronting the atmosphere of our university hall.

But no concert by Edward Johnson was complete without a ritual which had become familiar. He sang 'Sunrise and You', because it was expected, and also, I am sure, because he liked doing so. I have not heard the song for many years. I wonder if anyone sings it now? Perhaps not, for it was, it must be said, a commonplace drawing-room ballad. Even at fourteen I was critical of the poetry:

> *Far in the East there's a soft crimson glow,*
> *The new day blushes at its dawning—*

Thus it began, and moved on to the refrain:

> *Sunrise and you,*
> *And the soft morning dew,*
> *Like the tears on your cheeks when we parted.*
> *My fond heart awakes*
> *When the glorious day breaks*
> *For the sunrise reminds me of you!*

Flat, isn't it? And the music did little to lift it. But Edward Johnson did what great artists can do, and used the ordinary little song as the foundation on which he raised a creation of romantic regret, and the fleeting nature of youth and love, which was entirely his own. And this, too, is great artifice, for though it is the singer's art to give fitting expression to the noblest music, it is also his artifice to make something out of nothing. When he does that, we see his personal quality more clearly than when he is the servant of a mightier creator.

Was that all? No, indeed. There was an odd incident after the interval. When Mr. Johnson reappeared on the stage, he told us that there was someone in the audience to whom he wished to pay a special tribute. It was a very old lady who was sitting in the front row, who had been his first music teacher, and she had written a poem for the occasion which she had asked him to sing. As there was no music, he could not sing it, but he would read it instead. And read it he did, with warmth and affection. It was not memorable verse, and we all knew it. But we knew that Mr. Johnson had been put on the spot by his old teacher—old teachers have these tricks—and we were more than willing to help him out of his predicament. And so, by an act of understanding and kindness, he turned what might have been an embarrassing incident into a triumph.

There was something princely about it, and as I look back I see that there was something princely about him. (For years afterward our local amateur singers attempted to face their audiences in his posture of repose, which was with his hands lightly resting one upon the other at the level of his waistcoast; they caught the posture, but, alas, they never achieved the effect.) It was not only that his platform demeanour was elegant and transfixing, it was that he had the truly princely gift of conferring distinction upon others.

There is a Kingston story about that. The concert took place in the early autumn, and when Mr. Johnson arrived in Kingston he wanted a button replaced on his overcoat. He took it to a tailor, whose mind was fixed on another great local event, and who therefore looked him up and down and inquired: 'Are you in town for the ploughing match?'

Edward Johnson told that story after his concert, at a party. He told it very well. And it had the extraordinary effect of making that tailor seem to be, not a clown, but a wit. Indeed, he enjoyed a reputation as a wit until his death, without ever, so far as anyone knew, saying another memorable thing.

As I say, this was princely. The little old lady was known to hundreds of Kingstonians until she died as Edward Johnson's Music Teacher, though we knew very well that she had taught him the elements of the piano, and nothing whatever about singing. The tailor was a character, and no trivial character, in the Johnson legend. And for all of us Edward Johnson was a splendid figure, because, to crown his other great qualities, he was one of us, and princes were in short supply in Canada in those days. Indeed, they have never been so numerous that we have grown tired of them.

There you have it: the recollections of one who heard Edward Johnson, for the first and only time, when he was fourteen. Do you scorn me because I was impressionable? I am sure you do not. If I had been blasé at fourteen, it is most unlikely that you would want to hear anything I have to say now.

The man, as I have said, was princely. And he was one of our own.

Sir Ernest
MacMillan

IT WAS MY GOOD LUCK *to belong to a generation in Canada whose musical taste was greatly influenced by Ernest MacMillan. I thought myself fortunate to be asked to speak at the Memorial Service that was held for him in Convocation Hall, in the University of Toronto, on May 15, 1973. To be able to thank a man publicly for what he has done for you is all too rare a pleasure, and it is a pity that it comes so often after his death. Can we do nothing to change this?*

I HAVE BEEN ASKED TO SPEAK for those who take great delight in music but whose place it is to face the music. We are not the performers, nor the scholars, nor the critics. We are the audience.

There are hundreds of thousands of us, some rather older than I, and many much younger, whose musical taste was formed in greater or less degree under the influence of Ernest MacMillan. When he appeared on the musical scene in the twenties he set new standards of taste, purged the repertoire, and demanded a new quality of attention from us. Inevitably my reminiscences must be my own, but I think they will touch the experience of many who are here at several points. We became aware of Ernest MacMillan. We became aware that we had to live up to him.

If this sounds severe, it is not meant to suggest that his personality as we encountered it was in any way minatory or forbidding. But unquestionably it was exacting. We, as well as the players, had to come up to the mark. We liked that, because so many of us were of the same stock as he, and we were used to having demands made on us. We found delight in music, but we were in no way hostile to being instructed as well. This educational process was rarely carried through by Sir Ernest himself but by people under his influence, who knew what he wanted, and who were in some respects, I now believe, more royalist than the king.

We learned quickly to reprehend musical customs which had not seemed objectionable to our parents. To signal the approaching end of a piece of music by a *rallentando*, for instance became, for us, an unpardonable affectation. Hymns that an earlier generation had loved for their easy, lilting rhythms were, we discovered, trivial and irreverent. Singers who were not above pleasing their hearers with a few easy ballads of the drawing-room variety either changed their ways, or sank in our esteem. The ominous name of Bach was often on our lips, and we spoke pityingly of Stainer. We discovered a good deal about complexities of rhythm. We learned to love folk-music for its beauty, now revealed by musical treatment very different from the patronizing Jolly-Miller approach of an earlier day. We became quite familiar with modes and music which occasionally had an unusual number of beats in a bar. We learned in time to forget about bars entirely when they were irrelevant. In fact, we grew up musically. We knew that a good musician expected a good audience, and we were eager to provide one.

We heard stories of the great man that gave us keen satisfaction. We heard that singers who had grown grey in the Mendelssohn Choir had been gently but firmly exposed to a voice and sight-reading test, and that some of them had been found wanting. We heard that the new Conductor described leading the Mendelssohn Choir as an experience comparable to coaxing a lobster over a rough road on the end of a long elastic band. We approved of this stringency. It made for a better choir. We learned to understand, and quite soon we learned to relish, organ recitals of demanding music. We were eager to acquaint ourselves with mighty works that had not been attempted in Canada before; a succession of increasingly fine performances of the *St. Matthew Passion* stands out in special relief. And we were content that these demands should be made on us, because they came from a man who laid the heaviest demands upon himself. To those who played the music he was the conductor, but to those of us who faced the music he was our leader, and we knew that he was leading us into new realms of pleasure not easily attained, but infinitely worth any exertions in the attainment.

It is on the achievements of such men that the culture of a country rests. To say that they teach us is a poor description of what they do, for in reality they reveal to us things that we are eager to know, but which we cannot understand unaided. Their work is not education, but revelation, and there is always about it something of prophetic splendour. Sometimes, before they die, they become heroes of legend, and when they die we are aware, not of loss, but only of a growing splendour in the legend. And that is how it is with those of us who are glad to think of ourselves as belonging to the audience that was shaped by Ernest MacMillan.

The Funny
Professor

WHEN McGILL UNIVERSITY *celebrated its 150th anniversary in 1971 they paid me the compliment of asking for a talk about Stephen Leacock, one of their most celebrated figures. I had in earlier years written a good deal about Leacock in the measured terms of literary criticism; it was a pleasure to praise him in the university he loved so well.*

So MUCH HAS BEEN SAID about Stephen Leacock during the past two years that I am at a loss to find any new way of presenting him to you. I feel my inadequacy particularly in these surroundings; I am elated to have been asked to speak on such a subject in Leacock's own university, but I am also troubled by a sense that—even if you never knew him—you proud partakers of the McGill tradition possess him in a sense that is denied to the rest of us. I must tread warily, and I shall therefore abandon any vain striving for novelty.

He was known here to successive generations of students and to more slowly rolling waves of faculty as a Funny Professor. At the beginning of his career this was an academic type virtually unheard of, and even when he laid aside his gown in 1938 it was not so common as it is now. Nowadays, of course, all professors are funny; it has been made clear to them that they are a special branch of the entertainment world; if they are not amusing, their students will not become involved with what they are teaching, and a professor whose students are not involved is a man in deep and probably irremediable disgrace. Nowadays the only professors permitted to be wholly serious are those so eminent that they have become, in effect, walking monuments to their own intellectual splendour. So professors are funny, and not only their students, but the whole world, knows it.

In 1903, when Leacock came to McGill, it was not so. I possess an encyclopaedia of humour that was published in 1913—ten years after Leacock had joined you—and in all its 791 closely printed pages there is not a single joke about a professor. Doctors, dentists, butchers, judges, barbers, drunkards, debtors—plenty of jokes about all of these. Even the animal and inanimate worlds were laughed at in 1913, for there are jokes about mosquitoes, dogs, mice, railways, poets, and tenors, but not even a smile about professors. They had no public status whatever either as the objects of wit or as the originators of it.

The reason was, of course, that until after the First World War the extraordinary funniness of the university world and its inhabitants was a closely guarded academic secret. Scholars have always had a plentiful store of wit, but they kept it for their own consumption, as the monks of the Middle Ages preserved the secret of distilling, so that laymen might not be corrupted. If a university joke was handed on other than orally, it was in a musty volume in Latin, or perhaps it was written as a gloss on some rare manuscript. Those were good, durable jokes, too—the kind of joke that wore well. Let me offer you an example, which dates from 1615. That is to say, it was committed to paper in 1615, but from what we scholars call 'internal evidence' it seems to belong to a much earlier era:

A scholar traveyling, and having noe money, call'd at an alehouse, and ask'd for a penny loafe, then gave his hostesse it again, for a pot of ale, and having drunk it off, was going away. The woman demanded a penny of him. 'For what,' sayes hee. Shee answers, 'For ye ale!'

Quoth hee, 'I gave you ye loafe for it.' 'Then,' said shee, 'pay for ye loafe.' Quoth hee, 'Had you it not again?' which put ye woman to a *non plus*, that ye scholar went free away.

You see? We can imagine academics at High Table roaring over that one, and explaining it to one another, and going into all the ramifications of the scholar's false logic, and quarrelling about whether it was a *hysteron proteron* or an *argumentum ad crumenam*, down through the generations.

But you must not suppose that all academic jokes date back to the reign of Henry the Eighth. Here is one that is barely a hundred years old:

> Shortly after Dr. Butler was appointed Master of Trinity College, Cambridge, he received a request from the Head of Newnham that the lady students might use certain lawns across the river on Trinity Backs for tennis. The Master replied that he regretted he could not accede to her request as the lawns in question were for purposes of *agriculture*, not of *husbandry*.

Think how Dr. Butler's nifty must have amused Cambridge—is probably amusing it still, I shouldn't be surprised.

Great numbers of academic jokes are founded, not surprisingly, on the humour of somebody not knowing something he ought to know. Mispronunciations figure heavily in these, and we know that Leacock despised this kind of fun. Here is a clerical example:

> A raw young curate, having read the second lesson from the account of St. Paul's shipwreck, stumbled on a false quaintity. 'When they were escaped, then they knew that the island was called Melĩta.' His rector, preaching from the same passage, gave out his text: 'Acts xxviii. i, When they were escaped, *they* knew that the island was called Melĩta.'

This is the fun of knowing best, and laughing at the embarrassment of the raw young curate, who never forgot it, and probably became a missionary to the Cannibal Islands, and was eaten to expunge his shame. We do not care for that kind of joke much in these times, when we cannot really be sure that anybody around a university will know everything. Everything we know, that is to say, for this is nothing if not an age of specialization.

Leacock was a specialist in humour. He not only knew how to make jokes himself: he knew how other people made them. Like all specialists, he sometimes went too far, and one of the few really melancholy passages in his writing is in the book called *How to Write*, where he explains how anybody can be funny in print if they will just follow his directions. This always seems to me to be like Jupiter writing a book to demonstrate that anybody can turn himself into a swan and be a great success with the ladies. If it lay in anybody's power to be as funny as Leacock, we wouldn't need Leacock—and we do, yes, indeed we do. But some of his other remarks about humour are much better, as for instance that well-known passage in which he explains the difference between the American and the English way of telling a joke.

The joke he chooses is not, in my opinion, a very funny one, but it was a great favourite of his. Leacock's joke went like this:

> A man entered a sleeping-car and said to the porter, 'At what time do we get to Buffalo?' The porter answered, 'At half-past three in the morning, sir.' 'All right,' the man said; 'now I want to get off at Buffalo, and I want you to see that I get off. I sleep heavily and I'm hard to rouse. But you just make me wake up, don't mind what I say, don't pay attention if I kick about it, just *put me off*, do you see?' 'All right, sir,' said the porter.
>
> The man got into his berth and fell fast asleep. He never woke or moved till it was broad daylight and the train was a hundred miles beyond Buffalo. He called angrily to the porter, 'See here, you, didn't I tell you to put me off at Buffalo?' The porter looked at him aghast. 'Well I declare to goodness, boss!' he ex-

claimed; 'if it wasn't you, *who was that man I threw off this train at half-past three at Buffalo?*'

The story has not worn well. Something to do with the increase in air travel, probably. But Leacock set it down in the form I have just read to you, and he asserted that this was the one, true, apostolic way to tell the joke about the man who wanted to get off at Buffalo.

Then he demonstrates how it would be told in England. Of course it would not be a joke existing simply for its own sake; it would be a personal anecdote, for the English only like funny stories if they are about people known to them, or at least people of whom they have heard. The story I told you earlier about Dr. Butler of Trinity is a case in point. And the story would probably be told by a woman, because, says Leacock, 'The English girl has a sort of traditional idea of being amusing; the English man cares less about it. He prefers facts to fancy every time, and as a rule is free from that desire to pose as a humorist which haunts the American mind.' So the Buffalo joke in England, says Leacock, would probably go like this:

> We were *so* amused the other night in the sleeping-car going to Buffalo. There was the most amusing old negro making the beds, a perfect scream, you know, and he kept *insisting* that if we wanted to get up at Buffalo we must all go to bed at nine o'clock. He positively wouldn't let us sit up—I mean to say it was killing the way he wanted to put us to bed. We all roared!

Leacock assures us that when the expression 'we all roared' occurs in one of these English anecdotes, it is a sign that the story is over and laughter is in place. The point of the story has vanished, and we have no reason to suppose that the experience was in any way amusing except for the bare assertion of the narrator. But when a lady says that she roared at some time in the past, it would be churlish not to roar ourselves.

There was one story that seems to have been near to Leacock's heart. He never says so, but the story turns up from time to time in his voluminous writings, so we may assume that it lingered in his mind for many years. It is rather an old story, for it concerns a man who died in 1837.

One day, in the city of London, a fashionable physician sat in his consulting-room, confronted by a wan and melancholy individual who had been pouring out a tale as familiar to physicians then as it is today; the patient was oppressed in spirit, wanting in energy, listless, hopeless, and utterly broken. 'My dear sir,' said the doctor, 'there is really nothing wrong with you except that you require something to raise your spirits. Now I suggest that you go to the theatre, and see this wonderful new clown, Joey Grimaldi. To see Grimaldi is to be borne aloft on such an irresistible cloud of drollery that you will understand at once that all your troubles are illusions—mere phantoms of the brain—and that life is, after all, great and boundlessly good.' 'Doctor,' said the melancholy patient, '*I* am Grimaldi.'

I think that this story lingered with Leacock because he, too, was Grimaldi. For one reason or another I have written a good deal about Leacock, and I have not done so without acquainting myself very thoroughly with his work—the best of it, and the substantial quantity that falls far below the best. He was a humorist whose best work is touched with genius—and by that I mean that it is so good and so utterly his own that we cannot imagine anyone else writing it. To be a genius, after all, is to be able to do without effort what other men cannot do by the uttermost exertion of their powers. Because his best was so fine, his large public continually demanded more from him, and like most writers he could not turn a deaf ear to those flattering demands. But I am sure it is not fanciful to suggest that he often despised and perhaps hated the public that expected him to be perpetually and unfailingly funny, and which was often so undiscriminating in its praise.

Why do I think so? Because I have given much attention to humorous writing, of our own time and of the past, and I have read a lot about the private lives of humorists. There was not one of them, I assure you, who did not have a strongly sardonic strain in his nature, and sometimes it became more than that—it became outright hatred for the cap and bells that his admirers had pressed down upon his head. If Leacock had been an exception to this general observation we should certainly know about it. Instead, we know that he was often morose and sometimes impatient with lesser people to a degree that might have been mistaken for cruelty.

Do not misunderstand me. I do not suggest that Leacock was more of a Jekyll and Hyde than most men, except in so far as the vigour of his character made all of his moods and caprices larger than life. But many of you, I am sure, have observed a psychological balancing process at work among the people you know, the effects of which are only surprising to the naïve. The philanthropist who shows a mean streak in some quite unexpected quarter; the loving and patient mother who sometimes blasts her children with her anger; the intelligent man who becomes an aggressive lowbrow in some area about which he knows nothing: we have all observed these, and many other examples of the balancing and compensating process. Is it a cause for amazement, then, if the humorist who seems to be brimming over with good humour, and who is almost too insistent on his assertion that real humour hurts nobody, should now and then have fits of melancholy, or show a ferocity of misanthropy that startles those who are near him?

We are now beginning to have quite a number of books about Leacock, some of them from relatives who knew him when they were children. Apparently he was not always and unfailingly kind to children. But why should Leacock, any more than the rest of us, be a saint in his dealings with a portion of mankind which is frequently obtuse, noisy, obstreperous, and detrimental? Everybody likes children—more or less—but most people can, at very infrequent intervals, get enough of them. Why should Leacock be exempt from a general rule of life?

He was the bearer of a distinction of a kind which is little understood: he was a humorist, and by that I mean that he was a man who saw life always in terms of a special temperament. A humorist is not a man who, under particular circumstances, says to himself, 'Let's see, now; what would be the funny side of this situation?' Rather, he is a man to whom the funny side is almost always, and immediately, apparent. Very often he sees the funny side at inappropriate times. He is a man under stress, and when the stress can discharge itself in humour he is greatly prized by his fellows. But the humorist pays a price for his gift; very often, in his own life, he is oppressed, and he is apt to be irritable with those who wonder why the clown does not shake his bells and laugh. The stress does not always find its outlet in humour, or at least in good humour. It can be savage.

It is a disability peculiar to the humorist. Nobody expects a specialist in tragedy to be perpetually gloomy. It is recorded of the late Eugene O'Neill—a serious playwright if ever there was one—that he was normally of a pleasant disposition, and dearly loved an evening of hilarity with his friends. If the writer of tragedy is not denied his fun, why should we deny the writer of comedy his gloom? But that is what we are apt to do, unless we think carefully about the matter.

Much of the difficulty, I think, springs from the absurd over-valuation of tragedy in our cultural atmosphere. I have met people, even in universities, who seriously assert that almost any miserable Jacobean who wrote blood-drenched tragedies was a man of greater genius than Cervantes, who wrote a book of immortal comedy. There are those who take it as obvious that Dostoevsky is a greater novelist than Dickens, though Dostoevsky himself makes it clear that he learned much of his melodramatic art from Dickens, and would have learned comic art too, if he had had the stuff of comedy in him. I do not want to get into the unprofitable and always rather silly business of grading writers as if they were first-year students in a university, but I want to call attention to the widespread idea that the production of tragedy depends on a deep and awesome gift, whereas the production of comedy is a kind of low cunning—a mere knack. It is, I suppose, because almost anybody can manoeuvre himself into a condition of low spirits which he mistakes for tragic feeling, but the golden sunshine of comedy is not so easily faked.

This is what Leacock had. At his best, his work has a radiance that is at once universal and individual. Of all the many subdivisions of comedy, he excelled in the one we call nonsense, although it often seems to pierce through appearances to a finer sort of sense than any we know in the world of everyday. Consider the quotation from *Gertrude the Governess*, which is the only piece of Leacock to get into both Bartlett's *Familiar Quotations* and *The Oxford Dictionary of Quotations:*

> Lord Ronald flung himself from the room, flung himself upon his horse and rode madly off in all directions.

It is so familiar that we are apt to miss the easy brilliance with which it impales and deflates a special kind of romantic posturing. But it does something more; it has an individuality of tone and a vigorous grace of cadence that lift it above a mere funny line in a funny story, and make it not just a criticism of a special kind of bad novel-writing, but a criticism of an aspect of youth and of life. This is not achieved by art or contrivance; it comes to those to whom it comes.

The best advice Leacock ever gave to those who want to write was: 'It is perfectly simple; you just jot down amusing things that occur to you. The jotting presents no difficulty; it is the occurring that is difficult.' He was the kind of man to whom special and amusing things occurred.

He was also a deceptively skilful jotter. Leacock reads so easily and colloquially that we may be deceived into thinking that he wrote the prose of ordinary speech. I think you will find that in spite of the apparent easy, unmeditated flow, Leacock is a very close-textured writer. There are no flabby passages, no extraneous words. And the vocabulary, though it is that of common speech, is disciplined by something that Leacock abused publicly but never escaped in his personal work, and that was a classical education. Latin and Greek, if they teach us anything, teach us compression, and compression is a form of elegance. The Greeks and Romans were concise because in their time writing was a laborious business: with us the task of recording and duplicating is fatally easy and we quickly yield to the temptation to blather. There is an elegance that shows itself in the masterly disposition of ornament, and there is another elegance that is plain but inimitable, and this latter form was the elegance of Leacock. He knew how to think, which is another product of a classical education. I am told by people who have examined his professional writing, in economics and political science, that he didn't always think very well, but in the best of his humorous writing we see the effects of classical style, and of the classical approach even when the subject appears to be frivolous.

This brings me to Leacock's ideas about education, and what place could be more appropriate for comment on that topic than the university he loved and served so well? Some of Leacock's best writing was about education, and it has sometimes been overlooked because of his great general popularity. His ideas on the subject are a curious mingling of what is old-fashioned with what is still ahead of our time, and an example is offered by his views on the education of women. He did not think a modern university was any place for a woman, and he thought women in university classrooms were distracting nuisances, most of whom were there in pursuit of a biological end contrary and hostile to the pursuit of real learning. Leacock, by the way, seems to have had strongly ambivalent ideas about women. We know that he was happily married and had a high regard for the intelligence, as well as the great charm, of his wife; we know that women admired him, and that he could be gallant and chivalrous in his relations with them. But he thought they had a place of their own in society, and it was by no means always very close to where serious men were doing serious masculine things.

We should never forget that Leacock was a Victorian. He was born in 1869, and by the time Queen Victoria died in 1901, many of his social attitudes were established and did not change. We might be tempted, therefore, to suppose that his notions about women were simply Victorian, but that would not be true. He thought women were out of place in a university that offered an education shaped by centuries for the development of men, but he also asks the question, which has never yet been satisfactorily answered, why women should not have advanced education rooted in their own needs, and shaped at every point to meet the demands of their own kind of intellect? Because, you see, Leacock was so far ahead of most of us that he understood what some of our most advanced psychologists have been saying, and saying in vain: that women are not simply creatures with an undeveloped masculine type of intellect, but the possessors of a type of intellect very much their own, which is complementary to that of the male. Religion, of course, has always recognized this, and has known that Man understands Law, but that Woman understands Mercy, or to put it differently, that Man is good at Civilization, but that Woman is good at Life itself. But universities still work on the assumption that a brain is a brain, whatever sort of psychological organism it is hitched to, and that all brains can be prepared for life in the same way. Why do universities believe this? Leacock had the answer. Co-education is cheap, he said, and it will always be a cheap way to silence woman's desire for a fulfilment which she is not likely to find in an education that is better suited to her brothers.

He was equally interesting, though not so revolutionary, in his concept of the purpose of education. Learning, he said, was not supposed to be of any material or commercial benefit to anybody; its use was in saving the soul and enlarging the mind.

How old-fashioned, how Victorian, how unpopular it sounds! But is it not right? In our time, if you speak to a university undergraduate about saving his soul, he thinks you want to lure him into a church. His soul, he assumes, once had something to do with God, but he has heard rumours that God is dead, and will doubtless tell you that if he has a soul at all—which he thinks unlikely—it is his own, to do with as he pleases.

As for a graduate student, if you tell him that learning has no material or commercial benefit, he will brighten up at once, and tell you how hard it is getting to step into a faculty job at $20,000 a year, with every second year a sabbatical, and tenure after six months. He knows that the marketing of his PH D is becoming harder every year, and he thinks this is what Leacock was talking about.

It wasn't, of course. Leacock was talking about becoming a man, and arriving at the latter part of life with a sense of having understood, and partaken of, and contributed to, many of the aspects of life one had encountered on the journey. That was saving one's soul to him, for he seems not to have been a formally religious man, and his thought about the deepest aspects of life was stoical and humanistic. He thought that enlarging one's mind was the best way to make sure one did not lose one's way on the journey through life, because the more one knew the better one was armoured against surprise and vicissitude, and the more one knew about a few things the more one was likely to understand about all things. Leacock was convinced in the old classical fashion that education is to make good men; if it should fail, at least the failure knows what good men believe and what good men are trying to bring about in the world in which he finds himself.

But how is it done? Again, Leacock has an answer and it is a very modern answer. All the modern complaint about the Generation Gap, and the inhumanity of universities, where students and faculty never meet on informal terms, would have found a sympathetic listener in him. He believed in education by the most personal kind of intellectual contact between the teacher and the taught. His words on the Oxford system are very well known:

> The key to this mystery is found in the operations of the person called the tutor. It is from him, or rather with him, that the students learn all that they know: one and all are agreed on that. Yet it is a little odd to know just how he does it. 'We go over to his rooms,' said one student, 'and he simply smokes and goes over our exercises with us.' From this and other evidence I gather that what an Oxford tutor does is get a little group of students together and smoke at them. Men who have been systematically smoked at for four years turn into ripe scholars. If anybody doubts this, let him go to Oxford and he can see the thing actually in operation. A well-smoked man speaks and writes English with a grace that can be acquired in no other way.

What he would have said about student parity in university government I do not know, for the idea seems never to have entered his head. I may say, however, that I would not envy a student who found himself on a faculty committee with Leacock; he would certainly have smoked at him, but I doubt if it would have been the kind of smoke that encourages ripeness.

Occasionally I am asked if people read Leacock as much as they once did. The answer must certainly be that they do not. Fashions in humour change, and much of his large output was merely fashionable—excellent, thoroughly professional work in a popular but not enduring mode. The significant fact is not that Leacock is read less than before, but that he is still widely read when so many of his contemporaries—once potent names like those of Irvin Cobb, George Ade, Donald Ogden Stewart, Robert Benchley, and Harry Leon Wilson—are scarcely read at all. He is read, moreover, in Canada, which was not the land of his birth but was certainly the land of his choice. Rarely does one glance at a well-stocked paperback display without seeing two or three of the Leacock titles in the excellent New Canadian Library edition. Young people read him, and some of them have told me that they like him, though they do not entirely understand his great reputation. But I think they will. There is always an awkward interval between the death of an author—a death which may have followed a long silence or the production of some minor work—and a strong revival of interest in him, if such a revival ever comes. But there are signs that it is coming with Leacock, and when readers have ceased to wonder why his work is not contemporary they will begin to understand why the best of it has great enduring worth.

Unquestionably he was one of the first of the Funny Professors, and as we survey the work of that class of humorists we recognize that he was unquestionably one of the best of them, and perhaps the best of all. Happy the students who worked with him! Lucky McGill to have commanded his loyalty and his love! Much of the atmosphere that gives splendour to a great university resides in the memory of its great men, and among great scholars great humorists are rarer still. So I, who come from another university—itself of no humble tradition, for after all, we claim him among our graduates—felicitate you on numbering among your brightest lights the special, heart-warming radiance that was Stephen Leacock.

Two:
Giving Advice

What Every Girl
Should Know

AS A SCHOOLBOY *I listened to many speeches on Prize Days from older persons whose good intentions were impeccable, but whose manner and matter were tediously patronizing and stuffy. When my own turn came I determined to be as honest as possible, not to talk down, and if possible to say something that was not usually said in schools. This is what I said to the girls of the Bishop Strachan School in June 1973.*

DURING THE YEARS when my own daughters were pupils in this school I attended many of these gatherings, and heard many speeches made by men who stood where I stand at this moment. They said all sorts of things. I recall one speaker who said that as he looked out at the girls who were assembled to receive prizes, and to pay their last respects to their school, he felt as though he were looking over a garden of exquisite flowers. He was drunk, poor man, and it would be absurd to treat his remark as though he were speaking on oath. I am not drunk, although I have lunched elegantly at the table of the Chairman of your Board of Governors; I have had enough of his excellent wine to be philosophical, but with me philosophy does not take the form of paying extravagant and manifestly untruthful compliments. Let me put myself on record as saying that I do *not* feel as though I were looking over a garden of exquisite flowers.

On the contrary, I feel as though I were looking into the past. You look uncommonly as the girls of this school looked when my daughters were of your number. And in those days I used to think how much you looked like the girls who were in this school when I was myself a schoolboy, just down the road, at Upper Canada College.

I remember that boy very well. He was a romantic boy, and he thought that girls were quite the most wonderful objects of God's creation. In these liberated days, when it is possible for anyone to say anything on any occasion, I may perhaps make a confession to you, and this is it: I never liked anything but girls. Nowadays it is accepted as gospel that everybody goes through a homosexual period of life. I cannot recall any such thing: I always regarded other boys as rivals, or nuisances, or—very occasionally—friends. I am rather sorry about it now, because in the eyes of modern psychologists and sociologists it marks me as a stunted personality. Nowadays it appears that there is something warped about a man who never had a homosexual period. But there it is. I stand before you with all my imperfections weighing heavily upon me. I always liked girls, and simply because of geography, the girls I liked best were the girls of B.S.S.

I have recovered from this folly. I have myself achieved some knowledge of psychology and sociology, and it tells me significant but not always complimentary things about you. I don't know how many of you are here today, but statistically I know that during the next ten years 58.7 per cent of you will marry, and that of that number 43.4 per cent will have two and a half children apiece, and that 15.3 per cent will be divorced. Of the remainder, 3.9 per cent will be dead, 14.5 per cent will have been deserted, 24.2 per cent will have spent some time in jail. One hundred per cent of those who have married will have given up splendid careers in order to do so, and of this number 98.5 per cent will have mentioned the fact, at some time, to their husbands. These statistics were compiled for me by a graduate student at OISE, and if you doubt them, you must quarrel with her, and not with me. I accept no responsibility for statistics, which are a kind of magic beyond my comprehension.

I have said that when I was a boy I entertained a lofty, uncritical admiration for the girls of this school. Our romantic approach in those days was more delicate than it is today, when sexual fervour has achieved almost cannibalistic exuberance, and I thought I was lucky when I had a chance simply to talk to one of the girls from this school. I never had enough of that pleasure; I yearned for more. Now here I offer my first piece of good advice to you: be very careful of what you greatly desire, in your inmost heart, because the chances are very strong that you will get it, in one form or another. But it will never be just the way you expected. You see what has happened? As a boy I wanted to talk to the girls of B.S.S., and I always thought of doing this to one girl at a time, in shaded light, with music playing in the distance. And here I am today, talking to all of you, in broad daylight. The things I planned to say when I was a boy would be embarrassingly inappropriate if I were to say them now. Indeed, I don't want to say them; they have ceased to be true or relevant for you or for me. I know too much about you to compliment you, and in your eyes I am not a romantic object. Or if I am, you had better put yourself under the treatment of some wise psychiatrist.

Here I am, after all these years, and Fate has granted one of my wishes, in the way Fate so often does—at the wrong time and in wholesale quantity. What am I to say to you?

The hallowed custom, at such times as these, is that I should offer you some good advice. But what about? It was easier in the days when girls like yourselves thought chiefly about marriage. Nowadays when little girls play

> *Rich man, poor man, beggar man, thief,*
> *Doctor, lawyer, Indian chief*

they are trying to discover their own careers, not those of their husbands. Quite recently a very young girl told me that she did not intend to bother with a husband; she would be content with affairs, because they would interfere less with her career. That remark showed how much she knew about it. A girl who thinks love affairs are less trouble than a marriage is probably also the kind of girl who thinks that picnics are simpler than dinner-parties. A first-class picnic, which has to be planned to the last detail, but which must also pretend to be wholly impromptu, is a vastly more complicated undertaking than a formal dinner for twenty guests, which moves according to a well-understood pattern. Personally I have always greatly liked dinner-parties, and hated picnics. But then I am a classicist by temperament, and I think the formality and the pattern, either in love or in entertaining, is half the fun.

But you may have different views, so we won't talk about that. Let us talk about something that will be applicable to your life, whether the love aspect of it takes the dinner-party or the picnic form. Let us talk about enjoying life.

Don't imagine for a moment that I am going to talk about that foolish thing happiness. I meet all kinds of people who think that happiness is a condition that can be achieved, and maintained, indefinitely, and that the quality of life is determined by the number of hours of happiness you can clock up. I hope you won't bother your heads about happiness. It is a cat-like emotion; if you try to coax it, happiness will avoid you, but if you pay no attention to it it will rub against your legs and spring unbidden into your lap. Forget happiness, and pin your hopes on understanding.

Many people, and especially many young people, think that variety of sensation is what gives spice to life. They want to do everything, go everywhere, meet everybody, and drink from every bottle. It can't be done. Whoever you are, your energies and your opportunities are limited. Of course you want to try several alternatives in order to find out what suits you, but I hope that ten years from today you will agree with me that the good life is lived not widely, but deeply. It is not doing things, but understanding what you do, that brings real excitement and lasting pleasure.

You should start now. It is dangerously easy to get into a pattern of life, and if you live shallowly until you are thirty, it will not be easy to begin living deeply. Whatever your own desires may be, the people around you won't put up with it. They know you as one sort of person, and they will be resentful if you show signs of becoming somebody else. Live shallowly, and you will find yourself surrounded by shallow people.

How are you to avoid that fate? I can tell you, but it is not a magic secret which will transform your life. It is very, very difficult. What you must do is to spend twenty-three hours of every day of your life doing whatever falls in your way, whether it be duty or pleasure or necessary for your health and physical well-being. But—and this is the difficult thing—you must set aside one hour of your life every day for yourself, in which you attempt to understand what you are doing.

Do you think it sounds easy? Try it, and find out. All kinds of things will interfere. People — husbands, lovers, friends, children, employers, teachers, enemies, and all the multifarious army of mankind will want that hour, and they will have all sorts of blandishments to persuade you to yield it to them. And the worst enemy of all—yourself—will find so many things that seem attractive upon which the hour can be spent. It is extremely difficult to claim that hour solely for the task of understanding, questioning, and deciding.

It used to be somewhat easier, because people used to be religious, or pretended they were. If you went to the chapel, or the church, or a praying-chamber in your own house, and fell on your knees and buried your face in your hands, they might—not always, but quite often—leave you alone. Not now. 'Why are you sitting there, staring into space?' they will say. Or 'What are you mooning about now?' If you say 'I am thinking' they may perhaps hoot with laughter, or they will go away and tell everybody that you are intolerably pretentious. But you are doing very much what you would have been doing if you were your great-grandmother, and said that you were praying. Because you would be trying your hardest to unravel the tangles of your life, and seek the aid of the greatest thing you know—whatever you may call it—in making sense of what will often seem utterly senseless.

I am not going to advise you to pray, because I am not an expert on that subject. But I do know that it is rather the fashion among many people who do pray to think that it is pretentious to pray too much for yourself; you are supposed to pray for others, who obviously need Divine assistance more than you do. But when I was a boy at the school down the road, we were taught that prayer has three modes—petition, which is for yourself; intercession, which is for others; and contemplation, which is listening to what is said to *you*. If I might be permitted to advise you on this delicate subject, I would suggest that you skip intercession until you are a little more certain what other people need; stick to petition, in the form of self-examination, and to contemplation, which is waiting for suggestions from the deepest part of you.

If I embarrass you by talking about praying, don't think of it that way. Call it 'pondering' instead. I don't know if you still learn any Latin in this school, but if you do, you know that the word ponder comes from the Latin *ponderare,* which means 'to weigh'. Weigh up your life, and do it every day. If you find you are getting short weight, attend to the matter at once. The remedy usually lies in your own hands. And in that direction the true enjoyment of life is to be found.

There you are. I promised your Headmaster I would not speak for too long. But I have done what a speaker on such occasions as this ought to do. I have given you good advice. It is often and carelessly said that nobody ever takes advice. It is not true. I have taken an enormous amount of advice myself, and some of it was extraordinarily helpful to me. I have passed on some of the best of it to you this afternoon, and I have enjoyed doing so. Because, as I told you, it was my ambition for years to have a chance to talk to every girl in B.S.S. and today I have achieved it. Not quite as I had hoped, but then, in this uncertain world, whatever comes about quite as one hopes? I have enjoyed myself, and for what I have received from you I am truly thankful.

What Will the Age of Aquarius Bring?

IT IS EASY FOR THE SPEAKER at a university Convocation to forget that he is talking principally to an audience of young people who are in high spirits—or would be in high spirits if their elders gave them a lead. Alas, Convocation speakers who are themselves receiving honorary degrees seem often to be wearily conscious that they have reached a time of life when there will be no more thrills, and where even a new honour cannot lift them out of the abyss. And what can one talk to university students about that they have not already heard discussed to the point of exhaustion? Well, astrology is one possibility, and that was what I spoke about at the University of Calgary in June 1975.

MR. CHANCELLOR, and Members of Convocation: I am deeply sensitive to the honour you do me today, by the conferral of this degree, *honoris causa*, which I interpret as 'a mark of our esteem'. I assure you that I shall strive to deserve it, and never disgrace it or forfeit your friendship and good-will, which you have manifested so handsomely.

I am an old hand at Convocations. Indeed, I might fittingly refer to myself as a Convocation-buff. I have attended scores of them, usually to watch others receiving degrees, sometimes — as is the case today — to be received into a friendly academic community in this special and delightful way. So as you see, I have heard a great many Convocation speeches. I once heard a poet acknowledge an honorary degree by reading a poem specially written for the occasion; that was admirable. I have often heard an honorary graduand, whose achievements had been amply rehearsed in the speech in which he was presented to the Chancellor, go over the whole of that ground again, explaining in detail how he took every step in his distinguished, and wearisomely long, career. I have heard honorary graduands who sought to be funny; there have been times when they sought in vain. And I have heard honorary graduands who strove to attain splendid and sublime heights of seriousness; not infrequently they got the laughs that eluded the aspiring comedians. So I approach my task this morning with caution and some alarm. What am I to say to you?

I have my directions from the Chancellor's office; I am not to talk too long. Twenty minutes would be ample, the letter said, and I thought I detected a suggestion that less than twenty would do. But how am I to fill in this obligatory period before I may decently sit down and allow the really important part of the proceedings—the conferral of degrees on you—to begin? I must say something; it is the worst sort of academic manners to grab one's scroll of honour and run. So I must call on past experience of Convocations. What was the usual thing in the many I have attended?

The usual thing—the statistically normal thing—is for the speaker to tell the graduating class that they are going out into a world torn by dissent, racked by problems of unprecedented knottiness and difficulty, and headed for the abyss of destruction unless the graduating class shoulders its burden and does something splendid to put everything right. The speaker generally admits that he is at the end of his tether: he is old, and broken on the wheel of Fate; his decrepitude and his wounds have been received in this great battle with the world's problems. Nothing—absolutely nothing—is to be expected of him in the future. From his failing hands he throws the torch; he plants the task of setting the world right square on the graduating class. He says that he does it with confidence. But he is usually so gloomy that one wonders how much his confidence is worth. Sometimes one gets the impression that immediately after Convocation he is going home to die.

I would talk like that, if I believed it, but I have other opinions and contrary beliefs, and I dare not speak against them. Although I am, in part, a university professor, I have always felt as if I were a fraud when I am in the company of really modern professors, because they are full of modern knowledge, and a great part of it is gloomy and uncomfortable. Gloom and despair are extremely fashionable in our time, and not to be gloomy and despairing is to run the risk of seeming frivolous. But I would be dishonest if I tried to play the role of a modern professor, full of modern knowledge. I am, I fear, a most unfashionable sort of professor, and I am full of old-fashioned knowledge—so old-fashioned as to seem utterly useless, if not ridiculous and even demented. Well, you may say, if that's the way it is, why don't you modernize your attitude, and get into the swim? My answer must simply be this: my very old-fashioned knowledge gives me hope and a considerable measure of cheerfulness. I do not despair. Oh, I know when the going is tough as well as anyone else, but I also know that better times are coming.

When are they coming? I think you may look for significant changes about the year 2000, or perhaps 2025. Fifty years from now, to put it at a round figure. By that time you will be middle-aged, and I shall be getting on toward old age, but I hope we shall see the new dawn together.

And how do I know this? Well, that is what I shall tell you now, and I shall be as quick as I can, because if I dawdle the Vice-Chancellor may be so outraged by what I say that he will summon the university police and have me whisked away to the nearest madhouse.

You see, for the whole of my adult life I have been interested in alchemy. You know what alchemy is: it is the discredited ancestor of modern science. Alchemists are usually remembered today as men who attempted to turn base metal into gold. That was not all they did, as I shall shortly explain, but that is all that is remembered now, except by a few people like myself. The scandalous thing is not that they failed, but that sometimes they succeeded. I have done it myself. I am, as you know, an author, and for forty years I have transmuted stories I write, which several Canadian critics regard as very base metal indeed, into a modest but welcome quantity of gold. Enough gold, that is to say, to make it possible for me to appear here today not positively clothed in rags and suffering from the final stages of starvation. But such transmutation of base metals was not by any means the principal pursuit of the alchemists. They were deeply interested in Time and they did a lot of work on Time which would not impress your Faculty of Science, but which has impressed me.

They knew a great deal about the past, but they were boundlessly curious about the future. They wanted to know what was going to happen. Well, now—if you lived in the twelfth century, and wanted to understand the future, what would you do? You would cast your own horoscope, because you would be well versed in the current science of astrology. But suppose you wanted to go beyond that, and find out what would happen to the world? What then? It's simple: you would cast the world's horoscope. And that is precisely what they did.

It isn't as simple as casting the horoscope of a man, because the world moves in a different kind of time from human beings. The alchemists said it moved in periods called Platonic Years, and each Platonic Year was divided into Platonic Months, of about two thousand years' duration. Once you had established that, the rest was easy. You applied what you knew of astrology, and it was a breeze.

I see a glint appearing in your eyes. I am strongly conscious that I am speaking not in the fogs and intellectual miasmas of Eastern Canada, but in the Canadian West, where your climate and your minds are clear. You are disposed to pragmatism. You want to know if it worked.

It worked as astrology does work—in a sort of lurching, flouncing, vertiginous fashion that sometimes seems to produce utter nonsense, and at other times comes up with a piece of blazing truth. We haven't time for many examples, but I must offer you at least one.

The alchemist-astrologers who devoted themselves to this sort of study were agreed that the end of a thousand-year

period, when it coincided with a Platonic Month, or half a
Platonic Month, was a very rough time for mankind. Why half
a Platonic Month, I see signalled to me from the eyes of that
young man in the middle of the hall, whom I sense as being a
thorough pragmatist. Because Platonic Months are modelled
on lunar months, and in the lunar month the great moments
are the New Moon, at the beginning, and the Full Moon, in the
middle. That's why.

Look what happened in the year 1000, as an example
of what happened at the Full Moon of the Platonic Month in
which we live now—the month astrologically named Pisces.
There were astonishing doings everywhere in the world of
which we have knowledge, and at least one great expectation in
the European and Eastern World caused infinite disturbance.
As the year 1000 approached, prophets arose everywhere who
predicted the End of the World. These were the Millennialists.
In the year 1000, said they, Christ would return to Jerusalem
and there He would conduct the Last Judgement. The Bible
was absolutely firm on this point.

What happened? People everywhere began, about the
year 975—one thousand years ago—to hasten to Jerusalem.
They wanted good seats for the great event. They didn't want
to be called to the Last Judgement from some far-away place,
and perhaps whirled through the air in the arms of a great
storm. Humble people walked across Europe; people of high
station—and there were many of them who took the
trip—went by ship and caravan. What became of them? Many
died. Many more were seized by pirates and land-robbers and
sold into slavery. Quite a few actually reached Jerusalem,
where they hung around, wondering what had gone wrong
with the world clock, until their money was exhausted,
and they fell into the hands of money-lenders. It was perhaps
the first instance in history of that familiar modern disaster,
the tour which goes bankrupt in the middle and leaves its
clients stranded.

Were the astrologer-alchemists to blame? They were
not. Their record is spotless. It was not they who predicted the
End of the World. What they said was that prophets would
arise speaking of doom, that thousands of people would meet

with disaster and disappointment, that there would be portents in the sky (and there were), and that there would be general economic upheaval (and there was).

It was foolish of the world to misinterpret the astrologer-alchemists, but when has the world not been foolish? It will be foolish again, as we approach the year 2000. Is there anything to be done about it? Perhaps.

I am not going to waste time trying to persuade you that we are now in the dark of the moon of the Platonic Month of Pisces. We have been there for many decades, as your studies of history since the Reformation will assure you. Wars, pestilence, dispersions of peoples, famine, the fall of states, and threats to everything that modern civilization holds dear are the common fare of our daily papers. We are in the Grand Finale of the Platonic Month of Pisces, which was always foreseen to be a two-thousand-year period of great contention. You know the sign of Pisces? It is two fish, one swimming upstream and the other downstream, but the tension between them is so equal that they are perpetually at odds; one never quite gains the ascendancy over the other.

Has it not been so for two thousand years? The extraordinary ameliorating effect of Christianity, with its gospel of compassion and inner reliance, has been in perpetual strife with the greed and cruelty which are such powerful, but not wholly triumphant, elements in the human spirit. The tension between the Fishes has been at its most powerful since 1840, and we are to be spectators of the final showdown.

What will that final showdown be like? Need you ask? My dear friends, you are bang in the middle of it. And what do you see in the world about you? Prophets are heard everywhere, speaking of doom; thousands of people have met with disaster and disappointment, and thousands more will follow in their unhappy footsteps; there are portents in the sky, and have been for twenty-five years or more, and calling them Unidentified Flying Objects does not make them a whit more scientifically respectable; as for general economic upheaval, I can tell you with unshakable authority that it has already reached the universities of Eastern Canada, and when last seen was making its way rapidly west.

Is this unavoidable? Indeed it is. But this is where my astrologer-alchemists provide me with some good news. The showdown will not be total disaster: the tension of the Fishes of Pisces will eventually give place—*must* give place, because that is what the Platonic Calendar ordains—to the new Platonic Month of Aquarius. Great changes impend, hard times cannot be fled, some of us will be unable to sustain the culture-shock of the dawn of a new age, but Aquarius will come.

Sounds like a crisis, doesn't it? It was a crisis in the year 1000, too. Isn't it strange how people—not people in universities, like you and me, but just people—keep forgetting that 'crisis' is Greek for 'judgement'.

But supposing we make it to Aquarius, what will it be like? Many of you will remember that a few years ago there was a great deal of popular hubbub about the Dawning of the Age of Aquarius. The sort of people who predicted that new dawn were not—I am putting it as kindly as I can—were not sinewy-minded. They would never have made alchemists. They saw the Age of Aquarius as an era that might have originated in the mind of a very young person who had been partaking unwisely of a feast of whipped cream complicated by several sharp snorts of cocaine. The Age of Aquarius was to be easy and woozy, with a great deal of soft-boiled sex in it.

That isn't the way my old alchemist-astrologers saw it. I expect you are all familiar with the real significance of the symbol of Aquarius. If you aren't, how come you to be getting a university degree today? It is what is called a fixed, watery sign, unlike the mutable, watery sign of Pisces. Aquarius is under the dominance of the planet Uranus, the father of Titans, and it is notorious among astrologers that more great men are born under the sign of Aquarius than at any other time of the year. Not all great men are good men; some Aquarians have been among the greatest roughnecks known to history; but great they unquestionably are and their influence is widespread. Aquarius is represented as a Water Carrier, a man bearing on his shoulder an enormous pot of water, from which flows a mighty stream to refresh and replenish the earth.

Refreshment and replenishment would be welcome, would they not? Shall we, at last, learn how to feed our fiercely increasing population, and may we perhaps learn to do it by usefully employing our vast wastes of water? Might we even give up the obscene madness of treating our waterways as sewers? I cannot say, for I am neither alchemist nor astrologer, and I have a well-grounded horror of prophets. Refreshment and replenishment, in an era of Titans and mighty ones? Does it sound attractive? If I wanted to be gloomy—and I don't, because this is a great day for you and I would not for the world depress you—I would suggest that the Age of Aquarius was unlikely to be an age of democracy, for if there is one thing democracy can't stand it is Titans and mighty ones. It can barely be induced to put up with its great men. But perhaps you have not been taught history, as was fashionable in my youth, as though modern democracy was the ultimate human blessing.

Sometimes I wonder if this age of Titans and mighty ones will be achieved by methods man has not scrupled to apply to domestic animals, but has so far balked at applying to himself. I mean selective breeding. Will only the best be permitted to breed, in order to improve mankind? It would be very Aquarian to attempt that. I wonder what would come of it? When I consider what the majority of people think of as a superior man I am filled with misgiving.

That reminds me that today is a centennial: the centennial of a really superior man. On June 6, 1875, Thomas Mann was born. You know his writings? Of course you do. A great man, unquestionably. But if Aquarian science and Aquarian social planning made it possible to have 200 Thomas Manns at once, would the world be benefited to the power of 200? The question is beyond me. And even if I live to be a very old person, I shan't know the answer. But I have my dark surmises.

There is no time to pursue this subject further. You can read up on the sign of Aquarius yourself, if you want to know more. Not, I hasten to add, in one of those trashy little books about astrology that are sold in airports and body-rub parlours. No, no: you must get a proper treatise on astrology out of your university library—one of those venerable volumes written on parchment, in Latin and Greek, and studded with dark nuggets of Hebrew. As you read—and that sort of reading cannot be rushed—I think you will find much that is refreshing and replenishing. The future is not all black, and the desperate, agonized appraisals of the world's condition that we have foisted upon us so often at present are conceived and uttered in the dark of the moon. Wait for the new moon, and she will be as beautiful, as hopeful, and as serenely ready to grant the heartfelt wishes of decent people as she has always been.

But—the new moon of the Age of Aquarius, you cry—I shall be nearing fifty, and sinking fast into senility!

Don't you believe it. You will have learned to live. You will have shed many follies and you will have found out many things of which you do not even dream, now. Have courage. Pluck whatever is hopeful out of the strange events that lie before us all. Have courage. For although alchemists and astrologers were agreed that the destiny of man did not lie wholly in his own hands, they were all assured of one thing: fortune is not immutable, and fortune favours the bold. *Volentem ducit; nolentem trahit*, they said. Courage leads on, but fear betrays. They knew what they were talking about, those almost forgotten old men. So: have courage.

The Deadliest
of the Sins

QUEEN'S UNIVERSITY, *in Kingston, put its mark on me in two inexpungeable ways; first, by its kindness in taking me in when I had no real right to expect it, and second, by strong moral doctrine that was implicit in all its teaching. To have attended Queen's during the Depression of the thirties was to know that life was stern in its exactions, and austere in its rewards. As the recipient of an honorary degree in 1962, it would ill become me to be frivolous, even though cheerfulness would keep breaking in. So I talked about one of the Deadly Sins—the deadliest, indeed, for it is such a slow and subtle killer.*

IT IS WITH A FEELING of very special pride that I stand here at this moment, for I have just received my first degree from Queen's University. Queen's, for the second time in my life, has shown extraordinary kindness toward me. Many years ago it looked as though I should never go to a university, because I had made a miserable hash of my Matriculation examinations. I had failed—not by a hair's breadth, but utterly, abysmally, and catastrophically—in both algebra and geometry. I can easily recall the exact mark I made on both those papers. It was zero. There was no question of having another try. I had been getting zero in mathematics for a full three years. I exhibited in an awe-inspiring degree that quality which theologians call 'invincible ignorance'.

I am now able to speak of this with calm, but at that time I was terribly depressed by my failure. It was not unexpected; indeed, I had foreseen it for months. Nevertheless, I was very miserable, because in those days it was necessary to pass in twelve papers to get into a university, and I wanted to go to a university very much. It seemed to me that if I could not go to a university I should undoubtedly drift into some despised employment, take to drink, and die by my own hand within a few years. My failure was abject, my condition was wretched, and the midnight sky of my prospects showed not a single star.

It was then that Queen's University took pity on me, and I recall my sense of relief and gratitude when Dr. W. E. McNeill, who was the vice-principal at that time, suggested that I might attend lectures and write examinations as something mysterious called a Special Student. I could not hope for a BA but I could learn what other BA students learned. So I passed three busy years here; I even became something called a Tutor. A Tutor is to a professor what the boy who cleans his brushes is to a painter. And at the end of my three years I had scraped together enough academic respectability to get me into another university which did not set great store by mathematics. It lay, I may tell you, beyond the shores of Canada, where mathematical enthusiasm burned with a kind of hellfire for several years afterward.

Queen's came to my rescue when my future was dark and forbidding, and treated me with royal generosity. And now Queen's has done so again. If ever a university showed itself a bounteous mother to a poor varmint, Queen's was so to me, and I can only say that I shall ever be grateful. In the words of the Presbyterian hymn, I stand before you —

Pavilioned in splendour
And girded with praise

—but I tell you most sincerely that I am the humblest man within these walls.

Allusion has been made to a university called Waverley of which I have written in some trivial and jejune productions of mine; certainly I have made merry at the expense of a university of that name. Nobody has ever successfully identified it with Queen's. Indeed, nobody who really knows Queen's could believe that the two were the same. Where does the resemblance lie? The whole suggestion is distasteful to people of refined feeling. Let us dismiss it.

What shall we talk about, you and I, who are getting our first degrees from Queen's today? The problem is a little easier than is usually the case, because we are both going into new jobs. I have been an author for many years, and I intend to go on being one. But being an author isn't a job—it is a state of mind; also, it is not a gainful occupation except in a rather restricted sense. I have been earning my living as a journalist for twenty years, and now I am giving up that sort of work to take a different sort of job in a university. I shall be very green at it, and I expect I shall do a lot of things the wrong way. Perhaps I shall be a failure, but I have failed at several things already, and somehow I have lived through it. Failure at a specific task is always disagreeable and sometimes it is humiliating. But there is only one kind of failure that really breaks the spirit, and that is failure in the art of life itself. That is the failure that one does well to fear.

What is it like, this failure in the art of life? It is the failure which manifests itself in a loss of interest in really important things. It does not come suddenly; there is nothing dramatic about it, and thus it works with a dreadful advantage; it creeps upon us, and once it has us in its grip, it is hard for us to recognize what ails us.

It is not for nothing that this failure was reckoned by medieval theologians as one of the Seven Deadly Sins. I suppose you know what they were. Wrath, Gluttony, Envy, Avarice, and Lechery are not very hard to recognize and are perilously easy to justify, by one means or another. Pride is an extremely subtle sin because it is so clever at disguising itself as something else, and those astute men St. Ambrose and St. Augustine thought it the most dangerous of all the sins. But it is the seventh which I think is particularly prevalent in our day; medieval theologians called it Sloth.

Sloth is not really a suitable name for it now, because the word has come to mean a sluggishness and inactivity which is chiefly physical. But the sloth the theologians meant, the sloth which can damn you in this world and perhaps in the next, is spiritual. There was a better name, a Latin name, for it; it was also called Accidie, and it meant intellectual and spiritual torpor, indifference, and lethargy.

To be guilty of Acedia it is not necessary to be physically sluggish at all. You can be as busy as a bee. You can fill your days with activity, bustling from meeting to meeting, sitting on committees, running from one party to another in a perfect whirlwind of movement. But if, meanwhile, your feelings and sensibilities are withering, if your relationships with people near to you are becoming more and more superficial, if you are losing touch even with yourself, it is Acedia which has claimed you for its own.

How can it be recognized? Anatole France said that the great danger of increasing age was that the feelings atrophied, and we mistook the sensation for the growth of wisdom. It is true that as one grows older, one's sense of proportion may become greater, and things which troubled us or wounded us deeply in our youth seem less significant. But that is a different thing from feeling nothing deeply, and leaping to the conclusion that therefore nothing is really very important. As one grows older, one learns how to spare oneself many kinds of unnecessary pain, but one is in great danger if one ceases to feel pain of any kind. If you cannot feel pain at some of the harsh circumstances of life, it is very likely that you have ceased to feel joy at some of the satisfactions and delights of life. When that happens, one lives at all times under a mental and spiritual cloud; it is always wet weather in the soul. That is Acedia, and it was called a Deadly Sin because it dimmed and discouraged the spirit, and at last killed it.

I am sure that all of you know some people who have yielded to Acedia. They are the dampers, the wet blankets of life. Unfortunately some of them have a great attraction for the young. Their chronic lack of enthusiasm looks so much like sophistication. They are often clever people, who are adept at putting a chilly finger on the weak spot in whatever attracts their friends. They seldom make mistakes, because they never put themselves in a position where they are not complete masters of the situation. They take a sly pleasure in the failure of others, and they are always ready to say 'I told you so'. They have made just one great—indeed monstrous—mistake: they have died to joy and pain, and thus to feeling.

The opposites of these people are not, of course, those who allow every enthusiasm to run away with them, whose hearts always rule their heads, who go a-whoring after everything that is new. They are, on the contrary, people who take pains to keep their common sense in repair, and who keep their intelligence bright, but who also make daily efforts to meet experience with a fresh vision, and to give to everything that comes their way the measure of feeling, of emotion, of charity and understanding—yes, and also of pain—that it needs in order to understand it.

Because you are university people, I assume that you are people in whom mind is more prominent and better trained than is feeling. If you had not had some intellectual bias—even of quite a mild sort—it is unlikely that you would be here today to receive a degree. Therefore you must take special care that, in the years ahead of you, feeling is not neglected.

The temptation to neglect feeling is strong. You see—I say this knowing that it is blasphemy within university walls—it is really very much easier to think sensibly than it is to feel sensibly. We all know what messes people get into when they feel too much and think too little; but those people do not compel my pity so much as the hundreds of thousands whose lives are cast in a mould of midget tragedy because they think a good deal, in a strangulated, ill-nourished fashion, but hardly feel at all. These are the victims of Acedia.

Therefore I charge you, whether you are struggling under the burden of a mighty intellect, or perhaps just shuffling along with a pretty well-trained mediocre brain, to take pains not to lose your capacity to feel.

How is it to be done? I have some practical advice for you in this struggle, which is one of the great battles of life. Take some time every day—*every* day—to examine what you have been doing in the light of feeling, rather than of intelligence. It may be before you fall asleep at night; it may be while you are walking to your work; it may be at any time when you can withdraw your attention from external matters: that is the time to ask yourself—What do I really feel about all this? Not, what should I feel about it, what does the world expect me to feel, but what do I truly feel about it? You must be honest with yourself, because self-deception is one of the commonest roads to Acedia.

Now it may happen that you will find that you are committed to some course of action which you do not like—which you may positively hate. And yet, for good reasons, it may be necessary to continue with it. We all have to do things we detest, at one time or another, because we are not free to consult our own wishes only. But if you know the truth, you are protected from Acedia.

Nor is it only the detestable things that should be carefully examined. You must look clearly at the things which make your life happy and enviable, and you must give yourself up to a grateful contemplation of them. Never take such things for granted. I have seen many a promising marriage shrivel and dry up because one or both of the parties to it assumed that happiness was something that came by right, and could never be diminished. Consciously summoning up, and consciously enjoying, the good things that life brings us is a way of preserving them. It is not in their nature to last forever; they will change, and if you cherish them gratefully, the change is much more likely to be a change for the better than if you accept them as gifts which a grateful providence has showered upon you as a recognition of your magnanimity in condescending to inhabit the earth.

I have never been able to make up my mind which it is that people fear to feel most—pain or joy. Life will bring you both. You will not be able to escape the pain completely, though Acedia will dull it a little. But unfortunately it lies in your power to reject the joy utterly. Because we are afraid that great exultation may betray us into some actions, some words, which may make us look a little foolish to people who are not sharing our experience, we very often stifle our moments of joy, thinking that we shall give them their outlet later. But alas, after a few years of that kind of thing, joy ceases to visit us. I seem to be quoting theologians this afternoon. There is an old saying of medieval teachers which I recommend to your special notice:

Time Jesum transeuntem et non revertentem.

I shall translate it thus: 'Dread the passing of Jesus, for He does not return.' And thus it is with all great revelations, be they religious or not. Seize them, embrace them, let them engulf you, draw from them the uttermost of what they have to give, for if you rebuff them, they will not come again. We live in a world where too many people are pitifully afraid of joy. Because I wish you well, I beg you not to add yourself to their number.

Do not put off the moment of decision. Begin now. This is your hour. You are shortly to receive one of the great distinctions of your lifetime. Don't worry about looking dignified; don't be afraid that your pleasure may betray you into some lapse from that nullity of demeanour which we so pathetically accept as a substitute for true dignity. Don't accept your BA as if it were one more padlock on the inmost chamber of your heart. Education, if it is real and not a sham, is a releasing, not an imprisoning, thing. If you wish it to be so, the achievement of your degree is a step toward a new freedom. What is the word in your heart as you accept your diploma? Is it No—or is it Yes?

Preaching
Selfishness

GIVING GOOD ADVICE *to those whose profession is—at least in part—that of giving good advice to others is more than a duty; it is a pleasure. Furthermore, it is deeply satisfactory to preach selfishness to those who are engaged in one aspect of unselfishness. This was a talk to the Ontario Welfare Council, given in 1966.*

FOR SOME YEARS PAST, whenever I have found myself on my feet, as I do now, about to make a speech, I have been troubled by two questions: Why have they asked me to talk to them? and Why did I say I would?

In the present case, I think that you have asked me to talk to you because, after two and a half days of listening to speakers who are in some ways experts in your profession, you want to hear the voice of inexperience. I said I would provide it because I am afraid of your Chairman, whose word, among her friends, is law.

The voice of inexperience is something I am richly qualified to exemplify on such an occasion as this. I know nothing about Welfare. I have not been the recipient of public Welfare since, when I was eight years old, a School Nurse discovered that I was underweight and put me on a roster of children who were to be provided with free milk by the School Trustees. This milk was delivered every morning at 9:15 in a tin pail, by the brother-in-law of the Chairman of the Trustees, who happened to be a dairyman. It stood on the school steps in the sun until eleven o'clock, by which time it was warmer than milk is usually served, and as the brother-in-law of the Chairman of the Trustees was a thrifty man, it was often milk which he had saved for some days. Each young recipient of this milk brought his own glass, and as the school had no running water—it was in the country—they could not be washed. I was, I suppose, a pernickety child—you all know the type— and sour milk out of a dirty glass did not appeal to me. I acquired a distaste for milk, and there was a sharp exchange between my parents and the School Nurse, which led to my being taken off the milk roster. The School Nurse regarded me forever after as an example of Black Ingratitude.

In my university days I became involved with Welfare again; this time I was on the giving end of the deal. I was persuaded to lend a hand at a club for underprivileged boys, in which my university was interested, and I did. But not for long. The underprivileged boys and I had no community of interest. All the things they wanted to do they could do much better than I: they did not want to do anything that I wanted to do, because they thought it foolish. They would not tell me what it was like to be in Reform School—which was what I wanted to know. I refused to tell them about the sexual habits of upper-class women—which was what they wanted to know, and a subject on which I was pitifully ill-informed. It was a deadlock, and the underprivileged boys and I parted with mutual ill-will.

This is my complete career in Welfare, and you can see it is ludicrously inadequate. Even now, living in the heart of the university, I do not seem to encounter anything that would be of professional interest to you. I do not know a single student who takes dope, though I meet a great many students and know some of them well. I do not know a single faculty member who is an alcoholic; on a professor's salary large-scale vice is out of the question. Of course it is true that academic salaries are constantly mounting, but so, unfortunately, is the price of liquor. A professor who wants to be an alcoholic is in pursuit of a perpetually receding goal. The Government of

Ontario must realize that if it wants drunken professors, it must stop pricing drunkenness out of the professorial market. But I have not come here to talk economics.

What is there, then, that I can say to you that will make any sort of sense? I have thought about the question carefully, and I have decided that the only useful thing I can do is preach at you.

I want to warn you about the dangers of your profession. It doesn't matter that I know nothing about your profession, for what I am going to say applies to all professions. The danger of a busy professional life is that it will eat you up. The more thoroughly and committedly you become a professional person, the greater is the danger that you will cease to be a private person. That is where the danger lies. One of the serious troubles with our modern world is that far too many people have become so identified with their public life and their public role that they have lost sight of the private person that they must also be. The public figure is a giant: the private person is a dwarf.

Is this serious? Am I not misunderstanding the devotion to duty and the self-denying attitude which makes so many worthy people cut down on the time and energy they give to their private life, so that they may more vigorously serve mankind? No, I am not misunderstanding it at all. I have seen this process at work in so many cases that I think I know what I am talking about.

We are all familiar with the obvious examples of the kind of unbalance I am talking about—the physician whose health is neglected until he has a heart attack; the lawyer who dies without a will, after a lifetime of drawing wills for others; the clergyman whose home life is bleak because he has given all his love and concern to his flock; the public benefactor who cannot see that his children need some money they can call their own—we know these. But do we ever look for the kind of unbalance our own public life may create? Do we ever seriously examine ourselves?

People used to do so. They kept diaries in which they examined their consciences, tried to find out what was wrong with them, and resolved to do better. Indeed, people still keep such diaries; some of you will be familiar with the diary of Dag

Hammarskjöld, which is principally an examination of conscience of the kind I am talking about.

But then, people used to be religious in a way they are not now. As religion becomes more and more a thing of the past, I find that people who are not concerned with it believe some very strange and foolish things about it. They attribute to religious people beliefs which are absurd—beliefs which nobody of strong intelligence could ever have accepted. Among students I find many—possibly a majority—who regard religion as a sort of feeble-mindedness which mankind has almost outgrown.

Of course there were many religious people who were not much better than feeble-minded, just as there are nowadays lots of rationalists and future-planners who are not much better than feeble-minded; the intellectually poor we have always with us. But religion also engaged the lifelong attention of men and women of the highest intellectual quality—not only saints but philosophers, historians, poets, and warriors who found in it a pattern for life, a form into which they could put life, an order which was not imposed upon life but which arose from it. I do not say that only religion can do this; but I think something should give form, purpose, and—if you like—style to our lives.

In talking thus about religion I have not wandered from my subject, which is the danger of professionalism. I am trying to make clear that unless we have something that continually warns us against the pitfalls of allowing the external and public life to devour and diminish the inner and private life, we are in danger of becoming lop-sided. We become professional figures, rather than real people who serve the world and ourselves by the possession of particular sorts of skill and knowledge.

You are professionally engaged in Welfare. I can tell from the program of your conference that you offer the world a great variety of skills, undoubtedly supported by expert knowledge. But what else do you offer? What is the basic thing, and potentially the best thing, you offer? Is it not yourself?

What is yourself? Is it a neglected mammal you wash and feed and endure until you can put on its professional personality, and transform it into something rather like a human being? Is it some unfortunate man or woman who gets on badly with his immediate family, and has no interests, no recreations, and no source of spiritual and intellectual refreshment apart from his work? Is yourself an unlovable dullard? If so, not all the professional skill and information in the world can make you seriously and growingly useful and helpful to the people you encounter in your professional life.

This is an age of specialization, you may tell me. Yes; that is one of the things that is wrong with it. We meet specialists, not people. We meet people who know all the answers, except the answer to the most important of all questions: Who am I? If you want to be a specialist, nobody can stop you, but don't be surprised when you find that specialization has limits, and you reach them long before you die. Don't be surprised if you find that nobody wants you except in your professional capacity. Don't be surprised if you see, some day, on the face of a fellow-creature, the unmistakable evidence that he finds you a bore and a fool. That will be the day when you will do one of two things: either you will decide that the rest of mankind is stupid, or you will try to find the road back to humanity. The latter is the more difficult course.

I have said all of this before, to other groups of people. Sometimes they shrug it off; 'He is preaching Selfishness,' they say. That is true. I am teaching an intelligent regard for the preservation and nourishment of the Self—not the professional self, but the human being who lurks in all of us, and whom we so often neglect and ill-use. If we pay any attention to this human being—this Self—at all, it is usually to scold the poor thing for not being more than it is—for not being saintly, or valorous, or untiring. We never seem to take time to feed it, clothe it, encourage it, love it, and forgive it.

I thought I would say this to you today because you are professionally engaged in helping and advising people who are less fortunate than yourselves. You get them out of messes; you try to improve their relation to the rest of mankind. Have you ever done the same thing for yourself?

Where do you get the wisdom you disperse? Out of books and pamphlets? How do you know what will be good for somebody who is in trouble? Is there some plan that informs you? What is your goal, and what is your reward, and what is the wellspring of your energy? Is it honourable retirement, perhaps with an illuminated address? I tell you that unless you bring a well-developed, strong, resilient personal Self to your work, you are nothing. You are working for mankind, are you? Well, the best thing you can do for mankind is to devote your best energies to making the best possible job of yourself; then you will have something to give mankind that will really rouse its attention.

I said that I was going to offer you an impertinent word about personal Welfare and that is what I have done. It is impertinent because nobody is supposed to talk to strangers about the state of their souls, and that is what I have been doing. You don't have to pay any attention, but if you don't—allow me the prophet's privilege of being not merely personal, but rude—if you don't, you will be dead, dead in every important way, many a weary year before you are buried.

How to Design a
Haunted House

IF ONE MAKES A LOT OF SPEECHES *one is sure to be seized at some point by the desire to stop posturing as an authority, and to borrow the motley of the clown. I yielded to this impulse when the Ontario Association of Architects asked me to speak in 1960. All artists like jokes about their work, but many people forget that architects are artists, and treat them rather as if they were monumental masons—dealers in heavy, inde-structible wares of awesome solemnity. From their reception I knew that my speech was a rest for the architects and it was also a rest for me. Of course one should not attempt too often to be funny in public, and one should certainly never strive to be one's funniest, because in such circumstances the psychological sanction known as the Law of Reversed Effort comes into play, and the funnyman is left diminished and covered with shame.*

YOU ARE KIND INDEED to ask me to be with you on this occasion, and I appreciate the honour you do me. You have completed three days of addresses, of boards, of panels, and yet here you are—only slightly tranquillized—to subject your-selves to yet another speech. I am not unaware that some of you, at any rate, expect me to make an *amusing* speech, and I truly wish that I could assure you that I am about to do so. But it is not in mortals to command success—especially funny success. Furthermore I have all my life suffered from the fact that I am a deeply—I might almost say a neurotically—impressionable person, and for the past month or so the thought of the professional eminence and personal distinction of this audience has weighed so heavily upon me that I now feel that it would be impertinent to offer you anything less than the most profound and solemn reflections of which I am capable. Further, as *you* so well know, every man cherishes in his heart the belief that, if fate had been kinder, he would himself have been a very great architect. So, if I should chance, however fleetingly, to be amusing, I assure you that it is entirely inadvertent, and has only happened because I can't help it, and I apologize for it in advance.

My subject, as you know, is 'Architecture, What Else...?' Who would pass up the chance to talk to a captive audience of architects about their own profession? To this topic, after some thought, I added the rider, 'Literature, of Course' because I lost courage and thought I might not be able to talk long enough about architecture to fill up the necessary time.

You are, I hope, breathless with excitement, wondering how I can possibly bring these two great arts together in a single after-dinner speech. It has been easier than you might suppose. I am going to talk for a little while about *the Drama and the Novel, and the influence of architecture on both.* And, as plays and novels are really distillments of life itself, I shall inevitably talk about the influence of architecture on life.

Of course I am going to find fault. You know that without telling. Nobody speaks to an architect except to find fault. It is an occupational hazard you share with newspaper editors.

Let us begin with the Drama. You people have just about killed it because of the revolution you have brought about in theatre design. There was a happy age when we had wonderful playhouses, with terrible scenery: now you have given us terrible playhouses with wonderful scenery.

When people went to the theatre in the eighteenth and early nineteenth centuries, they bought an uplifting sense of personal splendour for the price of admission. Yesterday you listened to a discussion of 'The New Sensualism'; those old theatres were packed to the doors with the Old Sensualism. To the doors? Yes, and outside the doors, as well. The playhouses looked like temples, and the audience approached them in a spirit they brought to no other building. Indoors, the playhouses were modelled on palaces, and every playgoer became a nobleman, or at least an associate of noblemen, when he took his seat. Many of those old buildings are still in existence in Canada, because even the most malignant and bloody-minded City Council cannot pull them all down at once, and when we visit them we are immediately impressed with their *remarkable sensuous plasticity of surface.* (You didn't know I could talk Architectese, did you? I have always been a good linguist and can pick up a smattering of any language, quite quickly.) In those old theatres there is ornament everywhere. In the meanest of them there is a frieze, or perhaps a statuary group, of the Nine Muses, and Apollo is usually somewhere to be found. There is nothing puts an audience in the right mood for a trivial farce about adultery so quickly as a good preliminary stare at the Nine Muses.

But it would be quite wrong to suppose that the baroque opulence of the old theatres meant that they were designed without taste. They were not, as foolish people suppose, all tawdry gold and garnet plush. There is a newly decorated theatre in New York—the Billy Rose—which has been refurbished on that principle, and it is a horror. I don't ask for barbaric colour, but especially in a climate like ours, colour, inside and out, is of the uttermost importance. The theatres I speak of were not garish or vulgar. No, those old theatre interiors were decorated in the most elegant combinations of fawn, brown, and gold, and in many of them a subtle use was made of a colour which modern decorators seem to shy away from—a wonderful olive green. Everywhere you saw combinations of richness and elegance of which the secret seems to be lost, for of late years there has been a widespread notion that the secret of elegance is austerity. Of course, in our saner moments we all know that the secret of elegance is taste. Austerity is what happens when people dare not trust their taste.

If you doubt what I say, visit the best remaining examples of theatre I speak of. Go to that beauty at Drottningholm, in Sweden. Go to the Old Vic, in London, or the Theatre Royal at Bristol. In this latter playhouse, even in the footmen's gallery, the elegance and excitement of the building is palpable, and I say, quite seriously, that it is easier to enjoy a play in such a theatre than it is in the modern theatres I shall speak of in a moment. The reason is that the building was designed with enjoyment—public pleasure—foremost in the architect's mind.

One of the charms of these theatres, which cannot be recaptured because of the change in our social structure, is the comfort and convenience of the boxes. People sat in boxes for privacy—and of course we all know that to desire privacy today is to show oneself unfriendly, and probably fascistic. But in those boxes one could see without having to be seen; the chairs were movable, which is a great comfort, because democracy has not yet reached the point where we are all born of one size; it was possible to flirt in them, which was a great addition to the entertainment, and if you had no taste for flirting, there was nothing to prevent you from taking a servant with a picnic basket, and having a light meal as you watched the play. Show me the theatre today when you can flirt and eat, either consecutively or at once!

Don't let us talk about the movies. I know what goes on there, and I don't think it can be described as either eating or flirting—unless you use those terms very loosely.

These were exquisite playhouses, designed to flatter and accommodate the audience in the greatest possible comfort. But on the stage—! The scenic art was in its infancy—and a very peevish, rickety infancy, too. The scenery showed rooms with no windows, and frequently with no doors. When people wanted to enter or leave, they walked through open wings at the sides of the scene—apparently right through the wall. The royal palace and the swineherd's hut were both of precisely the same size. The effect of this scenic poverty on playwrights is of course familiar to you all; they couldn't depend on really handsome scenery, so they had to fall back on substitutes—like poetry. It was out of the question for them to write a play which depended on any circumstance of architecture. One of the great revolutionary plays of our time was *A*

Doll's House, written by Ibsen in 1879; the climax of the action comes when the oppressed wife, Nora, leaves her husband's house and *slams the door*. With that play, Ibsen brought architecture and modern scenic design into the theatre: if anybody could have found a door on a stage before that time, and had been so foolhardy as to slam it, everything behind the proscenium would have fallen down.

When Nora slammed the door, the modern theatre was born. And what a house you have provided for it! Where's the sensuous plasticity now? Where's the stimulating visual sensuous delight you hypocrites were talking about yesterday? Do you see it in our modern playhouses? You were in the O'Keefe Centre earlier today for what your program calls, with admirable restraint, a 'pre-lunch aperitif'. I was not with you, and I am curious about your experiences. Did you happen to notice Apollo anywhere? How many Muses were there after you had finished your aperitif—nine, or thirteen? I don't know. I wasn't there. I'm only asking for information.

I know nothing about the O'Keefe Centre, but I have been in a lot of other new theatre buildings in Canada. I call them that, because I was in them on theatre business, but they were really high schools or hockey arenas, or multi-purpose auditoriums which had, clinging about them, the fetid stench of secondary education and economical community planning. They were not temples. They were not dedicated to any of the gods, and they certainly had nothing to do with any of the rowdy, jolly demigods, like Folly or Pleasure. Maybe they had Stereo-Structural Sensualism; there seemed to be an awful lot of naked steel showing in some of them. I am so old-fashioned that it still makes me ashamed when I can see what holds a building up. It is honest, I know, but where is its charm? Such painfully honest architecture might perhaps be called the New Immodesty.

But on the stage of these places! What elegance of design! What breathtaking splendour! And what practicality! Windows that open and shut at the touch of a finger; doors that never stick; taps that squirt water without fail—all the things, in fact, that you can't get in your new $170,000 house. There is always, and necessarily, an air of fantasy, of a splendour beyond ordinary life, about the stage. Nowadays it reveals itself, strange to relate, in the perfection of the carpentry and plumbing. And as for design—those of you who saw the Comédie Française when it last came to Toronto will remember the setting for *Le Bourgeois Gentilhomme*, which was the work of Susanne Lalique. Which of us would not have a house like that, if it could be built anywhere except in a theatre?

You will notice that I have said nothing about accommodation for the actors. Of course it is always terrible, but even here there has been a change. In the old theatres they had smelly kennels in which to change their clothes. But nowadays, after the School Board has cut the estimates and changed the plans, they have nothing at all. Have you ever tried to transform yourself into a great character of drama in a schoolroom? The ghosts of dead mathematics teachers clutch at your costume and smear your make-up. Actors of an earlier day dressed in bad conditions too, even in barns. But the barns were unmistakably associated with Life; those schoolroom dressing accommodations speak of education, of repression, of being kept in after four, and their air vents whisper of lingering and chalky death. Humour is put to silence, Passion is rebuked, and Imagination is made to dance in chains.

Gentlemen, I appeal to you with all the force of which I am capable: give us back a theatre which it is a pleasure to be in! Give us colour, give us Muses, give us Joy! Oh, I know how much trouble you take to get the right seats, but you are caressing us at the wrong end. The *spirit* also demands its satisfactions, and man cannot live by foam rubber alone. Give us a whisper of grandeur, of excitement. Without it the theatre perishes. And that means that you must feel something of the spirit of the theatre in your own breasts. When you design an auditorium or a theatre, I beg you to banish the puritanism which seems to be the fashion in modern architecture, and invoke a vastly more appropriate spirit. I mean the spirit of one of the great ornaments of your profession, Sir John Vanbrugh.

Now let us turn to Architecture and the Novel. Modern novelists have turned their backs on architecture—except in detective stories, where it is absolutely essential to prove that nobody could have entered the room where the beautiful blonde was murdered. But the great novelists of the past leaned very heavily on architectural devices, usually of a kind not found in modern building. You know the kind of thing I mean. In countless novels written fifty years ago the heroine, having discovered that her husband was deceiving her with the beautiful brunette, crept away to the *nursery* to weep over her beloved children.

How is she expected to do that in a house which hasn't any nursery? No woman of ordinary sensibility can creep away to weep in the *rumpus-room*. The thing is a psychological absurdity, and by making it so you have contributed to the break-up of the modern home.

And the *study*—how many modern houses have a study? Yet every man needs a study. Not to study in, of course, but to retire to when the pressure of domestic life is too great. He summons the other members of the family to meet him there. 'George, I should like to see you in my study,' he says to his son, when he wants to tell him to stop spending so much money. 'Mary, come to my study,' he says when he wants to tell his daughter to break off her affair with that beatnik she has been meeting on the sly. 'My dear, will you come into my study,' he says, when he wants to tell his wife that he knows what she has been up to with that handsome Mexican dentist. But most of all he needs his study to *sulk* in. Every man must have a private sulking-place, and as his wife always wants the bedroom for that purpose, he must have a study, or bottle up his sulks. And if he bottles his sulks, it won't be long before he has to be taken away in a strait-jacket. How can he sulk in the living-area, which his children are using as the play-area, while his wife is right beside him in the kitchen-area, without so much as a screen to divide them? By forgetting the study you have struck an underhand blow at the mental health of the nation.

His wife, as I have said, sulks in the bedroom. I wish I could call it a *boudoir* but those wretched little boxes in modern houses cannot rise to the dignity of such a term. You know what a boudoir is. It's a bedroom that you can pace in. Consider this passage, from a very fine novel, written not quite a century ago by Mrs. Henry Wood:

Scarce able to see through the mist of tears that clouded her violet eyes, Lady Maude sought her boudoir. There, among the treasures she had brought from her childhood home, she paced the floor, lost in sombre reverie. Had I but known, she mused as she walked toward the window, had I but known when I gave my trust, my hand—yea, all that a woman holds in store of love and tenderness—to Cyril, that a day might come when I should wish,nay,implore Almighty God,for the power to recall every gift, I should have ended my life rather than yield to his suit. Yes, all of this, these broad acres, this stately mansion, yes, and—O God, be merciful!—even my children, I should have wished undone....She turned at the window and continued her weary pacing.

Do you see what I am getting at? She said all of that while making one trip from the door to the window. The book tells us that Lady Maude was tall—say five foot eight—and therefore one of her paces might be estimated at twenty-five inches. Everybody knows that when you are pacing and regretting at the same time, you take a step to every word. Therefore Lady Maude took 85 paces of 25 inches apiece, which is 2,125 inches or 177 feet from door to window. Assuming that the room was a double cube, and that she was walking the long way of it, that means that the dimensions of her boudoir were 177 by 88, giving her a floor space of 15,576 square feet. No wonder she was able to keep the treasures of her old home in it. If they had included a couple of racehorses she could have kept them in it, without serious inconvenience.

But the important point is that she was able to pace in her boudoir, and the novel has a happy ending. I put it to you, gentlemen, would it have had a happy ending if Lady Maude had been cooped up in one of the bedrooms of which the Canadian Council of Women have been complaining to Mr. John C. Parkin?

If we are to believe the evidence of literature, the houses in which people have lived greatly, and sinned nobly, were all big. Evidence in support of what I say crowds into the mind. What were the words of King Duncan as he greeted Lady Macbeth at the entry to Glamis?

> *This castle hath a pleasant seat. The air*
> *Nimbly and sweetly recommends itself*
> *Unto our gentle senses.*

However, that is getting into the realm of public health and town planning, and I won't press it.

However, I would like to urge upon you the convenience and charm of an amenity which was to be found in virtually every house described by Sir Walter Scott. I refer, of course, to the Secret Passage. Time and again in Scott's novels somebody reveals that a secret passage leads from the castle to the shepherd's hut, and as it inevitably led also from the shepherd's hut to the castle, it meant that both the shepherd and the lord of the manor had the good of it. It made life much simpler at all kinds of junctures when simplicity was needed. You could escape from the castle in a hurry, and you could also get into the castle unseen. In cases of murder or abduction this was invaluable. In ordinary domestic crises it meant that somebody could slip down to the hut and borrow a bottle of whisky if guests came unexpectedly. Still more often, it meant that the shepherd could sneak up to the castle and steal a bottle of whisky when he wanted one. It provided that element of surprise, of the unexpected, which modern domestic architecture so noticeably lacks.

How long is it since any of you included a Secret Passage in a new house? Of course I realize the difficulties you work under. Modern contractors don't know how to keep a secret. The union would certainly object to the old custom of cutting out the tongues of all the men who had worked on the job. The building inspector—they never have any imagination—would insist that it be equipped with electric light, drainage, and an air-changing system, because he would not realize that the essence of a secret passage is darkness, dampness, and a seepage of natural gas.

If you want to know what happens when somebody tries to build a secret passage today, just look at the mess on University Avenue at Bloor. The only secret is when it will be finished.

Yet another household convenience made familiar to us in historical novels is the *oubliette*. The works of Dumas are full of oubliettes. In its simplest terms, an oubliette is a very deep, dry well, or perhaps a disused privy, down which you can push people. Because the oubliette is deep and made of stone, they reach the bottom in a damaged condition, and there is no way out. A well-used oubliette can become rather objectionable, and ought to be located as far as possible from the boudoir. Among other things, the screams can be very trying to delicate nerves.

Please do not suppose that I am encouraging crime. The oubliette was not an instrument for settling family quarrels, or dismissing unwelcome guests. And—this is very important—no oubliette was ever built simply to be an oubliette. It became one when you threw really bad people—criminal, depraved people—into it. This circumstance, of course, has given rise to the proverbial saying that *you can't make an oubliette without breaking yeggs.*

I could continue in this strain for some time. There are countless amenities which every house needs, for literary uses, and which have been allowed to disappear from modern domestic design. The attic, for instance—invaluable for nostalgia; it is a proven psychological fact that you can't be nostalgic on the ground floor. And the cellar—admirable for murders, for knife-fights in the dark, for the walling-up of wives who have not worn well. Your objection, I know, is that a house equipped with all these handsome comforts would be rather large. True, but when the owners have finished with it, no ingenuity at all is needed to convert it into a first-class Funeral Home. The boudoir is of ample size for a chapel, you can garage the hearse in the Secret Passage, and the oubliette provides ample, cool accommodation for Unfinished Business.

I have spoken of Drama and Fiction as they relate to architecture, and I hope that I have reminded you of the fact that you, gentlemen, are the designers of the scenery against which we act out the drama of our personal lives. What our personal lives are you know only too well, and I really think that you must bear some measure of blame. If we are dull, who knows what a livelier setting might not do to improve our performances? If we lack splendour, is it because we live in circumstances where a single splendid gesture might knock the place down? Don't suppose that I blame you entirely. You are what we have made you, fully as much as we are what you have made us. But would it not be possible for some of us—a few of you architects, and a handful of us ordinary people—to conspire to bring a whisper of magnificence, a shade of lightheartedness, and a savour of drama into the settings of our daily lives? I think it would. Anyhow, I think we should try.

Three:
Jeux d'Esprit

Lines Written in Dejection After Seeing a Performance of 'Hair' on Epiphany, 1970

LIKE MOST WRITERS, *I produced some verse when I was young, but it was of such an unfashionable sort nobody wanted it. I liked strict forms, and rhymes, and showed what was considered an unpoetic tendency to be cheerful. Even now I write poetry on the sly, so to speak, when it seems to be the obvious form for what I have to say. Here is an example.*

AQUARIUS! AQUARIUS!' the hoarse young voices sang,
Heralding a new era in the world's horoscope
As Pisces wanes and the ambiguous sign rises.

So what, Aquarius, do *you* bring?
New Ice Age?
New Spring?
Anything for us
Born at the end of Pisces?
Any new virtue,
Or the sour stench of old vices?
(We haste to the theatre
As the Magi sought the Star,
Seeking an epiphany in HAIR:
Finding that most of the cast
Depressingly pronounce it HA'R.)

89

'A cold coming we had of it
Just the worst time of the year
For a journey, and such a journey;
The ways deep and the weather sharp,
The very dead of winter.'

        But we hoped for a dawning of youth
        In the fine old playhouse;
        Such renewal as the Magi found,
        Or Simeon, in the Temple.
        But alas, not a Babe, but babes were on view
        (Some, very recently, sucklings)
        And the whole possessed crew
        Shouting F U C K!
          (Had they, we wondered, known Love.)
        Shouting S H I T!
          (Whatever that word may have meant
          To those who seemed never to have heard that
          'Love has pitched his mansion
            in the place of excrement'.)

They offered us two great revelations:
First — THAT NAKEDNESS IS INNOCENCE.
        (There they stood, for us to see,
        With drooping breasts and pubic hair like
                      Highlanders' sporrans;
        Or else with narrow chests, shrivelled privates,
        And incipient varicose veins.
        Gothic was this nakedness, not Greek.)
Thus was innocence manifested nightly and twice on
        Wednesdays and Saturdays, for a figure not lower
        than the Equity minimum.

Second — THAT WAR IS A HORRIBLE BUSINESS.
        (Which we, who had been born into one war
        And worn through another,
        Already knew with the thoroughness of those
        Who have chewed and gagged down bitter herbs.)

These were their revelations.

Of course there were many false epiphanies;
The Magi made many fruitless journeys ere they died.

So, Aquarius, what else is new?

Animal U.

THIS WAS WRITTEN as a story for children, but several people assured me that children would find it difficult. I have a better opinion of children than that. They are, after all, adults in the making, and those who will have a sense of humour when they grow up have it when they are small. I wrote the story because when my wife and I and our daughters moved into Massey College in 1963, the building was full of animals that had lived on the land where the building now stood, and they were very hard to dismiss. It seemed almost as if they were determined to join the College community, and if they had done so, the consequence might well have been like this.

ONCE UPON A TIME in a great university, a new college was built. It was a beautiful building, with lots of studies and bedrooms, a library and a dining-hall, and a large garden.

The builders worked as hard as they could to finish it. 'The students will fill it as soon as autumn comes,' they said.

The builders did not know that it was full already. The college was built on a vacant lot, and as the walls went up and the rooms were finished, animals came down from the trees, and out of the sky, and up out of the earth, and took possession of the building. There were tribes of squirrels and chipmunks, mice, a skunk, two families of moles, a whole nation of rabbits, a fox, and a raccoon, not to speak of birds.

'How kind of these men to build us a college,' they said. 'It is really very unlike humans to understand our place in the university so well.'

'But the college is *not* for us,' said a large Hare. 'You have all made a terrible mistake. The college is for humans. I have been listening to the builders, and I know.'

All the other animals laughed cruelly. 'You think you know all about humans,' said they. 'We shall have to call you Human Hare.' And they laughed and rolled on the grass and sharpened their fingers at the Hare, who felt very badly, but did not change his mind.

'Waste no time on him,' said Richard Raccoon, who had taken charge of the big meeting of the animals in the College Library. 'This is a great moment in animal history. For the first time we have a university of our own. We must find a great name for it.'

'That's easy,' said a young Rabbit who was particularly clever because he ate the crocuses at the Law School every spring. 'Let's call it Animal University; it shortens down nicely to Animal U.'

He spoke so impressively that all the animals cheered without being sure why.

'Excellent!' said Richard Raccoon. 'And now we must choose our university staff. I do not think we could do better than to appoint Mr. Reynard Fox to the important position of President. Three cheers for President Fox!'

All the small animals began to cheer, because they were getting the habit. But the Hare interrupted.

'I am just an old grey Hare,' said he, 'but I am not a fool, and I warn you that this college is not for us.'

'Boo!' shouted all the small animals. 'Shut up, Human Hare! Hurrah for President Fox.'

'Thank you, thank you, my dear friends,' said Reynard Fox, waving his paw with easy grace. 'You may rely upon me to serve the interests of animal education with all my well-known artfulness. But I always say that a university president is no better than his teaching staff. Therefore it gives me the greatest pleasure to appoint all crows to the position of Full Professor. And as for my dear old friend Socrates Owl, I beg him to accept the position of Dean.'

Socrates Owl opened his beak, then closed it, as though his feelings were too much for him. He said nothing because he could think of nothing to say.

Poor Human Hare groaned, but nobody heeded him, because they were cheering.

'Let us not dilly-dally,' barked President Fox. 'Let us begin our university work at once.'

'One moment,' said Dean Owl, who had understood the expression on the face of his friend Richard Raccoon. 'We have forgotten the most important thing of all. Who is to be our Chancellor?'

'What's a Chancellor?' asked a little Fieldmouse, who did not mind appearing ignorant.

'A Chancellor is the highest official in any university,' said Dean Owl. 'The wisest, the best-loved, the most dignified, and'—he rolled a big eye at the Raccoon—'the biggest.'

'Richard Raccoon for Chancellor,' shouted President Fox, and seized the Raccoon by the paw. 'Our Chancellor!' he cried, waving encouragingly at the other animals who cheered wildly, because they were anxious to do the right thing.

'You make me feel very humble,' said Chancellor Raccoon. 'This is certainly the greatest day in animal history. My students—rabbits, skunks, moles, mice, all birds who are not black—let us hurry off at once and improve our minds!'

They did. The mice rushed to the kitchen and began research into all kinds of food, to see what tasted best. The rabbits set to work on a fine set of tunnels in the garden, to study earth science. The moles studied the college wiring, and sometimes got electricity in their teeth, and had to lie down for a while, till it went away. The squirrels and chipmunks rode up and down in the elevator that took things to the kitchen, studying engineering. The skunk spent hours every day studying garbage disposal. The rats worked very hard in the library, devouring books and sometimes spreading paste on the leaves with their tails, if the books seemed very dry.

The Professor Crows had a fine time, arguing all day, and laughing at jokes the student animals did not understand. President Fox sat in his office, worrying about money and eating chicken sandwiches. Dean Owl found a room with no light in it at all, and sat in it all day, sometimes sending for a fat mouse whose work was unsatisfactory. Such mice must have been expelled, because whenever anybody disappeared forever, the little animals whispered: 'He's been to the Dean!'

Happiest of all was Chancellor Raccoon. When the smaller animals had learned as much as they could hold, he held grand ceremonies in which he touched these animals on the shoulder saying, 'Hokus, pokus, skilamarokus' (which is animal Latin), 'Arise, BA' (which meant BETTER ANIMAL). Then the small animals went away to learn some more, and were very grateful to Animal U.

All this time poor Human Hare hung around the university, looking gloomy. Most of the animals sneered at him, but some of the nicer ones said, 'Cheer up! we forgive you for being wrong.'

Then one autumn day a lot of young people came into the College and moved books and suitcases and guitars into the lovely rooms. After them came some old men with even more books, and a lot of middle-aged men with brooms and lawn-mowers, who were very unkind to the students and professors of Animal U.

'It's an outrage,' shouted the animals, at a great meeting they held in the garden. 'It can't be ALLOWED!'

This was President Fox's greatest moment. 'It's no good saying something can't be ALLOWED when we have no way of stopping it,' said he. 'These young people have honoured us by coming to Animal U; it shows they know that animals are wiser than they are; they want to learn from us.'

'But what are we to do?' said Chancellor Raccoon.

'We do what any good university does,' said President Fox. 'We get advice from our greatest expert on Human Behaviour. Professor Human Hare, will you have the goodness to address the meeting?'

Human Hare, who had been standing nervously at the back of the crowd, was astonished at becoming a Professor so suddenly. But he drew himself to his full height, and spoke:

'It is simple,' said he. 'The Humans like to work by day; it is just as easy for us to work at night, and as a courtesy to them, that is what we shall do. Also, when human universities want to be specially nice to somebody they give him something called an LLD. As all you intelligent animals can see, those letters are simply a short form of aLLoweD, and they mean the person is aLLoweD to come to the university as much as ever he likes. We must give each of these humans an LLD from Animal U.'

So that very night, when all the young people were asleep, a splendid procession tiptoed through the College, led by Chancellor Raccoon in his black and silver gown, and President Fox in his red gown, and that very distinguished scholar in Human Behaviour, Professor Human Hare. Into each room they went, and after Professor Human Hare had assured Chancellor Raccoon that each sleeping young creature was really human (which he did by peeping under the blankets), the Chancellor touched him on the brow, saying, 'By my power as Chancellor I create you an LLD of Animal U. Hokus, pokus, skilamarokus! You are aLLoweD to stay here.'

When it was all over, the student animals danced around Human Hare in the moonlight, singing:

For he's a jolly good animal!
For he's a jolly good animal!
For he's a jolly good animal!
Which nobody can deny!

And Human Hare smiled gently, thinking how like human beings they were, to forgive him at last for being right.

The Cat that Went to Trinity: A College Ghost Story

Every christmas at Massey College we have a party called a Gaudy, which is what college parties have been called since the Middle Ages. We have music, and poetry, and of course food and drink, and since 1963, when the College was founded, I have written a Ghost Story, or a tale of mystery and imagination: a Christmas party without such a story is unthinkable, and I read it as part of the Gaudy. This is the tenth College Ghost Story, written for reading at Christmas, 1972.

Every autumn when I meet my new classes, I look them over to see if there are any pretty girls in them. This is not a custom peculiar to me: all professors do it. A pretty girl is something on which I can rest my eyes with pleasure while another student is reading a carefully researched but uninspiring paper.

This year, in my seminar on the Gothic Novel, there was an exceptionally pretty girl, whose name was Elizabeth Lavenza. I thought it a coincidence that this should also be the name of the heroine of one of the novels we were about to study—no less a work than Mary Shelley's celebrated romance *Frankenstein*. When I mentioned it to her she brushed it aside as of no significance.

97

'I was born in Geneva,' said she, 'where lots of people are called Lavenza.'

Nevertheless, it lingered in my mind, and I mentioned it to one of my colleagues, who is a celebrated literary critic.

'You have coincidence on the brain,' he said. 'Ever since you wrote that book—*Fourth Dimension* or whatever it was called—you've talked about nothing else. Forget it.'

I tried, but I couldn't forget it. It troubled me even more after I had met the new group of Junior Fellows in this College, for one of them was young Einstein, who was studying Medical Biophysics. He was a brilliant young man, who came to us with glowing recommendations; some mention was made of a great-uncle of his, an Albert Einstein, whose name meant nothing to me, though it appeared to have special significance in the scientific world. It was young Mr. Einstein's given names that roused an echo in my consciousness, for he was called Victor Frank.

For those among you who have not been reading Gothic Novels lately, I may explain that in Mrs. Shelley's book *Frankenstein, or The Modern Prometheus,* the hero's name is also Victor, and the girl he loved was Elizabeth Lavenza. This richness of coincidence might trouble a mind less disposed to such reflection than mine. I held my peace, for I had been cowed by what my friend the literary critic had said. But I was dogged by apprehension, for I know the disposition of the atmosphere of Massey College to constellate extraordinary elements. Thus, cowed and dogged, I kept my eyes open for what might happen.

It was no more than a matter of days when Fate added another figure to this coincidental pattern, and Fate's instrument was none other than my wife. It is our custom to entertain the men of the College to dinner, in small groups, and my wife invites a few girls to each of these occasions to lighten what might otherwise be a too exclusively academic atmosphere. The night that Frank Einstein appeared in our drawing-room he maintained his usual reserved—not to say morose— demeanour until Elizabeth Lavenza entered the room. Their meeting was, in one sense, a melodramatic cliché. But we must remember that things become clichés because they are of frequent occurrence, and powerful impact. Everything fell out as a thoroughly bad writer might describe it. Their eyes met across the room. His glance was electric; hers ecstatic. The rest of the company seemed to part before them as he moved to her side. He never left it all evening. She had eyes for no other. From time to time his eyes rose in ardour, while hers fell in modest transport. This rising and falling of eyes was so portentously and swooningly apparent that one or two of our senior guests felt positively unwell, as though aboard ship. My heart sank. My wife's, on the contrary, was uplifted. As I passed her during the serving of the meal I hissed, 'This is Fate.' 'There is no armour against Fate,' she hissed in return. It is a combination of words not easily hissed, but she hissed it.

We had an unusually fine autumn, as you will recall, and there was hardly a day that I did not see Frank and Elizabeth sitting on one of the benches in the quad, sometimes talking, but usually looking deep into each other's eyes, their foreheads touching. They did it so much that they both became slightly cross-eyed, and my dismay mounted. I determined if humanly possible to avert some disastrous outcome (for I assure you that my intuition and my knowledge of the curious atmosphere of this College both oppressed me with boding) and I did all that lay in my power. I heaped work on Elizabeth Lavenza; I demanded the ultimate from her in reading of the Gothic Novel, as a means both of keeping her from Frank, and of straightening her vision.

Alas, how puny are our best efforts to avert a foreordained event! One day I saw Frank in the quad, sitting on the bench alone, reading a book. Pretending nonchalance, I sat beside him. 'And what are you reading, Mr. Einstein?' I said in honeyed tones.

Taciturn as always, he held out the book for me to see. It was *Frankenstein*. 'Liz said I ought to read it,' he said.

'And what do you make if it?' said I, for I am always interested in the puny efforts of art to penetrate the thoroughly scientific mind. His answer astonished me.

'Not bad at all,' said he. 'The Medical Biophysics aspect of the plot is very old-fashioned, of course. I mean when the hero makes that synthetic human being out of scraps from slaughter-houses. We could do better than that now. A lot better,' he added, and I thought he seemed to be brooding on nameless possibilities. I decided to change the line of our conversation. I began to talk about the College, and some of the successes and failures we had met with in the past.

Among the failures I mentioned our inability to keep a College Cat. In the ten years of our existence we have had several cats here, but not one of them has remained with us. They all run away, and there is strong evidence that they all go to Trinity. I thought at one time that they must be Anglican cats, and they objected to our oecumenical chapel. I went to the length of getting a Persian cat, raised in the Zoroastrian faith, but it only lasted two days. There is a fine Persian rug in Trinity Chapel. Our most recent cat had been christened Episcopuss, in the hope that this thoroughly Anglican title would content it; furthermore, the Lionel Massey Fund provided money to treat the cat to a surgical operation which is generally thought to lift a cat's mind above purely sectarian considerations. But it, too, left us for Trinity. Rationalists in the College suggested that Trinity has more, and richer, garbage than we have, but I still believe our cats acted on religious impulse.

As I spoke of these things Frank Einstein became more animated than I had ever known him. 'I get it,' he said; 'you want a cat that has been specifically programmed for Massey. An oecumenical cat, highly intelligent so that it prefers graduates to undergraduates, and incapable of making messes in the Round Room. With a few hours of computer time it oughtn't to be too difficult.'

I looked into his eyes—though from a greater distance than was usual to Elizabeth Lavenza—and what I saw there caused a familiar shudder to convulse my entire being. It is the shudder I feel when I know, for a certainty, that Massey College is about to be the scene of yet another macabre event.

Nevertheless, in the pressure of examinations and lectures, I forgot my uneasiness, and might perhaps have dismissed the matter from my mind if two further interrelated circumstances—I dare not use the word coincidence in this case—had not aroused my fears again. One autumn morning, reading *The Globe and Mail*, my eye was caught by an item, almost lost at the bottom of a column, which bore the heading 'Outrage at Pound'; it appeared that two masked bandits, a man and a woman, had held up the keeper of the pound at gun-point, while seizing no less than twelve stray cats. Later that same day I saw Frank and Elizabeth coming through the College gate, carrying a large and heavy sack. From the sack dripped a substance which I recognized, with horror, as blood. I picked up a little of it on the tip of my finger; a hasty corpuscle count confirmed my suspicion that the blood was not human.

Night after night in the weeks that followed, I crept down to my study to look across the quad and see if a light was burning in Frank Einstein's room. Invariably it was so. And one morning, when I had wakened early and was standing on my balcony, apostrophizing the dawn, Elizabeth Lavenza stole past me from the College's main gate, her face marked, not by those lineaments of slaked desire so common among our visitors at such an hour, but by the pallor and fatigue of one well-nigh exhausted by intellectual work of the most demanding sort.

The following night I awoke from sleep at around two o'clock with a terrifying apprehension that something was happening in the College which I should investigate. Shouts, the sound of loud music, the riot of late revellers—these things do not particularly disturb me, but there is a quality of deep silence which I know to be the accompaniment of evil. Wearily and reluctantly I rose, wrapped myself in a heavy dressing-gown, and made my way into the quadrangle and there—yes, it was as I had feared—the eerie gleam from Frank Einstein's room was the only light to guide me. For there was a thick fog hanging over the University, and even the cruel light through the arrow-slits of the Robarts Library and the faery radiance from OISE were hidden.

Up to his room I climbed, and tapped on the door. It had not been locked, and my light knock caused it to swing open and there—never can I forget my shock and revulsion at what I saw!—there were Frank and Elizabeth crouched over a table upon which lay an ensanguined form. I burst upon them.

'What bloody feast is this?' I shouted. 'Monsters, fiends, cannibals, what do I behold?'

'Shhh,' said Elizabeth; 'Frank's busy.'

'I'm making your cat,' said Frank.

'Cat,' I shrieked, almost beside myself; 'that is no cat. It's as big as a donkey. What cat are you talking about?'

'The Massey College cat,' said Frank. 'And it is going to be the greatest cat you have ever seen.'

I shall not trouble you with a detailed report of the conversation that followed. What emerged was this: Frank, beneath the uncommunicative exterior of a scientist, had a kindly heart, and he had been touched by the unlucky history of Massey College and its cats. 'What you said was,' said he to me, 'that the College never seemed to get the right cat. To you, with your simple, emotional, literary approach to the problem, this was an insuperable difficulty: to my finely organized biophysical sensibility, it was simply a matter of discovering what kind of cat was wanted, and producing it. Not by the outmoded method of selective breeding, but by the direct creation of the Ideal College Cat, or ICC as I came to think of it. Do you remember that when you talked to me about it I was reading that crazy book Liz was studying with you, about the fellow who made a man? Do you remember what he said? "Whence did the principle of life proceed? It was a bold question, and one which has ever been considered as a mystery; yet with how many things are we upon the brink of becoming acquainted, if cowardice or carelessness did not restrain our enquiries." That was written in 1818. Since then the principle of life has become quite well known, but most scientists are afraid to work on the knowledge they have. You remember that the fellow in the book decided to make a man, but he found the work too fiddly if he made a man of ordinary size, so he decided to make a giant. Me too. A cat of ordinary size is a nuisance, so I decided to multiply the dimensions by twelve. And like the fellow in the book I got my materials and went to work. Here is your cat, about three-quarters finished.'

The fatal weakness, the tragic flaw, in my character is foolish good-nature, and that, combined with an uninformed but lively scientific curiosity, led me into what was, I now perceive, a terrible mistake. I was so interested in what Frank was doing that I allowed him to go ahead, and instead of sleeping at nights I crept up to his room, where Frank and Elizabeth allowed me, after I have given my promise not to interfere or touch anything, to sit in a corner and watch them. Those weeks were perhaps the most intensely lived that I have ever known. Beneath my eyes the ICC grew and took form. By day the carcass was kept in the freezer at Rochdale, where Elizabeth had a room; each night Frank warmed it up and set to work.

The ICC had many novel features which distinguished it from the ordinary domestic cat. Not only was it as big as twelve ordinary cats; it had twelve times the musculature. Frank said proudly that when it was finished it would be able to jump right over the College buildings. Another of its beauties was that it possessed a novel means of elimination. The trouble with all cats is that they seem to be housebroken, but in moments of stress or laziness they relapse into an intolerable bohemianism which creates problems for the cleaning staff. In a twelve-power cat this could be a serious defect. But Frank's cat was made with a small shovel on the end of its tail with which it could, once a week, remove its own ashes and deposit them behind the College in the parking-space occupied by *The Varsity*, where, it was assumed, they would never be noticed. I must hasten to add that the cat was made to sustain itself on a diet of waste-paper, of which we have plenty, and that what it produced in the manner I have described was not unlike confetti.

But the special beauty of the ICC was that it could talk. This, in the minds of Frank and Elizabeth, was its great feature as a College pet. Instead of mewing monotonously when stroked, it would be able to enter into conversation with the College men, and as we pride ourselves on being a community of scholars, it was to be provided with a class of conversation and a vocabulary infinitely superior to that of, for instance, a parrot.

This was Elizabeth's special care, and because she was by this time deep in my course on the Gothic Novel she decided, as a compliment to me, to so program the cat that it would speak in the language appropriate to that *genre* of literature. I was not so confident about this refinement as were Frank and Elizabeth, for I knew more about Gothic Novels than they, and have sometimes admitted to myself that they can be wordy. But as I have told you, I was a party to this great adventure only in the character of a spectator, and I was not to interfere. So I held my peace, hoping that the cat would, in the fulness of time, do the same.

At last the great night came, when the cat was to be invested with life. I sat in my corner, my eyes fixed upon the form which Frank was gradually melting out with Elizabeth's electric hair-dryer. It was a sight to strike awe into the boldest heart.

I never dared to make my doubts about the great experiment known to Frank and Elizabeth, but I may tell you that my misgivings were many and acute. I am a creature of my time in that I fully understand that persons of merely aesthetic bias and training, like myself, should be silent in the presence of men of science, who know best about everything. But it was plain to me that the ICC was hideous. Not only was it the size of twelve cats, but the skins of twelve cats had been made to serve as its outer envelope. Four of these cats had been black, four were white, and four were of a marmalade colour. Frank, who liked things to be orderly, had arranged them so that the cat was piebald in mathematically exact squares. Because no ordinary cat's eyes would fit into the huge skull the eyes of a goat had been obtained—I dared not ask how—and as everyone knows, a goat's eyes are flat and have an uncanny oblong pupil. The teeth had been secured at a bargain rate from a denturist, and as I looked at them I knew why dentists say that these people must be kept in check. The tail, with the shovel at the end of it, was disagreeably naked. Its whiskers were like knitting needles. Indeed, the whole appearance of the cat was monstrous and diabolical. In the most exact sense of the words, it was the damnedest thing you ever saw. But Frank had a mind above appearances and to Elizabeth, so beautiful herself, whatever Frank did was right.

The moment had arrived when this marvel of science was to be set going. I know that Frank was entirely scientific, but to my old-fashioned eye he looked like an alchemist as, with his dressing-gown floating around him, he began to read formulae out of a notebook, and Elizabeth worked switches and levers at his command. Suddenly there was a flash, of lightning it seemed to me, and I knew that we had launched the ICC upon its great adventure.

'Come here and look,' said Frank. I crept forward, half-afraid yet half-elated that I should be witness to such a triumph of medical biophysics. I leaned over the frightful creature, restraining my revulsion. Slowly, dreamily, the goat's eyes opened and focussed upon me.

'My Creator!' screamed the cat in a very loud voice, that agreed perfectly with the hideousness of its outward person. 'A thousand, thousand blessings be upon Thee. Hallowed be Thy name! Thy kingdom come! O rapture, rapture thus to behold the golden dawn!' With which words the cat leapt upon an electric lamp and ate the bulb.

To say that I recoiled is to trifle with words. I leapt backward into a chair and cringed against the wall. The cat pursued me, shrieking Gothic praise and endearment. It put out its monstrous tongue and licked my hand. Imagine, if you can, the tongue of a cat which is twelve cats rolled into one. It was weeks before the skin-graft made necessary by this single caress was completed. But I am ahead of my story.

'No, no,' I cried; 'my dear animal, listen to reason. I am not your Creator. Not in the least. You owe the precious gift of life to my young friend here.'

I waved my bleeding hand toward Frank. In their rapture he and Elizabeth were locked in a close embrace. That did it. Horrid, fiendish jealousy swept through the cat's whole being. All its twelve coats stood on end, the goat's eyes glared with fury, and its shovel tail lashed like that of a tiger. It sprang at Elizabeth, and with a single stroke of its powerful forepaws flung her to the ground.

I am proud to think that in that terrible moment I remembered what to do. I have always loved circuses, and I know that no trainer of tigers ever approaches his beasts without a chair in his hand. I seized up a chair and, in the approved manner, drove the monstrous creature into a corner. But what I said was not in tune with my action, or the high drama of the moment. I admit it frankly; my words were inadequate.

'You mustn't harm Miss Lavenza,' I said, primly; 'she is Mr. Einstein's fiancée.'

But Frank's words—or rather his single word—were even more inadequate than my own. 'Scat!' he shouted, kneeling by the bleeding form of his fainting beloved.

Elizabeth was to blame for programming that cat with a vocabulary culled from the Gothic Novel. 'Oh, Frankenstein,' it yowled, in that tremendous voice; 'be not equitable to every other and trample upon me alone, to whom thy justice and even thy clemency and affection is most due. Remember that I am thy creature; I ought to be thy Adam; dub me not rather the fallen angel, whom thou drivest hence only because I love—nay, reverence—thee. Jealousy of thy love makes me a fiend. Make me happy, and I shall once more be virtuous.'

There is something about that kind of talk that influences everybody that hears it. I was astonished to hear Frank—who was generally contented with the utilitarian vocabulary of the scientific man—say: 'Begone! I will not hear you. There can be no community between thee and me; we are enemies. Cursed be the day, abhorred devil, in which you first saw the light! You have left me no power to consider whether I am just to you or not. Begone! Relieve me of the sight of your detested form!'

Elizabeth was not the most gifted of my students, and the cat's next words lacked something of the true Gothic rhetoric. 'You mean you don't love your own dear little Pussikins best,' it whined. But Frank was true to the Gothic vein. 'This lady is the mistress of my affections, and I acknowledge no Pussikins before her,' he cried.

The cat was suddenly a picture of desolation, of rejection, of love denied. Its vocabulary moved back into high gear. 'Thus I relieve thee, my Creator. Thus I take from thee a sight which you abhor. Farewell!' And with one gigantic bound it leapt through the window into the quadrangle, and I heard the thunderous sound as the College gate was torn from its hinges.

I know where it went, and I felt deeply sorry for Trinity.

Dickens Digested

THE FOLLOWING STORY, *like its predecessor, was told on Gaudy Night. In 1970, the centenary of Charles Dickens' death, I decided to honour the great man's memory. He seems not to have liked scholars; they rarely figure in his novels. What he would have made of a modern graduate student—well, that is the theme of this College Ghost Story.*

IN THIS, the centenary of his death, I should like to speak well of Charles Dickens; the literary world has united to do him honour as one of the half-dozen foremost geniuses of our great heritage of poetry, drama, and the novel. That I should have to stand before you tonight and direct at that Immortal Memory a charge of—the word sticks in my throat, but it must be given voice—a charge of Vampirism, repels and disgusts me, but when Dickens has cast this hateful shadow across the quadrangle of Massey College, I have no other course.

This is what happened.

It was the best of times, it was the worst of times, it was the age of wisdom, it was the age of foolishness, it was the epoch of belief, it was the epoch of incredulity—in short, it was the beginning of the Autumn Term, and the year was 1969. I met the incoming group of Junior Fellows, and among the

thirty-five or so new men were some who immediately at-
tracted my attention—but the subject of my story was not one
of these. No, Tubfast Weatherwax III had nothing about him
to draw or hold one's interest; he was a bland young man, quite
unremarkable in appearance. Of course, I was familiar with his
dossier, which had been thoroughly examined by the Selec-
tions Committee of the College. He came to us from Harvard,
and he was a young American of distinguished background—as the dynastic number attached to his name at once
made clear. His mother, I know, had been a Boston Winesap.
But young Weatherwax bore what one politely assumed to
be—in republican terms—a noble heritage lightly, and indeed unobtrusively.

He was a student of English Literature, and he sought
a PH D. When I asked him casually what he was working at, he
said that he thought perhaps he might do something with
Dickens, if he could get hold of anything new. I considered his
attitude rather languid, but this is by no means uncommon
among students in the English graduate school; hoping to
encourage him I said that I was certain that if once Dickens
thoroughly took hold of him, he would become absorbed in
his subject.

Ah, fatal prophetic words! Would that I might recall
them! But no—I, like poor Tubfast Weatherwax, was a pawn
in one of those grim games, not of chance but of destiny, which
Fate plays with us in order that we may not grow proud in our
pretension to free will.

I saw no more of him for a few weeks, until one day he
came to see me, to inquire about Dickens as a dramatist. I am
one of the few men in the University who has troubled to read
the plays of Charles Dickens, and relate them to the rest of his
work, so this was normal enough. He knew nothing about the
nineteenth-century theatre, and I told him I thought Dickens'
drama unlikely to yield a satisfactory thesis to anyone but an
enthusiastic specialist. 'And you, Mr. Weatherwax,' I said, 'did
not seem very much caught up in Dickens when last we spoke.'

His face changed, lightening unmistakably with enthusiasm. 'Oh, that's all in the past,' he said; 'it's just as you said
it would be—I feel that Dickens is really taking hold of me!'

I looked at him more attentively. He had altered since first I saw him. His dress, formerly that elegant disarray that marks the Harvard man—the carefully shabby corduroy trousers, the rumpled but not absolutely dirty shirt, the necktie worn very low and tight around the loins, in lieu of a belt—had been changed to extremely tight striped trousers, a tight-waisted jacket with flaring skirts, and around the throat what used to be called, a hundred and fifty years ago, a Belcher neckerchief. And—was I mistaken, or was that shadow upon his cheeks merely the unshavenness which is now so much the fashion, or might it be the first, faint dawning of a pair of sidewhiskers? But I made no comment, and after he had gone I thought no more about the matter.

Not, that is, until the Christmas Dance.

There are many here who remember our Christmas Dance in 1969. It was a delightful affair, and, as always, the dress worn by the College men and their guests ran through the spectrum of modern university elegance. I myself always wear formal evening clothes on these occasions; it is expected of me; of what use is an Establishment figure if he does not look like an Establishment figure? But somewhat to my chagrin I found myself outdone in formality, and by none other than Tubfast Weatherwax III. And yet—was this the ultimate in modern fashion, or was it a kind of fancy dress? His bottle-green tailcoat, so tight-waisted, so spiky-tailed, so very high in the velvet collar, and so sloping in the shoulders; his waistcoat of garnet velvet, hung all over with watch-chains and seals depending from fobs; his wondrously frilled shirt, and the very high starched neck-cloth that came up almost to his mouth; his skin-tight trousers, and—could it be? Yes, it certainly was—his varnished evening shoes, were in the perfection of the mode of 1836, a date which—it just flashed through my mind—marked the first appearance of *Pickwick Papers*. And his hair—so richly curled, so heaped upon his head! And his sidewhiskers, now exquisite parentheses enclosing the subordinate clause which was his innocent face. It was—yes, it was certainly clear that Tubfast Weatherwax III had got himself up to look like the famous portrait of the young Dickens by Daniel Maclise.

But his companion! No Neo-Victorian she. I thought at first that she was completely topless, but this was not quite true. Braless she certainly was, and her movement was like the waves of ocean. As for her mini, it was a *minissima*, nay, a *parvula*. She was a girl of altogether striking appearance.

'Allow me to present Miss Angelica Crumhorn,' said Weatherwax, making a flourishing bow to my wife and myself; 'assuredly she is the brightest ornament of our local stage. But tonight I have tempted her from the footlights and the plaudits of her ravished admirers to grace our academic festivities with beauty and wit. Come, my angel, shall we take the floor?'

'Aw, crap!' said Miss Crumhorn, 'where's the gin at?'

I knew her. She was very widely known. Indeed, she was notorious, not as Angelica Crumhorn, which I assume was her real name, but as Gates Ajar Honeypot, star of the Victory Burlesque. She was the leader of an accomplished female group called the Topless Tossers.

If there is one point that has been made amply clear by the university revolt of the past few years, it is this: students will no longer tolerate an educational institution which professes to stand *in loco parentis*; good advice is absolutely *out*. Therefore I did not call young Weatherwax to me the following morning and tell him that he stood on the brink of an abyss, though I knew that this was the case. It was not that, at the dance, he had eyes for no one but Gates Ajar Honeypot; in that he was simply like all the rest of us, for as she danced, Miss Crumhorn gave a stunning exhibition of the accordion-like opening and closing of her bosom by means of which she had won the professional name of Gates Ajar. No, what was wrong was that when he looked at her he seemed to be seeing someone else—some charming girl of the Regency period, all floating tendrils of hair, pretty ribbons, modest but witty speech, and flirtatious but essentially chaste demeanour. I saw trouble ahead for Tubfast Weatherwax III, but I held my peace.

I thought, you see, that he was trying to be like Charles Dickens. This happens very often in the graduate school; a young man chooses a notable literary figure to work on, and his subject is so much more vital, so infinitely more charged with life than he himself, that he begins to model himself on the topic of his thesis, and until he has gained his PH D—and sometimes even after—he acts the role of that great literary man. You notice it everywhere. If you were to throw an orange in any English graduate seminar you would hit a foetal Henry James, or an embryo James Joyce; road-company Northrop Fryes and Hallowe'en versions of Marshall McLuhan are to be found everywhere. This has nothing to do with these eminent men; it is part of the theopathetic nature of graduate studies; the aspirant to academic perfection so immerses himself in the works of his god that he inevitably takes on something of his quality, at least in externals. It is not the fault of the god. Not at all.

Very well, I thought. Let Tubfast Weatherwax III take his fair hour; he has heard of Dickens' early infatuation with Maria Beadnell; let him try on Dickens' trousers and see how they fit.

This meant no small sacrifice on my part. Whenever I met him, I said, as I should, 'Good-day, Mr. Weatherwax,' and then I had to listen to him shout, 'Oh, capital, capital! The very best of days, Master! Whoop! Halloo! God bless us every one!' Or if perhaps I said, 'Not a very fine day, Mr. Weatherwax,' he would reply: 'What is the odds so long as the fire of soul is kindled at the taper of conviviality, and the wing of friendship never moults a feather!' I began to avoid encounters with Weatherwax. The only Dickensian reply to this sort of thing that I could think of was 'Bah! Humbug!' but I shrink from giving pain.

But I saw him. Oh, indeed, I saw him crossing the quad, his step as light as a fairy's, with that notable strumpet Gates Ajar Honeypot upon his arm. 'Angelica' he insisted on calling her, poor unhappy purblind youth. I longed to speak, but my Wiser Self—who is, I regret to tell you, a cynical, slangy spirit whom I call the Ghost of Experience Past—would intervene, snarling, 'Nix on the *loco parentis*,' and I would refrain.

Even when he came, last Spring, to ask permission to marry Angelica Crumhorn in the Chapel, late in August, I merely gave formal assent. 'I shall fill the little Chapel with flowers,' he rhapsodized; 'flowers for her whose every thought is pure and fragrant as earth's fairest blossom.' I repressed a comment that a bridal bouquet of Venus' fly-trap would be pretty and original.

I prepared the required page in the College Register, but August came and went, and as nothing had happened I made a notation 'Cancelled' on that page, and waited the event.

Poor Weatherwax pined, and I ceased to avoid him and began to pity him. I inquired how his Dickens studies went on. He asked me to his rooms in the College, and when I visited him I was astonished to find how Victorian, how like chambers in some early-nineteenth-century Inn of Court, he had contrived to make them. He even had a bird in a cage: inevitably it was a linnet. The most prominent objects of ornament were a large white plaster bust of Dickens—very large, positively dominant—and a handsome full set of Dickens' Works in twenty-four volumes. I recognized it at once as the Nonesuch Dickens, a very costly set of books for a student, but I knew that Weatherwax had money. He languished in an armchair in a long velvet dressing-gown, his hair hanging over his face, the picture of romantic misery. I decided that—prudent or not—the time had come for me to speak.

'Rally yourself, Mr. Weatherwax,' cried I; 'marshal your powers, recruit your energies, sir!' I started to hear myself give utterance to these unaccustomed phrases, but with that bust of Dickens looking at me from a high shelf, I could not speak in any other way. So I told him, in good round Victorian prose, that he was making an ass of himself, that he was well quit of Gates Ajar Honeypot, and that he must positively stop trying to be Charles Dickens. 'Eating your god,' I cried, raising my hand in admonition, 'cannot make you into your god. Stop aping Dickens, and read him like a scholar.'

To my dismay, he broke down and wept. 'Oh, good old man,' he sobbed, 'you come too late. For I am not eating my god; I fear that my god is eating me! But bless you, bless your snowy locks! You have sought to succour me, but alas, I know that I am doomed!'

I rose to leave him, and as I did so—I tell you this knowing how incredible it must seem—the bust of Dickens seemed to smile, baring sharp, cruel teeth. I shrieked. It was a mental shriek, which is the only kind of shriek permitted to a professor in the modern university, but I gave a mental shriek, and fled the room.

Of course I returned. I know my duty. I know what I owe to the men of Massey College, to the spirit of university education, to that sense of decency which is one of the holiest possessions of our changing world. And as autumn wore on—it was this autumn just past, but as I look back upon it, it seems far, far away—the conviction grew upon me that Weatherwax's trouble was greater than I had supposed; it was not that he thought he was Dickens, but that he thought he was one of Dickens' characters, and by that abandonment of personality he had set his foot upon a shadowed and sinister path. One of Dickens' characters? Yes, but which? One of the doomed ones, clearly. But which? Which? For me this past autumn was a season of painful obligation, for not only had I to care for Weatherwax—oh yes, it reached a point where I took him his meals, and fed him such scant mouthfuls as he could ingest, with my own hands—but I had to adapt myself to the only kind of language he seemed now to understand.

One day—it was in early November—I took him his usual bowl of gruel, and found him lying on his little bed, asleep.

'Mr. Weatherwax,' I whispered, 'nay let me call you Tubfast; arouse yourself; you must eat something.'

'Is it you, Grandfather?' he asked, as he opened his eyes, and across his lips stole a smile so sweet, so innocent, so wholly feminine, that in an instant I had the answer to my question. Tubfast Weatherwax III thought he was Little Nell.

His decline from that moment was swift. I spent all the time with him I could. Sometimes his mind wandered, and seemed to dwell upon Gates Ajar Honeypot. 'I never nursed a dear gazelle, to glad me with its soft black eye, but when it came to know me well and love me, it was sure to prefer the advances of a fat wholesale furrier on Spadina Avenue,' he would murmur. But more often he talked of graduate studies, and of that great Convocation on High where the Chancellor of the Universe confers PH D's, *magna cum* angelic *laude*, on all who kneel before his throne.

When I could no longer conceal from myself that the end was near, I dressed his couch here and there with some winter berries and green leaves, gathered in a secluded portion of the parking-lot. He knew why. 'When I die, put me near to something that has loved the light, and had sky above it always,' he murmured. I knew he meant our College quadrangle, for though the new Graduate Library will shortly throw upon our little garden its eternal pall of shadow, it had been while he knew it a place of sunshine and of the laughter of the careless youths who play croquet there.

Then, one drear November night, just at the stroke of midnight, the end came. He was dead. Dear, patient, noble Tubfast Weatherwax III was dead. His little bird—a poor slight thing the pressure of a finger would have crushed—was stirring nimbly in its cage; and the strong heart of its child-owner was mute and motionless for ever.

Where were the traces of his early cares, the pangs of despised love, of scholarly tasks too heavy for his feeble mind? All gone. Sorrow was dead indeed in him, but peace and perfect happiness were born; imaged in his tranquil beauty and profound repose. So shall we know the angels in their majesty, after death.

I wept for a solitary hour, but there was much to be done. I hastened to the quad, lifted one of the paving stones at the north-east end, where—until the Graduate Library is completed—the sun strikes warmest and stays longest. For such a man as I, burdened with years and sorrow, the digging of a six-foot grave was heavy work, and it took me all of ten minutes. With the little chisel in my handy pocket-knife it was the work of an instant to inscribe the stone—

Hic jacet

STABILIS WEATHERWAX TERTIUS

and then, as my Latin is not inexhaustible, I continued—

He bit off more than he could chew

It was my intention to place the stone over the grave, with the inscription downward, so that no unhallowed eye might read it. Now all that remained was to wrap the poor frail body in the velvet dressing-gown and lay it to rest. Or rather, I should be compelled to stand it to rest, for the grave had to be dug straight down.

It was only then I raised my eyes toward the windows of Weatherwax's room, which lay on the other side of the quad.

What light was that, which flickered with an eerie effulgence from the casement? Had I, stunned by my grief, forgotten to turn off the electricity? But no; this light was not the bleak glare of a desk-lamp. It was a bluish light, and it seemed to ebb and flow. Fire? I sped up the stairs, and threw open the door.

Oh, what a sight was there revealed to my starting eyes! My hair lifted upward upon my head, as if it were fanned by a cold breath. The bust of Charles Dickens, before so white, so plaster-like, was now grossly flushed with the colours of life. The Nonesuch Dickens, which had hitherto worn its original binding of many-coloured buckram was — oh, horror, horror!—bound freshly in leather, and that leather—would that I had no need to reveal it—was human skin! And that smell—why did it so horribly remind me of a dining-room in which some great feast had just been completed? I knew. I knew at once. For the body—the body was gone!

As I swooned the scarlet lips of the Dickens bust parted in a terrible smile, and its beard stirred in a hiccup of repletion.

It was a few days later—last Friday, indeed—when a young colleague in the Department of English—a very promising Joyce man—said to me, 'It is astounding how Dickens studies are picking up; quite a few theses have been registered in the past three months.' I knew he despised Dickens and all the Victorians, so I was not surprised when he added, 'Wonderful how the old wizard keeps life in him! Upon what meat doth this our Charlie feed, that he is grown so great?'

He smiled, pleased at his little literary joke. But I did not smile, because I knew.

Yes, I knew.

Four:
Thoughts
About Writing

The Conscience
of the Writer

MANY YOUNG PEOPLE who want to write, or who have already begun to write, appeal to me for advice about what it is to be a writer, and what keeps a writer going through what may be a long life in a solitary profession. The writer's work, however prompt his publisher may be, does not reach his public until several months after he has finished it; before that time he has worked, necessarily in solitude, cheered by no one except perhaps a faithful and long-suffering wife. What makes him do it? How does he bear up during the long wait before some echo reaches him from his readers? How does he keep on into the latter part of his career? When in 1968 Glendon College in York University asked me to speak, I decided to try my best to put such advice as I had into a single utterance, and here it is.

MY SUBJECT IS 'The Conscience of the Writer', and I have accepted your invitation to speak not because I think I have anything new to say about it, but because I think that the familiar and basic things demand constant repetition, in an age when familiar and basic things are so often cast aside, as if we had outlived them. The writer's calling has been greatly romanticized—more so, I believe, than that of any other artistic creator. Painters, sculptors, and composers are regarded with a degree of awe by the public in general, but writers possess a special sort of magic, and I believe that in part it is the magic of what seems to be a familiar and attainable, yet somehow unrealized, element in the lives of many people who are not artists of any kind. Anybody can see that he is not going to paint like Picasso, or write music like Benjamin Britten; he is not so sure that he is not going to write like somebody whose writing he admires. He has learned the humblest techniques of the writer at school; he can put down words on a page; he has some idea of grammar, or he may have decided that grammar is an unworthy shackle on his inspiration; he is constantly meeting with experiences, or observing people, that seem to him to be the stuff of writing. But somehow he never writes.

He could do so, of course. Every writer is familiar with the person who buttonholes him and tells him about the book he would write—if he had the time. Or else they have fathers or uncles who are screamingly funny characters whose lives ought to be written at once. These people sometimes offer to collaborate with the author, providing the raw material if he will do the actual work of writing.

Such people are usually middle-aged. Younger people with the urge to write do not want to collaborate; they are, on the contrary, often suspicious that older writers will snatch their splendid inspirations and capitalize on them. These young people are often daring experimenters in technique, because their ideas can only be given adequate form in some wholly new way of writing—leaving out all the verbs, or perhaps writing nothing but verbs, but most often in the present day by describing, with gloating particularity, various sexual acts which they have just discovered, and of which they wish to make the innocent old world aware. But after a few months during which they burn with a hard, gem-like flame, these people cease to write.

The world is full of people who think they could write, or who have, at some time, written. But they do not stay with it. Why?

Is it because the real writer, the serious writer, who is a writer all his life, is a special kind of person? Yes, it is. And what kind of person is he? I do not pretend to be able to answer that question fully, for there are many kinds of writers, some of whom I do not understand at all, and some whom I understand but do not admire, although I am well aware of their talents. But they all have a characteristic—indeed a distinguishing trait in their psychological make-up—which makes them recognizable, and it is this that I have called the writer's conscience, although that is not a very satisfactory name for it. I use that phrase to describe the continuing struggle that goes on in the psyche of every writer of any importance. And by that expression 'of any importance' I exclude the journalistic word-spinners, the ghost-writers, the concocters of literary confectionery, although some of these are remarkable technicians. I am talking about the writers who try—perhaps not all the time but certainly during the greater part of their careers—to write the best they can about the themes that concern them most.

This is not a moral judgement, and has nothing to do with the themes that writers choose. Perhaps I can make myself clear by instancing two books—Dostoevsky's *Crime and Punishment* and Max Beerbohm's *Zuleika Dobson*. One is an agonized exploration of the psychology of a criminal intellectual; the other is a charming joke about youth and love. One is clumsily written, with long passages of over-heated and perversely sensitive emotion; the other is elegantly and exquisitely written, in a fashion so subtle that it yields up its secrets only after several careful readings. Both are great books, and I think it is foolish to say that one is greater than the other, as if one were marking an examination, and giving Dostoevsky higher marks because he tries harder. He didn't try harder. He just wrote the best book he could in the circumstances in which he found himself. So did Max Beerbohm. Both books appeal strongly to large numbers of readers, who encounter them at particularly fortunate moments in their lives. And I believe that it is because both writers wrote under the domination of conscience, and it is the subsequent revelation that gives the books their particular weight and value.

There are no absolutes in literature that can be applied without reference to personal taste and judgement. The great book for you is the book that has most to say to you at the moment when you are reading. I do not mean the book that is most instructive, but the book that feeds your spirit. And that depends on your age, your experience, your psychological and spiritual need. These days I find myself reading poetry rather a lot. But when I was ten what I liked to read best were bound volumes of a boys' paper called *Chums*. It had just what I needed, and it extended my world remarkably; however, when I looked at some of that stuff recently I could not endure it. But I am sure I should not be reading what I read now if I had not read *Chums* then, and I am grateful. We do not read to make ourselves cultured, but to nourish our souls. Real culture is the evidence, not the reality, of the fully realized spirit.

This is one of my great quarrels with university courses in English; they require students to read lists of fine books, and to profess a knowledge of them that is usually superficial, though even this sort of knowledge is better than none at all. But for every masterpiece that is on the reading-list, there are five that are not, and many students fall into the trap of thinking that anything that is not on the list is not Blue Brand Literature, and may be disregarded. This is not the intention of English courses, but it is what happens. The great difficulty is that the emphasis in universities is likely to be on criticism of literature, rather than on delighted discovery and surrender to it. Every student — BA, MA, or PH D — knows what is wrong with Charles Dickens, though they have probably read nothing but *Great Expectations*, and read it once, when they were too young to understand it. The reason for this is perfectly clear: criticism is comparatively easy in its showy but superficial aspect. Anybody can pick up its techniques and use them with a display of skill, just as anybody can make a spectacular cut with a surgeon's scalpel, simply because it is so sharp. But the vastly more difficult business of discovering literature, and giving oneself wholly into its embrace, and making some of it part of oneself, cannot be done in large classes, and not everybody can do it even in small classes. A surprising number of people can get PH D's in criticism; to be a worthy reader of what writers of conscience have written is a very different matter.

Which brings us back to our theme — the writer and his conscience. Moral judgements based on the themes a writer chooses, I have said, are irrelevant. Evelyn Waugh was a writer of extraordinary conscience, and his novels, even when most serious, have a comic guise, and are spare and elegant in form. Tolstoy was similarly a writer of extraordinary conscience, but *Anna Karenina* and *War and Peace* are solemn and almost portentous in tone, and their greatest admirers will admit that they might have been the better for the cutting of large passages. It is of little use to say that *War and Peace* is a masterpiece because it tells us all there is to say about war; it tells us wonderful things, but Waugh's little novel *Scoop* tells us something that Tolstoy did not. This is not to say that the two books are equally 'great' or 'good' but only that every good book is good in its own way, and that comparisons are of extremely limited value. Unless, of course, you are a superficial critic, in which case you had better banish all humility in the face of genius and get on with your self-appointed task of awarding marks and establishing hierarchies. But if you want to know and feel what genius knows and feels, you must be a reader first, and a critic a very long way afterward.

Now—what is this conscience I have been talking about? It is the writer's inner struggle toward self-knowledge and self-recognition, which he makes manifest through his art. Writers, and artists generally, are notoriously resistant to psycho-analysis, and to put hundreds of thousands of words by both Freud and Jung into a nutshell it is because they are continuously psycho-analysing themselves in their own way, which is through their work, and it is the only way to peace of mind, to integration, open to them. It is a life process, and in the work of a writer of great abilities who has been so fortunate as to live long it presents an awesome achievement. Consider the case of Thomas Mann; from *Little Herr Friedemann*, which he published when he was twenty-three, and *Buddenbrooks*, which appeared when he was twenty-five, the succession of his books reveals to us, beneath the themes, the fables, and the philosophical explorations, the development of an extraordinary spirit: *The Magic Mountain* (1924), the great *Joseph* tetralogy, which was sixteen years in the writing, *Lotte in Weimar* (1939), *Doctor Faustus* (1948), and that extraordinary book which appeared when the writer was eighty, *The Confessions of Felix Krull*—these are a few mountain peaks in a career of an artist's self-exploration. And what is revealed? A deep preoccupation with themes of death and disease, of sin and remorse and redemption, of myth and the irrationalities of life, of the wellsprings of the creative spirit, and at the last, in *Felix Krull*, a triumphant return and exploration of one of Mann's lifelong preoccupations, which was the link between the artistic and the criminal instinct, embodied in what I regard as quite the subtlest and most hair-raisingly erotic novel I have ever read. A concern, as you see, with some of the deep and continuing problems of human life.

Here we have what the great literary artist does; he explores his own spirit to the uttermost, and bodies forth what he finds in a form of art that is plain to anyone who can read it—though not necessarily to anyone who picks up his books.

The struggle is not easy and its results are sometimes disastrous, for reasons that we shall explore a little later. Psycho-analysis is notoriously demanding and disagreeable, when undertaken by a sympathetic and skilled physician: consider what it means when it is a solitary venture, undertaken as a life sentence and carried out under the circumstances in which most authors live. Is it any wonder that the domestic lives of some of them are rumpled and unseemly? Or that many of them take to drink? Or that others escape into that attractive world of action where they can get so much easy acclaim by protesting or sitting-in or freaking-out or setting themselves up as great friends and patrons of youth, or whooping it up for the Pill or LSD—doing anything, in fact, except getting on with the laborious task to which their gift and their temperament calls them?

Henrik Ibsen knew all about it, and he was one of the heroes who remained chained to his task until finally it broke him; for the last years of his life he toiled painstakingly every day over a copybook, trying to force his hand to learn, for the second time, the skill of making readable writing. Did you know that Ibsen was a poet? Here is a translation of one of his verses, full of meaning and of warning for writers:

> *To live—is a battle with troll-folk*
> *In the crypts of heart and head;*
> *To write—is a man's self-judgement*
> *   As Doom shall judge the dead.*

'A man's self-judgement'—that is the conscience of the writer.

Whatever he writes, and whatever the summing-up of that mysterious inner court may be, if it is carried through truthfully and manfully, we shall sense in it that quality that makes literature one of the greatest of the arts, and well worth the sacrifice and the frequent misery of a writer's life.

Sometimes I laugh when aspiring writers assure me that if they could get enough money—usually in the form of a grant from some handout agency subsidized by the government—they would go to Mexico, or the Mediterranean, or to Capri, and there they would be able to write—so readily, so fluently, so happily. Fools! 'A man's self-judgement' will go with him anywhere, if he is really a writer, and he will not be able to command either inspiration or happiness or serenity. Of course if he is a mere scribbling tourist, or a work-shy flop, or both, it does not really matter much where he goes. But if he is a writer he will be wise to write wherever he finds himself. The history of literature is full of writers who have thought that the judgement of the inner court would be easier in some country outside his own.

This is not to say, of course, that a writer should not travel or gain experience. But if he is really a writer his task may be, not to seek experience, but to survive the experience that crowds upon him from every quarter. As Aldous Huxley has written, 'experience is not a matter of having actually swum the Hellespont, or danced with the dervishes, or slept in a doss-house. It is a matter of sensibility and intuition, of seeing and hearing the significant things, of paying attention at the right moments, of understanding and co-ordinating. Experience is not what happens to a man: it is what a man does with what happens to him.' Many years ago I read a book by the travelling journalist Richard Halliburton; he had climbed a very high mountain somewhere—I forget where because the book was not of the sort that sticks in the mind—and he recorded the reflection of his companion at the top. It was 'Now I can spit a mile!' We are familiar with the reflections of Wordsworth, who climbed a few quite unremarkable hills in the Lake District. There is the contrast in what experience meant to a man of trivial mind, and to a poet.

Let us continue the theme of the writer's artistic experience considered in terms of psycho-analysis. To do so, I want to talk from the standpoint of C. G. Jung, rather than that of Sigmund Freud. Great as Freud was, and unassailable as his position is among the great liberators of the human mind, his actual technique seems more suited to the consulting-room than to the university lecture-room; his mind dealt more strikingly with problems of neurosis than with matters of aesthetics, and his cast of mind was powerfully reductive. After the Freudian treatment most things look a little shabby—needlessly so. Jung's depth psychology, on the other hand, is much more aesthetic and humanistic in its general tendency, and is not so Procrustean in its effect on artistic experience. The light it throws on matters of literature and on the temperament of the writer is extremely useful and revealing.

Jung is insistent on a particular type of development in the mind of anyone who meets the problems of life successfully; it is the change, the alteration of viewpoint, that transformation of aims and ambitions, that overtakes everybody somewhere in the middle of life. In women this change is physiological as well as mental, and consequently it has always been a matter of common observation. But in men the change is an intellectual and spiritual one of profound consequence, and this is something observable in the careers of virtually all writers of the kind we are talking about here—the committed writers, the servants of the writer's conscience.

Example is probably better than explanation at this point. The career of the late Aldous Huxley will be familiar to many of you. During the early part of his career his work was remarkable for its strongly satirical edge, for the brilliance of its wit, for its concern with matters of morality and especially morality as it relates to sex, which seemed to many people revolutionary and perhaps dangerous and destructive. He is rather out of fashion at present, but when the usual slump in reputation that follows a writer's death is over—it takes about ten or fifteen years—I think these novels will be prized for their stringent charm. But I well remember the surprise and excitement that was caused by the appearance of *Eyeless in Gaza* in 1936; it seemed to be a work by a new man, for its tone was inquiring, mystical, and tormented beyond anything we had found in him before. Of course the fashionable people chattered about his probable conversion to Roman Catholicism, and those who had chiefly valued the bitterness of the early books thought that he had 'gone off' terribly, and lamented him as one lost. But the change in direction had been heralded for anybody with eyes to see it in his earlier book *Point Counter Point*, which was a tortured and questing book; the bitterness in it was born of revulsion rather than glee at the follies of mankind. And what was significant about *Eyeless in Gaza* was that it was written when Huxley was forty-two, and ripe for a change. If there had been no change, we should soon have tired of the old Huxley wearing the young Huxley's intellectual clothes. And from that time until the end of his life his exploration of mystical religion and his discussions of morality were at the root of everything he wrote.

Much the same sort of foolish hubbub broke out when Evelyn Waugh wrote *Brideshead Revisited* in 1945. Has our favourite jester gone serious on us, cried the people who admired his earlier books only because they were funny, and not because they were wise. But Waugh was forty-two, and his point of view had changed.

What is the nature of this change? It is part of intellectual and particularly spiritual growth. As Jung explains it, in the early part of life—roughly for the first half of it—man's chief aims are personal and social. He must grow up, he must find his work, his must find out what kind of sex life he is going to lead, he must achieve some place in the world and attempt to get security within it, or else decide that security is not important to him. But when he has achieved these ends, or come to some sort of understanding with this part of existence, his attention is turned to matters that are broader in scope, and sometimes disturbing to contemplate. His physical strength is waning rather than growing; he has found out what sex is, and though it may be very important to him it can do little to surprise him; he realizes that some day he is really going to die and that the way he approaches death is of importance to him; he finds that without God (using that name to comprehend all the great and inexplicable things and the redemptive or destructive powers that lie outside human command and understanding) his life lacks a factor that it greatly needs; he finds that, in Jung's phrase, he is not the master of his fate except in a very modest degree and that he is in fact the object of a supraordinate subject. And he seeks wisdom rather than power—though the circumstances of his early life may continue to thrust power into his hands.

Now, the paradox of this change is that it does not make him an old man. What will make him an old man is a frightened clinging to the values of the first half of life. We have all seen these juvenile dotards whose boast is that they are just as young as their sons or their grandsons; they do not realize what a pitiful boast that is. They prate about their sympathy with youth, but they mean only the superficialities and ephemera of youth. Many of the sad smashups in marriages that we all see among middle-aged people have their origin in this attempt to dodge an inescapable fact. The values that are proper and all-absorbing during the first half of life will not sustain a man during the second half. If he has the courage and wisdom to advance courageously into the new realm of values and emotions he will age physically, of course, but his intellectual and spiritual growth will continue, and will give satisfaction to himself and to all those associated with him. And such courage and wisdom are by no means rare; they may show themselves among many people who have never thought along these lines at all but who have a knack for living life wisely; and they also are to be found among those who regard self-awareness as one of the primary duties of a good life. Paradoxically, such people are on better terms with youth than the shrivelled Peter Pans who dare not be their age.

How does this affect the writer, who is our chief concern here? It is important to him to manage this change in outlook with skill and humility, for a failure to do so can be his ruin. He may be one of those whose special gifts fit him for the kind of writing a man does before middle life. This has been the case with many poets, who appear to have lost everything but technical skill after the appearance of a number of fine—perhaps great—early works. One wonders what Byron would have been like after forty-five. One regrets that Keats did not live to give us the mature works of one of the greatest geniuses of youth. On the other hand, we recall that Cervantes, whose works written during his early life were capable, but not the sort of thing that it would occur to anybody to translate, astonished the world with *Don Quixote* when he was fifty-eight, and wrote the second part of it ten years later. We think of Goethe, who wrote the first part of *Faust* when he was fifty-six, and completed the mighty second part of that play between his seventy-fifth and his eighty-second year. I have already spoken of Thomas Mann, whose genius survived triumphantly until his death at the age of eighty, and I do not suppose it is necessary to point out that all the finest work of Bernard Shaw belongs to the second half of his life.

There are those who do not choose to make this necessary advance, or who repress evidence of it in their writing. It would be impertinent to speculate superficially on such a subject, but one may wonder if that is not what happened to Ernest Hemingway. And certainly if we examine the works of our own best-known writer, the late Stephen Leacock, with care, we wonder whether he was not trapped in the manner of his earliest writing. He did not set out on his career until he was in his early forties, but it was in the manner of his youth; his success was so great that he may have hesitated to introduce a new and deeper note into what was so gratefully accepted by his readers. The result is writing that is often thin and perfunctory. But in one of his last books—the short autobiographical sketch called *The Boy I Left Behind Me*—we are given a tantalizing sample of what he might have done if he had chosen.

There are exceptions to all rules, and you may be surprised to hear me name a writer who is one of the greatest technicians of the last fifty years, P. G. Wodehouse, who continues to produce novels—they have been discerningly called 'musical comedies without music'—that are much like his earlier successes in tone, and are so brilliantly adapted to his aims that they continue to astonish us. He is in his eighty-seventh year and still writing. But he invented a highly artificial mode which no one has successfully imitated. Wodehouse, however, is no case of arrested development; if you think him immature, read his autobiographical volume called *Performing Flea*, which he wrote in 1951. Sean O'Casey, with characteristic spleen, had referred to Wodehouse as a performing flea, and in this book Wodehouse makes it plain that he is certainly no trivial entertainer, but a man of maturity, irony, and keen perception —qualities not overwhelmingly demonstrated by O'Casey, whose best work was done by the time he was forty-four.

How does the real writer—the man with the writer's conscience, or temperament, or whatever label you choose—set about his work? There are as many ways as there are writers, but there are a few well-worn paths, and of these I can only speak with certainty about the path I have chosen for myself. It would be more correct to say, the path my temperament has chosen for me. I combine writing with other sorts of work. For twenty-eight years I have been a journalist—not just a writer, but an editor, an employer, a man who had to make sure that his newspaper did not lose money, who had to worry about new machinery, new buildings, new contracts with unions, and continually to be concerned with an obligation to a community. When I had spent the day doing this I went home and wrote, altogether, works that fill eighteen volumes; I am at work on the nineteenth, and the twentieth exists in the form of extended notes. I am not counting four full-length plays that were produced but are not yet in print. I am not saying this to dazzle you with my industry, but to tell you how I do my work. I have always been grateful for my journalistic experience, which amounts to millions of words of writing, because it kept my technique in good muscular shape. I can write now without that humming and hawing and staring at the ceiling which plagues so many writers who have trouble getting started.

I have of late become a university professor and head of a college, and these tasks can hardly be regarded as a rest-cure. My most difficult work in this realm is the correcting of student essays and marking examinations. Reading inexpert writing is deeply exhausting. It is like listening to bad music.

I have also had the ordinary family experiences. I am married and have three children, now all grown up, and I have spent countless happy hours in domestic pursuits—gardening, family music-making, getting together some modest but pleasant collections of things, amateur theatricals as well as some professional theatre-work, and a kind of family life that seems perhaps to be more characteristic of the nineteenth century than of our streamlined era. I have sat on committees, and boards; I have made a great many speeches, and I have listened to what seem, in recollection, to be millions of speeches.

All of this I consider necessary to my life as a writer. It

has kept me from too great a degree of that fruitless self-preoccupation which is one of the worst diseases of the literary life. It has provided me with the raw material for what I write. The raw material, you observe; before it becomes the finished product it must undergo a process of distillation and elimination. An author is a very different thing from a reporter, or an autobiographer. This way of living has confirmed a theory I formed many years ago, when I was at the age you have reached now, that myth and fairy-tales are nothing less than the distilled truth about what we call 'real life', and that we move through a throng of Sleeping Princesses, Belles Dames sans Merci, Cinderellas, Wicked Witches, Powerful Wizards, Frog Princes, Lucky Third Sons, Ogres, Dwarves, Sagacious Animal Helpers and Servers, yes and Heroes and Heroines, in a world that is nothing less than an enchanted landscape, and that life only seems dull and spiritless to those who live under a spell—too often a spell they have brought upon their own heads.

Do not misunderstand me. I am not being whimsical, and my world is not the cosy nursery retreat of Winnie-the-Pooh. It is a tough world, and it only seems irrational or unreal to those who have not grasped some hints of its remorseless, irreversible, and often cruel logic. It is a world in which God is not mocked, and in which a man reaps—only too obviously—what he has sown. I do not think I understand it all, but I think I am acquainted with a few corners of it. And I may as well tell you that I regard the writing I have done as little more than a preparation for the work I mean to do.

Although I have been telling you about what I have done that is not the primary work of a writer, I would not have you believe that I have merely fitted my writing into odd corners of my life. Writing has always been central to my life, and my real work. But I said that I was glad to have the ordinary occupations of a busy man to protect me against that self-preoccupation that is one of the worst diseases of the literary life. Let me explain: I do not write in my spare time, I write all the time; whatever I may be doing, the literary aspect of my mind is fully at work: it is not only the hours at the desk or the typewriter, but the hours spent in other kinds of work and in many kinds of diversion when I am busily observing, shaping, rejecting, and undergoing a wide variety of feelings that are the essential material of writing. Notice that I said feelings—not thoughts, but feelings. One of the burdensome parts of the writer's temperament, as I understand it, is that one feels quite strongly about all sorts of things that other people seem to be able to gloss over, and this can be wearisome and depleting. This is the famous 'artistic sensitivity' that one sometimes hears people boasting about—very often people who show no other awareness of it. It is not a form of weakness. A writer is very rarely a wincing, delicate kind of man; in my experience he is often rather a tough creature, though given to hypochondria and sudden collapses of the spirit. I rely on a routine of daily work, and the necessities of a busy life, to keep me from succumbing too completely to the demands of a particular kind of temperament. My kind of writer—I can speak for no other—needs other work and a routine to keep him sane.

Let me return once again to the emphasis I laid on feeling, rather than thinking, in the writer's temperament. All sorts of people expect writers to be intellectuals. Sometimes they are, but it is not necessary to their work. Aldous Huxley was an intellectual, but he was not so good a novelist as E. M. Forster, who is not and does not like to be considered one. The writer is necessarily a man of feeling and intuition; he need not be a powerful original thinker. Shakespeare, Dickens, Dostoevsky — we do not think of them as intellectuals ; Tolstoy's thinking was vastly inferior to his fiction; Keats was a finer poet than Arnold, though no one would deny Arnold the title of intellectual. I do not say that writers are child-like creatures of untutored genius; often they are very intelligent men: but the best part of their intelligence is of the feeling and intuitive order. Sometimes they are impatient and even rude with people who insist on treating them as intellectuals. It is not pleasant to be treated like a clock by some clever but essentially unsympathetic person who wants to take you apart to see what makes you tick. But the modern passion for this sort of thing has led to the establishment on many campuses of a man called the Writer in Residence, who is there, in part at any rate, for intellectuals to pester, take apart, and reassemble, under the impression that they are learning something about writing.

As I draw to a conclusion, I want to return to something I said at the beginning of this address, which is that the life of a writer may be likened to a long self-analysis. I suggested that the process was painful, and indeed it frequently is so. But it is something else—something that Freud never mentioned, because of his preoccupation with neurosis, but which Jung suggests: it is sometimes joyous, victorious, and beautiful. It is not fashionable nowadays to say that one's life has moments of piercing beauty, or that it brings hours which are not merely recompense, but ample and bounteous reward for all the anxieties and dark moments. But I am not a fashionable person, and I am saying that now.

The degree of self-examination that is involved in being a writer, and the stringency of the writer's conscience, which holds you to a path that is often distasteful, necessarily takes you on some strange journeys, not only into the realm of the personal Unconscious, but into the level below that. It is assumed, by many people who have read Freud and Jung, that these descents must always be alarming experiences, because Freud and Jung were so much occupied with people who were very seriously disordered. But the writer is not necessarily disordered, and great rewards await him in this realm, if he approaches it with decent reverence. He will have serious struggles, but sometimes his struggles are like those of Jacob when he wrestled with the angel at Peniel, and cried in his extremity, 'I will not let thee go, unless thou bless me.' And he received the blessing, and bore it all his life. That realm of the Unconscious, which is the dwelling-place of so many demons and monsters, is also the home of the Muses, the abode of the angels. The writer, in his traffic with that realm in which dream, and myth, and fairy-tale become mingled with the most ordinary circumstances of life, does not lack for rewards and very great rewards. Self-examination is stern and often painful, as Ibsen tells us in the verse I quoted to you, but it is not all bitterness.

I have spoken to you seriously, because I presume that you are serious people. Certainly I am one, though such reputation as I have as a writer rests—rests perhaps a little too heavily—on my qualities as a humorist. Never be deceived by a humorist, for if he is any good he is a deeply serious man, moved by a quirk of temperament to speak a certain kind of truth in the form of jokes. Everybody can laugh at the jokes; the real trick is to understand them.

I have spoken of the conscience of the writer, trying to give you some insight into what it is that distinguishes the writer by temperament, the writer who cannot help being a writer, from someone who may write very well, but who writes for a different purpose—to instruct, to explain, to criticize— and for whom therefore writing is a necessary technique rather than an all-absorbing art. If I have discouraged anyone, I am sorry, but honesty comes before even courtesy in such matters as this. And if I have made anybody look searchingly into himself, to determine whether or not he has the kind of artistic conscience I have described, I shall think myself greatly rewarded.

What May Canada Expect from Her Writers?

THE PERSONAL STRUGGLE *of Aleksandr Solzhenitsyn and his utterances when he had at last been permitted to leave Russia affected me deeply, and made me think afresh about what it means to be a writer. Personal ambitions are given great importance in North America, and attempts to take writing with a more than personal seriousness—to regard it in fact as a vocation and a trust—may gain the writer a reputation for inflation of the ego. Canada is no friend to seriousness of this kind, among writers or, indeed, among people in public life. A profoundly Canadian story was told me by a friend who was at a party in Vancouver in 1957 when someone came in with the news that Lester B. Pearson had been awarded the Nobel Peace Prize. There was silence for a moment, broken by an elderly lady who spoke, trembling with indignation: 'Well—just who does he think he is?' she demanded. Mr. Pearson had offended against her Canadian demand for the appearance (not necessarily the reality) of humility. . . . The speech that follows was made in 1972 to a society of Industrial Accountants, who had asked me to say something about writing.*

SINCE 1901, when it was founded, the Nobel Prize for Literature has carried greater distinction than any other international literary award. It never fails to arouse widespread interest, even among people whose concern with literature is slight. Never did it give rise to so much discussion as in 1970, when the award was made to Aleksandr Solzhenitsyn, the Russian novelist.

Much of this excitement was created by the refusal of the government of the USSR to permit Solzhenitsyn to go to Stockholm to accept the prize, and by a later refusal to grant a travel visa to a representative of the Swedish Academy who sought to visit Russia in order to award the prize on the spot. The Russian government does not like Solzhenitsyn, and with reason; he is unquestionably one of its most outspoken critics. Being a novelist of sombre emotional power, whose work is translated and read everywhere in the Western world, he is something more than just a nuisance; he is a protesting voice, heard everywhere. He enjoys the special immunity of the great artist—for any attempt to get rid of him or silence him would bring about an international outcry.

Nor is Solzhenitsyn crippled by modesty in the claims he makes for himself. The splendid confidence in his own greatness that is exhibited by some European writers—the name of the late Thomas Mann comes to mind, as well as that of Solzhenitsyn—speaks of a culture very different from our own. A great writer, he has said, is like a rival government in an oppressed country, and the official government cannot be expected to like him. He knows himself to be a man of heroic courage, living constantly under threat; a single unwise move on his part, or a failure of discretion on the part of Russian authority, could bring about his death. He has no wish to die; he wants to go on living, and writing, and making his widely read protests against the tyranny that would reduce him to silence, or compel him to join that group of biddable writers who ensure a safe and profitable career by working within the limits considered permissible to artists in the USSR.

Because of his special status, people everywhere who are interested in the cause of literary freedom waited anxiously for what Solzhenitsyn would say about the award of the Nobel Prize for Literature to himself. It was only within the last few weeks that his speech of acceptance could be made public. On August 25 it was released to the world, and, as was expected, it was yet another powerful protest, not so much against the

Russian government as against all forces, everywhere, that seek to harness, censor, and diminish the opinions of men of letters, who must, above all artists, have freedom to say what they have to say without hindrance. For the work of the writer, whose medium is words, may come under fire from any government official who thinks he understands words, and is ready to excerpt passages which he considers, for one reason or another, to be offensive or dangerous.

Solzhenitsyn's speech caused little stir in Canada. For indeed, when has anything concerned with the world of literature ever caused a stir in our somnambulistic country? There may have been some comment in our press; if so, I did not see it. But I read some newspapers that come to me from outside Canada, and there the speech was reported, discussed, and sifted for what this extraordinary, courageous being had dared to say in the teeth of a government which might crush him, and where, as he said, 'a whole national literature was buried, cast into oblivion not only without a grave, but without even underclothes, naked, with a number tagged onto its toe.'

What I have said up to now may strike you as a rather ominous beginning for a speech which you may have hoped would be light in tone—perhaps even funny. Don't worry: the funny part is coming now. As I read, and reread, what Solzhenitsyn had risked his freedom and possibly his life to say to the writers of the world, and to people who value the free exchange of ideas, and not only of ideas but of feelings, emotions, and shades of sensibility, I asked myself again and again: 'What does this say to me? I am a Canadian writer; this man is talking to writers; what do his words mean to a Canadian?' There were two possible responses: laughter or tears. I chose to laugh, but it was not what people mean when they speak of 'a good laugh'. It was a bad laugh—one of the very worst laughs I have ever had in my life. For I realized that my own country had not yet progressed to that point of development where literature is a serious matter.

Do not misunderstand me. I do not long to live dangerously. I do not want to lie awake at night wondering if the soft knock of the agents of the secret police will come before dawn. I have no yearning to see in Canada any increase in what we already have of the violence of which Solzhenitsyn says that it 'is brazenly and victoriously striding across the whole world.' But I should like to think of myself as a writer in a country which demonstrably and undeniably had a serious concern with serious things, which saw itself from a world view and not from a parochial view, and which could distinguish between what things in life are serious and what things are merely solemn. I should like to think of myself as a writer in a country where a writer is recognized as a man with a vocation and not merely as a man with a hobby. I should like to think of myself as writing for fellow-countrymen in whose personal consciousness I might hope to form a part, however humble, and not simply as an entertainer whose value rises or falls by the estimation in which he is held by the New York Times Book Review or the Book-of-the-Month Club. Are these desires of mine unrealistic? I read and reread what Solzhenitsyn had written to the world and I realized that he and I were worlds apart. He, living in a country where to be a writer was as dangerous as to be a spy in the employ of a foreign power: I, living in a country where to be a writer is as innocuous, as laudable without being in the least significant, as being a man-ufacturer of yoghurt.

I spoke of Solzhenitsyn as living in the USSR as a spy in the employ of a foreign power. But every writer of any significance in any country is a spy in the employ of a foreign power, and that power is the supra-national power of free, unresting, probing intelligence. If that power is foreign to Russia, is it not also foreign to Canada? But Russia seems to know that it exists and dreads it: Canada has but dimly guessed that such a power exists. When I speak of Canada I speak of the educated and intelligent men and women of the whole coun-try: I do not speak of a few hundred intellectuals who are indeed aware of this external world power, and who owe it their chief allegiance. A few hundred quiet intellectuals do not make an awakened country; only an aware, alert, tirelessly curious middle class can do that, and it is greatly to be feared that in our country the middle class rarely stirs in its sleep. And yet to say that as a nation we sleep is not really accurate, for to sleep is often to dream, and Canada, in the national sense, does not dream. Our condition is stuporous; dully contented and stuporous.

Did I say that Canada does not dream? That again is not *quite* true. Canada does dream, but it pays very little heed to its dreams. I do not know how much attention you pay to modern advances in the investigation of the mind, in health and in sickness; the people who are engaged in that work pay great attention to dreams, and they are familiar with the patient who, when asked if he dreams much, replies, 'I dream now and again, but I don't remember what I dream.' Not to remember one's dreams can be a danger-signal, because it means that one of the routes by which the deepest promptings of the spirit reach the intelligence has been closed off. Not by accident but because of indifference or, worse, fear as to what the dreams might hint at, or give a riddling voice.

The literature of a country is in many ways like the dreams of a man. Some dreams are so fleeting, or so trivial, or so obviously caused by a draught from the open window, or an unwise snack before going to bed, that we quickly put them aside. Similarly some books are so inconsiderable, or so obviously touched off by some trivial circumstance, that we are quickly tired of them. But there are other dreams which cannot be attributed to external causes, and which are so vivid in their purposeful statement that we puzzle over them, and remember them for years afterward. Sometimes, if we are persistent, they yield up a secret; they tell us something about ourselves that we are well advised to heed, and grateful to learn.

So it is with books. There are even dreams which, without being themselves prophecies, contain the form of something that is yet to come. The writers of such books are not prophets, except in the sense that they are sensitive to national attitudes and generally accepted points of view in a way that most men are not. They can, as the saying goes, see through a brick wall. The reason is simple: the wall has long since ceased to exist, but it is the writer, rather than some other man, who notices when it came down.

I hope you will not think me immodest if I offer an example that concerns myself. For many years the question occurred to me at intervals: What would Canada do with a saint, if such a strange creature were to appear within our borders? I thought Canada would reject the saint because

Canada has no use for saints, because saints hold unusual opinions, and worst of all, saints do not pay. So in 1970 I wrote a book, called *Fifth Business*, in which that theme played a part. Several people suggested to me that I misjudged Canada in supposing that it would not know a saint when it saw one. But only last summer it was drawn forcibly to the attention of the people of Canada that they had possessed one man, Dr. Norman Bethune, who was certainly considered a great humanitarian, of virtually saint-like stature, in Red China. Canada had pretty well succeeded in ignoring Dr. Bethune, who unquestionably held unusual opinions. But all of a sudden Dr. Bethune began to pay; he was the strongest sympathetic link between Canada and a country with which Canada hoped to do some profitable business. And as soon as Dr. Bethune began to pay, political figures hastened to the scene of his birth, a memorial plaque was unveiled there, and Canada was assured from several sources of undoubted respectability that Dr. Norman Bethune had been a Great Canadian, and that we had at last overcome our natural modesty about saying so.

I told you that there would be some funny parts in this speech, and that is one of them. I was understandably pleased that a book of mine had dwelt, certainly not in a prophetic but in an allusive manner, with a theme which so soon asserted itself in our national life. A new novel of mine appeared on October 20, and I can hardly wait to see if anything I have written in it will make a subsequent appearance in the daily news.

I said that I would talk on the theme: What Does Canada Expect from Her Writers? The question is easily answered: Canada expects nothing from her writers. Let us rephrase the question to read: What May Canada Expect from Her Writers?

Canada may reasonably expect what other countries expect and get from a national literature. First, a sense of national character. Not, I hasten to say, of aggressive nationalism, of scorn-Britainism, of anti-Americanism, for these are negative qualities upon which nothing can worthily be built. Nor do I mean a projection of the picture of a typical Canadian of any kind, for literature of the first order does not deal with types, but with individuals. But as a people we are neither

Englishmen who have been exported to the new world, nor are we Americans who, having been assembled on Canadian soil, pass as a native product while still looking like something conceived in Detroit. We have our own concerns, our own secrets, and our own dreams. Sometimes, to the Canadians who remember and ponder them, these dreams are restless, disquieting, and fearsome; sometimes they are foreshadowings of what is yet to be; sometimes they are assurances of personal conquests and new heights seized and held. It is upon these deeply personal things that our national character rests.

Second, we may expect from our writers that vigilance on behalf of intellectual freedom and moral vigour which Aleksandr Solzhenitsyn has shown heroically and in isolation in a country where those qualities are endangered. Endangered, as I have pointed out, because the government of his country fears them. Endangered and abraded in our land because it appears so often that Canada hardly realizes that these qualities exist, and does not know where to look for help in making them matters of acute and untiring national concern.

Last, we may expect from our writers a true depiction of what our life in Canada is. And of course I speak of the essence of that life, not its externals. That life cannot be described in terms of the problems of other countries, for even when we share those problems, they appear in our country as Canadian matters. Nor can our national life be described without saying some things that will distress tender-minded people who shrink from what is disagreeable. A great poet has said:

If way to the better there be
It exacts a full look at the worst.

But not, of course, at the worst alone. There is much in our life that lies in realms that can brace us, elate us, and make us laugh.

Canada has a literature now, and some parts of it may well be objects of national pride, and as I am myself a novelist, and must not therefore speak of the work of novelists, let me refer you to the work of some of our poets, which is poetry of a special fragrance, for it is our own. And in the future, we may, if Canada asks for it, expect from our writers works of the kind Solzhenitsyn speaks of in the great declaration to the world of which I have already spoken. They are, he says, works of pungence and luminosity, with completely irrefutable power to convince, works which cause the reader to be visited, dimly, briefly, by revelations such as cannot be produced by rational thinking.

Works like the looking-glass in the fairy tale, he says; you look into it and you see not yourself but, for one second, the Inaccessible, whither no man can ride, no man can fly. Ah, yes, but to have glimpsed the Inaccessible is, however imperfectly, to have gained access to it. Once we have *found* the mirror, we can return to it again and again.

And that, ladies and gentlemen, is what your writers can give you, if you want it, and let them know that you want it. But that decision rests not with the writers, but with you. And before you can ask us for what we have, it is first necessary to understand what we are.

Jung and
the Theatre

WHEN I AM ASKED *why I have spent so much time, over the past twenty-five years, in the study of the work and thought of Dr. C. G. Jung, I reply that it is because Jung's discoveries and speculations throw so much light on my work as a student and teacher of literature. Jung always insisted that he was a scientist, and unquestionably that was true; but he was also a great humanist, and although I deplore partial and facile application of Jungian ideas to literary criticism, I know that a serious study of Jungian thought is one fruitful path of literary study. What follows is a suggestion, necessarily brief and incomplete, of what a Jungian approach reveals about some plays of the nineteenth century whose literary value is not of the first order, but whose appeal to large audiences over a long period is explicable on grounds of their relevance to some matters of deep human concern. This speech, somewhat varied in form, has been given to the Analytical Psychology Society of Ontario in 1973, to the Analytical Psychology Club of Chicago, and to the C. G. Jung Foundation of New York in 1977.*

DURING THE PAST FIFTY YEARS we have grown accustomed to the use of Sigmund Freud's attitude toward life, or some version of it, as an instrument of artistic criticism. But

143

criticism of the arts springing from the thought of C. G. Jung has been much less familiar. Jung was drawn toward literary criticism himself: it creeps into his scientific writing repeatedly and we may ask ourselves how much he may have repressed in order that the ideal of science might be served. Herbert Read has written interestingly about painting and sculpture from a Jungian point of view; there has been some useful and stimulating criticism of the sculpture of Henry Moore—who seems very often to be seeking to give archetypes a shape—along Jungian lines. Of late years a renewed interest in the painting of some of the Romantics has brought forth Jungian explications; I am thinking especially of some books written about the Swiss-English painter Henry Fuseli. Jungian comment on literature has come from a somewhat unsuspected source, for one would not immediately have thought of J. B. Priestley as a Jungian; but he acknowledges a great debt to Jung, and some of the best passages in his much underrated book *Literature and Western Man* are Jungian in inspiration and method. Indeed, I have sometimes thought that the sheer weight of common sense in that book, and its Jungian bias, are what have put conventional critics so much against it. For Jungian thought, although it looks at common sense through a prism that splits it into many facets, leaves it common sense still, and much of the reluctance of conventional people to recognize it as such is no more than the ordinary disposition of the intellectual to prefer the complex to the simple, and the distant vision to what is directly under his nose. In Jungian terms it might be described as an over-valuation of the Thinking Faculty.

In attempting to talk to you about Jung and the Theatre I must at once admit to having bitten off far more than I can chew. There is enough material in the subject to engross the attention of a year-long weekly seminar, and anything that I can do tonight must be confined to a hop-skip-and-jump. Was Jung interested in the theatre? It seems that he was not, and in all the *Collected Works* I can find only two references in the Indexes to either Theatre or Drama. These references are, however, strongly suggestive. It goes without saying that they are the comments of a writer who seems to regard the theatre, as so many people do, as primarily a branch of literature. I disagree with that point of view, for the theatre was already old when what we generally call literature was still unheard of. The theatre is as old as Prophecy and the Epic, and to look upon it as the bastard sibling of such Johnny-come-latelies in the arts as the Novel or Lyric Poetry is to do it a grave injustice. The appeal of the Theatre is primal, and it continues to be so even in its most modern forms. The more it partakes of primal quality in feeling, the more effective it is as theatrical art.

Jung gives me courage. He writes: 'One might describe the theatre, somewhat unaesthetically, as an institution for working out private complexes in public.' I may as well jump in with both feet and mark out my ground at once: in my opinion the theatre is a house of dreams, in which audiences gather to share a dream that is presented to them by a group of artists who are particularly skilled in bodying forth dreams. The script of the play is at best no more than the plan from which they work; it may be a plan of unique literary value, but it is not and cannot be the whole of the dream which is presented on the stage, because many other artists may bring their contributions to that completed artistic whole. There are the actors, who are skilled in the crafts of making themselves vivid and attractive in roles which present characters often at variance with their private personalities; in great plays these actors must also be highly skilled speakers, who give point and cogency to the words they say which cannot be rivalled by the person who reads a play to himself. And there is the designer, who offers a splendid *milieu* for the dream, aided by a designer of lighting who may claim to be an artist in his own right. And there is the composer, whose music supports the play and intensifies the feeling it evokes. And there is the audience itself, which provides each of its members with a sense of sharing the experience of the play, which also heightens the effect of that experience. A fine performance of a great play is one of the most compelling and rewarding experiences our culture provides, and it is also a highly sophisticated version of that experience of which anthropologists have written, where members of the tribe gather together to be told a great dream which is of importance to the tribe.

Do you think I am making extreme claims for the theatre? Certainly I am talking about the theatre at its best. I am thinking of certain performances of great plays I have seen during my lifetime, such as a thrilling performance of Goethe's *Faust*—the whole of it—presented on two successive nights at the Salzburg Festival. I am thinking of a magnificent performance of *The Magic Flute* which I once saw at Covent Garden —because I include opera under my general heading of theatre. I am thinking of certain performances of Greek plays, of Shakespeare, of Ibsen, of Chekov, and certainly of some splendidly life-enhancing performances of superb comedies, such as *The Way of the World*, *The Country Wife*, *The School for Scandal*—performances which were great experiences of what G. K. Chesterton so finely called 'the mysticism of happiness'.

I am not talking only about television serials, or B-movies, but television serials and B-movies have their place, as well, because those who claim to experience and value art only on the highest level know nothing whatever about art; television serials and B-movies body forth the dreams of a large number of people, or else money-greedy entrepreneurs would not continue to manufacture them. Art is not democratic; it is aristocratic, and to suggest that everybody will love the highest when they see it is demonstrably rubbish. They won't. But they will love what reaches them, and the human need which is satisfied by television serials and B-movies is nearer to the human need which feeds on *Hamlet* and *Oedipus* than either of them is to the psyche of the person who cannot dream, or does not dare to dream, and who is bored by the theatre.

What we expect to find in a dream, of course, are dream-figures and archetypal involvements. It is for this reason, I believe, that Realism in the theatre is a dead end. When I was a very young man a play visited Toronto that was, at that time, the very pinnacle of Realist drama. It was Elmer Rice's *Street Scene*. The stage setting was of a group of houses in a New York slum. The windows opened, and could be shut. Garbage cans containing real garbage stood at the front doors. Some of the garbage had fallen on the pavement, and occasionally people slipped on it. A woman was having a baby in one of the upstairs flats, and her groans and occasional piercing shrieks punctuated the play. A policeman passed up and down the street, and children jeered at him. Morning gave place to mid-day, which in its turn gave place to dusk; one marvelled at the cleverness of the man on the switchboard. It was all quite wonderful. You could almost smell it. But to save my life I cannot remember what the play was about, and I have not since cared to read it to find out.

In that same autumn, however, I saw *A Midsummer Night's Dream* for the first time. The company had little money, but they had a good deal of talent and they acted the play in a setting which was simply curtains. The magical flower which figures in the action was obviously a paper flower, and when Bottom appeared in the ass's head it was plain that it was a head made of *papier mâché*. This was the very opposite of Realism. But it was a great dream, and nobody in the audience cared a damn about Realism after the first ten minutes. I have seen that play, I suppose, at least a dozen times since, sometimes sparely set on the stage, and sometimes very lavishly and beautifully mounted. Every time I respond in the same way: I am the Duke, I am both the male lovers, I am all the clowns, I am Bottom the Weaver making a glorious ass of himself in the enchanted wood. Because, you see, this is one of the very greatest dreams of the tribe, and whenever I see it I feel both immeasurably enriched in myself and also very much more a member of the tribe. Here, in the present, the past has spoken to me, as I know that it will speak to the future when I am no more. And this is not Realism which is an imitation of surfaces; it is the vast, complex panorama of life itself, of which I am a part, and which the great dream permits me to experience, for the duration of the play, at the very centre.

I feel, however, that it would be unfair if I spoke to you now solely in terms of Shakespeare and Goethe and the mighty Greeks, because supreme works of art are themselves convincing arguments in favour of any theory to which they can be attached, however frail the attachment may be. So in order to demonstrate my ideas about the Jungian content of effective drama I am going to confine my examples to the popular drama of the nineteenth century—to what is called—usually with an undertone of contempt—melodrama. Nobody can then say that I am marshalling an army of great writers on my side in order to cloud my argument. Melodrama has, until quite recently, been considered beneath serious criticism, because its literary content is not arresting. Its theatrical—or, if you think the word more impressive, its dramatic—content is, however, indisputable. Melodrama was a theatrical mode which filled the theatres of the nineteenth century, and if we despise it, we would do well to remember that there were people in those audiences whose taste we admire in matters of the novel, of poetry, of all the arts, of statesmanship, and of philosophy; if they were not fools in these things, why should we assume that they were fools when they went to the theatre?

When people speak of melodrama, however, they are often referring to the worst examples of the *genre*, and surprisingly often they are referring to plays they have never seen seriously and well presented. One of the greatest and most successful writers of melodrama, Douglas Jerrold, described it in a government report as a type of play having a great many telling situations, with a physical rather than a mental appeal. Well, it depends on what you mean by 'mental'; certainly we do not go to the theatre in order to hear philosophers debate, but neither do we go to see nothing but physical action. We go, most of the time, for emotional experience; the theatre is a temple of art, and that means a temple of feeling.

If we are to talk about melodrama, I must describe a few examples to you. I should like to begin with a play which I regard as a very great melodrama, and which has had considerable success on the stage. The name of its author is not wholly unknown, either. I speak of Lord Byron's play *Manfred.*

Byron himself described *Manfred* as 'very wild, metaphysical and inexplicable'. Briefly described, it is about a nobleman who is in despair because he has, in some manner which is not specified, destroyed the woman he loved. It is made abundantly clear that this woman who is given the name of Astarte was his spiritual likeness, his feminine self—as we should say in our Jungian vocabulary, she was his Anima. Listen to the words in which he describes her:

> She was like me in lineaments; her eyes,
> Her hair, her features, all to the very tone
> Even of her voice, they said were like to mine;
> But soften'd all, and tempered into beauty:
> She had the same lone thoughts and wanderings,
> The quest of hidden knowledge, and a mind

> To comprehend the universe: nor these
> Alone, but with them gentler power than mine,
> Pity, and smiles and tears—which I had not;
> And tenderness—but that I had for her;
> Humility—and that I never had.
> Her faults were mine—her virtues were her own—
> I loved her, and destroyed her!

WITCH: With thy hand?

MANFRED: Not with my hand, but heart, which broke her heart;
> It gazed on mine, and wither'd. I have shed
> Blood, but not hers—and yet her blood was shed;
> I saw—and could not stanch it.

Separation from her is intolerable, and Manfred seeks the aid of magic to recall her spirit. He is confronted by terrifying apparitions of many kinds, and at last he is confronted by Rhadamanthus himself, the great Judge of the Underworld; in answer to the emotional power of his demand the Phantom of Astarte appears, and though he begs in agony for her forgiveness, she speaks only to predict his death. And, at the end of the play he does indeed die, refusing spiritual comfort and unrepentant of his pride and his sins, defying the evil spirits that seek to possess him, and hopeful that the mercy of Astarte will lead him to bliss—which means reunion with her.

Byron told a friend in a letter that the germs of *Manfred* were to be found in a journal which he had sent to his half-sister, Augusta Leigh. This was the sister whom it was pretty generally asserted that he had loved incestuously, and who bore what was believed to be his child. The mainspring of the plot of the play is incest. It does not much matter that Augusta Leigh was rather a silly little woman, and that her fate was not that of the heroine of the play. What matters is that Byron has written a very fine play about a man who is divided from his soul, who seeks reunion with it, and gains it at a terrible cost.

The Jungian elements in this play are easily identified. Manfred is the Fatal Man, the incubus-devil who destroys what he loves but who seeks Redemption; the consulting-rooms of analysts are crowded with such people, though they do not describe their plight in Byronic verse. The Phantom of Astarte is the lost Anima, 'whose voice was like the voice of his own soul, heard in the calm of thought'. There is also a Wise Old Man in the play, the Abbot of St. Maurice, whose advice Manfred scorns; there is an archetypal Friend, who saves Manfred from self-destruction before he receives Astarte's promise of redemption. And there is the Witch of the Alps, a figure of the dark side of the Anima, whom one is sometimes inclined to think might have been a better match for Manfred than the beautiful Astarte. There they all are, the Jungian Theatre Company of the Archetypes, acting out their accustomed roles, and speaking in Byronic verse of a high order. In *Manfred*, the date of which is 1816, we have a drama which deals with a splendid, passionate grappling with the dark side of man's nature, in a dramatic *milieu* where only death may be accepted as the settlement of all debts.

Not every writer of melodrama was a Byron, of course, and during the nineteenth century we often see this great theme degenerate in lesser hands into the struggle of Virtue against Vice, where both Virtue and Vice have been reduced from aristocratic, heaven-storming dimensions to merely *bourgeois* conflicts. But let us not be superior, for the *bourgeoisie* has its soul struggle as well as the poets and the aristocrats, and things must be described in terms which are congruous and comprehensible to those who wish to understand them.

The drama of the Redeemed Man is common enough in the nineteenth century. There were several versions of *The Flying Dutchman*, condemned to sail the seas until he is freed by the love of a pure woman. We know it still, and respond to it still, in Wagner's powerful opera of that name. The man who kills his soul appears again and again. In Victor Hugo's play *Le Roi s'amuse* it is the savage jester who, in his desire to avenge himself on an enemy, kills his own daughter—the only creature he loves. That story persists, too, in Verdi's *Rigoletto*. And there is the drama of the Lost Lady, the woman who seems to be of doubtful virtue, but whose nobility of soul is far above the understanding of the lover who turns against her. It has had many versions, of which the most famous was the younger Dumas's *La Dame aux Camélias*, once again preserved for us—and still doing sell-out business—in Verdi's *La Traviata*.

Why do we continue to respond to these figures and the dramas in which they appear? Because they are of archetypal power. It is beside the point to say that they are not 'like life'. Which life are you talking about? The life of the daily papers, or the inner life of the psyche? Indeed, does it matter, for it is unusual to read the daily papers without finding at least one news report in which, beneath the surface, we detect an archetypal strain in some crime of vengeance, or wounded pride, or despair because a spiritual treasure has been lost. In the theatre, understandably, such stories are presented in a heightened form, in which all the tedium and apparent irrelevance of everyday reality has been set aside. But if you strip tedium and irrelevance away from many painful and arresting human predicaments you arrive at an essence which we may call melodrama, and its simplified form is dream-like.

Consider, for instance, the most commonplace of plots, which was used for a thousand melodramas, and which occurs to many people whenever the word melodrama is used. I mean the plot where an Innocent Village Maiden is loved by a Worthy Young Man, but whose virtue is menaced by the Villainous Squire. Eventually there is a showdown, in which the Squire is worsted, but before that happens both the young people have felt the weight of his oppression. The plot became a melodramatic cliché simply because it was also a cliché of human experience. In a highly stratified society a man of wealth and position can, if he wishes, rob a girl of inferior station of her virtue, and social historians have made it plain that in the nineteenth century it was by no means usual for a humble girl to reach the age of sixteen with her virginity intact.

It is no use saying that in such cases the girl may have been a wholly or partly willing party to her seduction, and that her humble lover accepted the situation as he found it. Whatever the facts of her own special case might have been, a humble female playgoer liked to think that she had been wronged; to present before her eyes the case of a girl who was an idealized version of herself, who struggled to maintain her virtue, and did so, was acceptable drama to her. It was as though she were living through her own drama again, in a greatly improved version. It was a dream of virtue, and who would be so hard-hearted as to deny her the satisfaction of that dream? Those to whom virtue is a luxury, dream of virtue. The aspirations of the psyche, and daily reality, are not identical.

In this century there have been several extremely popular plays which are based on the notion that love, and goodwill—but especially Love—will overcome all difficulties, and bridge all chasms of social or cultural difference. Such a play was the immensely successful *Abie's Irish Rose*, in which Love overcame the gulf between Catholicism and Judaism. A more recent example was the play called *A Majority of One*, in which a Jewish lady of no particular culture but a rich folk-wisdom discovered that she and a Japanese gentleman of substantial wealth and rather advanced culture were soul-mates. These plays succeed because people wish that the ideas they put forward were true. They are wish-fulfilments. They are, in fact, dreams which millions of by no means simple people cherish in their inmost hearts.

But to return to nineteenth-century melodrama, and the archetypal figures it presents, is there anyone here who knows Dion Boucicault's famous play *The Colleen Bawn*? Probably not, but it had a successful stage life of more than fifty years, beginning in 1860. Very briefly, the story is about a young Irishman of aristocratic birth, Hardress Cregan, who loves a girl who is distinguished by her beauty and goodness, Eily O'Connor, known as the Colleen Bawn, which means the Beautiful Maiden. But Eily is of humble birth, and Cregan soon finds that his family look down on her, and he thinks he cannot accept her as his wife. The plot is subtle and complex, but in a few words, he conspires at her murder, although it is his mother who actually sets the machinery of the murder in motion. What is interesting to us is that the murderer, who fails in his attempt, is a hunchbacked servant named Danny Mann, who loves Hardress like a brother; in fact, they are foster-brothers. Precisely what he is we are told in the first few lines of the play. A friend says to Cregan:

Hardress, who is that with you?
HARDRESS: Only Danny Mann, my boatman.
KYRLE: That fellow is like your shadow.

DANNY: Is it a cripple like me, that would be the shadow of an elegant gentleman like Mr. Hardress Cregan?

The author of *The Colleen Bawn* was no Jungian, but he was a very able playwright, and in the characters of Hardress and Danny Mann he gives us a Hero and his Shadow, and it is the task of the Shadow to do the evil deed which the Hero desires but does not like to contemplate. When Danny has been killed, Hardress is redeemed, and we are led to believe that he is wholly reconciled to his humble sweetheart.

But there is more to concern us in this deeply interesting play. Who kills Danny Mann, sparing the heroine from death and redeeming the hero? He is a delightful rogue called Myles-na-Coppaleen, who is a horse-breaker, a poacher, a distiller of illegal whisky, and unquestionably the largest spirit and most able man in the play. He is, indeed, its Hero in a very special sense, for he loves Eily O'Connor deeply—though not silently, for he is eloquent and witty—but knowing she loves Hardress and knowing himself to be something of a scoundrel, he gives her up at the end to the man she loves.

In Myles-na-Coppaleen we have a figure who is easily recognizable in Jungian terms as the Mercurius, the rogue who is sometimes benevolent and sometimes a trickster, an enemy to the law and the revenue officers, but a great friend to people of noble spirit, and to lovers. This Mercurius figure is by no means confined to this play alone; it is part of the apparatus of melodrama. Not infrequently the part was represented as being an Irishman, and much of the character that Irishmen have in popular opinion for being witty and irresponsible is the result of these stage representations. Boucicault created several of them, though they occurred before him, and after he had ceased to write.

But there is another element in Myles's character to which I call your attention. He loves the girl, but he does not get her. She goes to another man whom he believes to be more worthy of her love than himself. This situation is a common one in melodrama. It is the theme of Renunciation. Perhaps you are familiar with it in one of the most celebrated of all melodramas, *The Only Way*. It is adapted from Charles Dickens'

A Tale of Two Cities. The drunken, dissolute, but noble-hearted lawyer Sydney Carton, loves Lucie Manette, but he knows himself to be unworthy of her: he contrives to die by the guillotine in the place of the man she truly loves, and who loves her, the French aristocrat Charles Darnay. His final words have become a melodramatic cliché: 'It is a far, far better thing that I do than I have ever done; it is a far, far better rest that I go to than I have ever known.' But I assure you stage speeches do not pass into the common speech because they are contemptible; they become clichés because they contain a truth. And what is the truth in this case? Is it, perhaps, that Sydney Carton loves Charles Darnay at least as much as he loves Lucie Manette? If so, I suppose we must call the emotion homosexuality, but it is certainly not homosexuality as it is presented by the Gay Liberation Movement. We must remember that the circumstance which made it possible for Sydney Carton to pass himself off as Charles Darnay was that they were uncommonly alike in appearance. Was Carton perhaps the Shadow of Darnay? Was he, in dying that Darnay might live, preserving whatever was best in himself? I do not want to push these Jungian explanations too far; they are too obvious to need feverish and insubstantial support. Let us suppose, therefore, that what lies behind the theme of Renunciation may sometimes be homosexual feeling. Surely we may admit that homosexuality, like heterosexual love, may lead to acts of nobility when it is associated with a noble spirit. And let us remember that a redeemed Shadow contains much that is of worth.

No discussion of this sort would be possible without some reference to the archetype of the Wise Old Man. He is a commonplace of melodrama, and sometimes he is presented with extraordinary power. A very popular play of the nineteenth century was *The Hunchback*, written by Sheridan Knowles, and first performed in 1832. Briefly, it is the story of a beautiful and accomplished girl named Julia, who has been brought up by the hunchbacked agent of the Earl of Rochdale. This strange, testy, but wise and good man brings to her Sir Thomas Clifford, who is noble and honourable, and they are betrothed. But when Julia discovers that Clifford has lost his fortune she rejects him, and accepts in his place a man who is obviously a fool. The plot is complex and interesting, but when at last it is resolved, we learn that Master Walter, the Hunchback, is the rightful Earl of Rochdale and also Julia's father; he had concealed his identity in order to spare her the ignominy of having to acknowledge a cripple. But he is able to make her rich and marry her to Clifford, and has the coolness to describe the agony of the young people, which he himself has brought about, as 'wholesome, though severe'.

The plot is manifestly absurd on the surface, but its appeal goes far below the surface. The theme of the proud girl who rejects the worthy but penniless suitor is a good one, and in another nineteenth-century favourite, *The Lady of Lyons*, by Bulwer-Lytton, it is exploited even more successfully than in *The Hunchback*. There is a special satisfaction for audiences —women as well as men—in seeing a beautiful and proud girl humiliated. But what interests us at the moment is the character of Master Walter; he is unquestionably one of those ambiguous monsters from fairy-tale—wise, uncanny, seemingly unkind, unpredictable, and extremely powerful—who puts the hero and the heroine through the fire of his trials so that they may prove themselves worthy of his eventual bounty.

This is the stuff of myth and fairy-tale, and certainly of archetype. I call your attention to the frequency with which disguise and concealed identity occur in these old plays. It is assumed that a great and wealthy man may conceal himself —and his very obvious humped back—for twenty years, without anybody spotting him. The only explanation for this absurdity is that people wish it were so. It is extraordinarily difficult to disguise oneself thoroughly, but much drama— some of the greatest drama—rests on the assumption that it can be done. And of course fairy-tale is full of it. And do we not all wish that it were so—that we might mix among our friends unknown, and live another life unsuspected? Part of the task of the theatre is to make wishes come true, and this is an instance of it.

Another and better play in which the archetype of the Wise Old Man is the mainspring of the plot is *Richelieu*, by Bulwer-Lytton, which was first seen in 1839, and held the stage for ninety years. The plot is about an attempt on the part of some French courtiers to lure the ward of the great Cardinal

Richelieu into a compromising situation, when she will become the mistress of the King, Louis XIII; there is also some political intrigue. But the play depends on the display of the many facets of the principal character, Richelieu himself. He is sometimes a worldly statesman; he has been a great lover and a warrior; in moments of moral fervour he remembers that he is still a priest.

I want to quote some lines of this play to you, because they are characteristically melodramatic. It would not do to speak of Richelieu without mentioning the scene which was most admired by audiences, and which very happily illustrates one aspect of the archetype of the Wise Old Man — the Wizard, the possessor of supernatural powers.

BARADAS: My lord, the King cannot believe Your Eminence
              So far forgets your duty and his greatness
              As to resist his mandate. Pray you, Madam,
              Obey the King — no cause for fear!
JULIE: My father!
RICH: She shall not stir!
BARADAS: You are not of her kindred —
              An orphan —
RICH: And her country is her mother!
BARADAS: The country is the King!
RICH: Ay, is it so;
              Then wakes the power which in the age of iron
              Burst forth to curb the great, and raise the low.
              Mark where she stands, around her form I draw
              The awful circle of our solemn church!
              Set but a foot within that holy ground,
              And on his head — yea, though it wore a crown —
              I launch the curse of Rome!
BARADAS: I dare not brave you!

The whole play is written in that sort of blank verse, and it is by no means bad. Indeed, it is immensely effective on the stage. And its secret, I think, is that it has the true archetypal ring. Do you remember that in *Memories, Dreams, Reflections* Jung writes: 'Archetypes speak the language of high rhetoric, even of bombast'? When he wrote that he was somewhat over-modestly trying to excuse the high tone which he himself had taken in the composition of the *Seven Sermons to the Dead*. Now the language of the *Seven Sermons* may be embarrassing if you are presenting yourself to the world, or even to yourself alone, as a man of science. But it would not come amiss in melodrama. What Jung says is quite true; elevated feeling expresses itself in elevated language, and if the writer does not happen to be a great poet—and they are few—the language of high rhetoric may serve him well and he may acquire a fine mastery of it. Repeatedly in melodrama the characters break into highly rhetorical language under emotional stress, and the audiences of the nineteenth century saw nothing wrong with it. In some unsophisticated plays very unlikely characters, soldiers or sailors, defend themselves against unjust reproach in language that shows extraordinary literary complexity. It was assumed by simple audiences that nothing but the best was good enough for the hero, and this inflated language was the best they knew. Similarly it is by no means uncommon in melodrama to find a young man or woman of humble birth, whose parents speak in a rural or lower-class dialect, expressing themselves in entirely correct, and even somewhat pretentious, upper-class English. One of the problems of the modern dramatist is that his characters are not permitted to be eloquent. We are at the moment in the grip of a resolute belief that nobody of any moral worth is able to express himself literately at all, and this shows itself not only in modern theatre dialogue, but in the public utterances of our politicians.

Other instances of the use of archetypal material in nineteenth-century plays could be brought forward, but I do not seek to weary you. I feel, however, that what I have to say would be incomplete even in this sketchy form if I did not make allusion to the figure of the Friend, the helper and server, who assists the Hero in time of need, but who does not seek to usurp the central role of the Hero. In melodrama it was by no means unusual for both the Hero and the Heroine to have a Friend of this sort, and it was an accepted convention that these friends should be comic characters. They were not strong in intellect, but they had mighty hearts; they said foolish things and worked themselves into foolish situations, but in the hour of crisis they could be counted on to do marvels. Not surprisingly, these Friends often served their employers as Valet and Lady's Maid. At the end of the play, when the Hero and Heroine were romantically united, or re-united, the Friends were comically united, to the delight of the audience. Because audiences for melodrama were very fond of symmetry, and had also a splendid Jungian feeling for quaternities, two marriages, uniting four people, was a conclusion greatly to their taste.

The other archetypal figure I must mention, however briefly, is the Miraculous Child. Two examples, from very famous and popular plays, will suffice. They are Little Willie in *East Lynne* and Little Eva in *Uncle Tom's Cabin*. When Little Willie dies we know—and we feel a chill at the knowledge —that the fortunes of his mother, Lady Isobel, have now reached a point of desolation from which they will never recover. And when Little Eva dies we recognize that the fate of the St. Clair family is sealed, and also that Uncle Tom's luck has gone into eclipse. It was my good fortune to see *Uncle Tom's Cabin* twice in childhood, and as I was a child myself, and a member of an unsophisticated audience, I felt the emotion without any interference from a superior critical faculty. When Little Eva died I knew that bad times were coming, and the light had gone out of the Hero's life. And when, in the final tableau, Little Eva appeared as an angel, and Uncle Tom's chains fell from his hands as he mounted into Heaven at her behest, I felt a great uplifting of the spirit, because I knew that his luck, or whatever you want to call it, had been restored to him, and that his salvation was assured. This was certainly primitive drama, but it was drama about a very big theme, presented in whole-hearted imagery; it was crude, but it was very much nearer to *Hamlet*, who also had flights of angels singing him to his rest, than it was to some trivial comedy about adultery or worldly ambition.

I began by saying that the theatre could be, and often is at its best, a place where an audience meets to experience one of the great dreams of the tribe. I have chosen my examples from an era of drama which I do not suppose is familiar to most of you, because it is not composed of plays which are read except by specialists in the history of the theatre. I did this purposely, so that you would not think that I was trying to support my case by references to masterpieces which carry great prestige. And I have talked about plays which all had great popular appeal, reaching not only playgoers of high cultivation, but also very simple people who went to the theatre for a night out, and a big value in emotional experience. They are not realistic plays, and it would not be far wide of the mark to call them dreams or fantasies.

Let me repeat what Jung said about his own encounter with by no means dissimilar experiences: 'I wrote down the fantasies as well as I could, and made an earnest effort to analyse the psychic conditions under which they had arisen. But I was able to do this only in clumsy language. First I formulated the things as I had observed them, usually in "high-flown" language, for that corresponds to the style of the archetypes. Archetypes speak the language of high rhetoric, even of bombast. It is a style I find embarrassing; it grates on my nerves, as when someone draws his nails down a plaster wall, or scrapes his knife against a plate. I had no choice but to write down everything in the style selected by the Unconscious itself....Below the threshold of consciousness everything was seething with life.'

It is from the source thus explored by Jung that much of the literature of Romance comes, but the melodramatic playwrights, many of them men of humble gifts and limited sensibility, seem often to have transferred the bombast of their inspiration directly to the stage without any of the alchemy observable, for instance, in the drama of Byron. But even at its worst, melodrama continued to draw on that realm where *'everything was seething with life'*, and to transfer as much as possible of that extraordinary psychic vitality to the stage. The plays, so neglectful of the externals of reality, were psychologically convincing because they spoke from these depths to corresponding depths in their audiences. However crude the effect might sometimes be, melodrama did not shrink from that battle with troll-folk, in the crypts of heart and head, which Ibsen said was the essence of life. So far as the conventions of the nineteenth century allowed, they tried to deal with much that was personal, subjective, and psychologically daring, and for the first eighty years of that century they made the essence of the Romantic Movement available to sections of the public that would be unlikely to encounter it in any other form.

Because I have drawn my examples from the nineteenth century I would not wish you to think that archetypal and dream material has no part in the drama of our time. Theatre, film, and television abound in it, but to trace its influence there would take more time than we have tonight. Permit me, instead, to point out that much of this melodrama of which I have been speaking, and the Jungian, archetypal material with which it deals, is still vital and popular in the opera houses and ballet theatres of the world, and that as opera and ballet they engage the deeply serious attention of some of the foremost theatre artists of our time, drawing large and by no means simple-minded audiences. It is only the emphasis that has changed; music has replaced language as the primary means of expression, and language supports music. A fine performance of *Rigoletto*, or *The Magic Flute*, or *Giselle*, or *Le Lac des Cygnes* is an experience in which we discern, and by no means dimly, the melodrama of the earlier day, and the mighty archetypal world from which it drew its themes. Nor is it irrelevant that opera and ballet are international in appeal.

If we seek the supreme genius in making the Jungian archetypal world manifest in the theatre of our time we shall find him in no playwright of the nineteenth century, but in Giuseppe Verdi, and in the works of Verdi we are transported immediately into that realm of phantasmagoria and dream-grotto where only the greatest artists are at home, and to which C. G. Jung, for a different purpose, has carried the illumination of his very different genius.

Insanity in
Literature

IT IS UNDERSTANDABLE *that insanity should be a frequent theme in poetry and fiction and drama; it is one of the most arresting evidences of the frailty of that reason on which civilized man so prides himself; we all stand much nearer to unreason than we suppose. The exploration of insanity that has taken place during the past century has told us much, and has offered some improvements in the alleviation, and sometimes the cure, of mental disorder. All my life I have been keenly interested in what medical science can do in this realm, and I have been greatly complimented by invitations to talk, first to the medical staff of the Clarke Institute in Toronto in 1976, and later to the Department of Psychiatry in the medical faculty of the University of Ottawa in 1977. On both occasions I was rewarded by the opportunity to talk to psychiatrists about their work, without being under the constraint of making them a professional visit.*

WHEN I WAS ASKED what I would speak about tonight, I suggested airily that 'Insanity in Literature' might provide a topic. It was not until I put myself to the task of composing an address that I realized that I had bitten off far, far more than I could possibly chew in the compass of an after-dinner speech; I had proposed a subject that would pro-

161

vide material for quite a thick book. As I toiled on, wondering what I might choose from the mass of material at hand, it occurred to me also that you might wonder why I had chosen such a theme. I know something about literature; that is how I get my humble living. But do I know anything about insanity? Anything, that is to say, that would entitle me to speak on such a subject to such an audience as this?

The truth is that I have been fascinated by insanity since I was a child. By the time I was three years old I was aware of it, because our village madwoman lived directly opposite my parents' house. Every village has its madwoman, and ours was of special consequence because she was also rich. Her heirs were waiting for her to die; they visited her frequently, and sometimes they might be seen coming down the steps in haste, followed by her abusive screams. She lived in a Victorian house—a tall house, painted grey, and with plenty of those ornamental windows which such houses have—windows that one cannot imagine opening inward into any pleasant or ordinary room. The heirs did not interest me, because I did not know what they were, but Miss Ferguson herself was the star of the drama of my childish world, because from time to time she would escape from the big, strong woman who was her keeper, and dash out into the road, throw herself down in the dust—because it was a dirt road—and throw up a cloud like a hen having a dirt-bath, meanwhile screaming in a terrified voice, 'Christian men—come and help me! Christian men—come and help me!' As indeed they did. Men—more or less Christian—used to assemble quickly and assist the keeper to get Aunt Ellen—which was what everybody called her—back into her Victorian Gothic prison. When you think of this drama you must imagine a small figure, transfixed in wonder, standing at one side of the wide movie screen with its back to the camera. Me.

I recall that once, when my mother was haling me off to bed at what I thought an unreasonably early hour, I threw myself on the floor and shouted 'Christian men, come and help me!' and my mother was displeased; she said I was not to make fun of Miss Ferguson, who was to be pitied. But it was not my intention to make fun of her; I simply wanted to be like her.

She was the most dramatic character in my world, and I accorded her the compliment of imitation.

My family had an insane member of its own, as I suppose many families do. He was a cousin of my mother's who had qualified as a medical doctor, but never practised, because he had fallen in love with a young woman who refused his suit, and he went strange for several months. Doc, as he was always called, was a victim of unrequited love, and you may judge how romantic a family mine was when I say that this was accepted as a perfectly valid reason for losing his wits. He recovered some of them in time, but never fully; he did not work in the ordinary way, but he devoted himself to mechanical and physical experiments, the purpose of which was to discover the principle of perpetual motion. He never found it, but he lived in a houseful of wheels and springs and water-engines, seeking for it, until he was almost ninety. He sustained life almost entirely on a diet of oatmeal porridge, and was buried in what was to have been his wedding suit. When I became a writer, he used to secure copies of all my books from the Public Library—because he was extremely tight with his considerable fortune—and would write to me, as each one appeared, a letter that never varied in form. It went:

> Dear Cousin—
> I have read your book. I presume
> you know that there are typographical
> errors on the following pages.
> Yr. affct. cousin,
> O. A. Langs

I used sometimes to wish that I could achieve the Nobel Prize, just to see if it would jolt a compliment out of Doc. But alas, he has gone where there are no typographical errors, and I shall never know.

You see that my interest in insanity began early, and it has never abated. When I was at Queen's University I was taught by a psychologist who later achieved a substantial reputation, and who was a wonderful instructor. His name was George Humphrey, and for many years he was Professor of Psychology at Oxford. I sometimes discussed with him an ambition I then held, which was to be a psychiatrist. He advised against it. Be a ditchdigger, he said, or make a profession of pulling up tree-stumps with your bare hands, but do not be a psychiatrist; the work is brutally hard, and the rewards are meagre. If you are a psychiatrist you will have to spend many hours each day talking to, and listening to, people whom nobody else can stand. I don't think you have the temperament for it. I heeded his advice, and became an author; the work is brutally hard and the rewards are meagre, but at least you can choose your own company.

Literature, however, only emphasized my concern with madness. Literature is full of it, and it is a matter of endless fascination to me to observe how various authors have dealt with it. Some of them know a great deal about the subject; the concern of others is merely romantic. They use madness to get rid of characters whom they cannot quite persuade themselves to kill. In my time I have read countless novels, usually from the Victorian period, in which characters succumb to an illness called 'brain-fever', which is usually brought on by overwork of an intellectual kind. Now I understand that there really is a brain-fever, more properly called encephalomyelitis, and if I am not mistaken it is truly an inflammation of the brain. But the brain-fever of the novelists sounds more like mononucleosis, accompanied by fatigue and depression which, under the care of a Victorian doctor who believed in a low diet, bleeding, and heavy purging, might very well present all kinds of distressing complications. But brain-fever was generally invoked by novelists when they wanted to get a character out of the way for an unspecified period of time. Recovery was common; the afflicted person reappeared in the novel, pale and interesting, in time to play his allotted part, which was frequently to reveal a secret known only to himself, which would have brought the novel to an abrupt end if it had been made known too early.

Shakespeare knew a great deal about madness, as he knew about so many things. His most famous madman is unquestionably Hamlet, and the fascination of Hamlet is that we cannot be sure whether he is mad or not. He pretends to madness, certainly, and talks irrationally in order to annoy people he does not like. Sometimes his despair—as for instance when he discovers that Ophelia is acting as an agent for the King and her father, in order to trap him into damaging confessions—verges on madness. When he has killed Polonius he exhibits symptoms that look like madness, but which are really a combination of despair and cunning. We who sit in the audience know that in whatever is of great importance Hamlet is not mad; he is the sanest person in the play. But I need hardly tell such an audience as this that keen insight may alternate with apparently irrational behaviour in people who are under extreme emotional stress, and that to call this madness is altogether too simple a solution to the problem.

The unquestionably mad character in *Hamlet* is Ophelia, and the reasons for her madness are plain: the man she has thought of as her lover rejects her and kills her father. In some modern productions of *Hamlet* it is also suggested that she is pregnant. This seems to me to be quite needless and unjustified. But what is of interest to us here is not the fact that Ophelia is mad, but the means Shakespeare uses to show us that she is so. He chooses a typically Shakespearean device, which is music. Ophelia does not rave, though she says some mystifying things; she sings, and it is the choice of her songs that tells us her story and the emotional confusion that has robbed her of her sanity.

Her songs are sharply contrasted, and have two themes, death and unfaithful love. One seems to spring naturally from her mourning for her father, because we have seen that she was an attached and dutiful daughter—more dutiful, perhaps, than was good for her. The other song is a rowdy piece about seduction, and for a moment we may wonder where such a girl would learn such a song. But as we all know, the most carefully brought up girls come to know things that we might imagine were unsuitable for them, and the song Ophelia sings she might easily have heard soldiers singing in the royal castle of Denmark. It is amazing how much we can forget, however often we are told, whereas a dirty limerick, once heard, clings to the mind like a burr. It satisfies something in us of which we may be ashamed, but which we disown at our peril. Ophelia in her madness displays the most touching pathos linked with a coarseness which is even more touching because it seems to be so much out of character. But is it? I do not need to tell you what jarring and extraordinary elements are to be found in apparently normal human beings.

But I must not tell you what madness is: that would be the grossest impudence on my part. I want to give you some instances of madness in literature, and in this case I am demonstrating the extraordinary art and compression with which Shakespeare has shown us the destruction of a mind, told us the reasons for it, and wrung our hearts in a scene of 219 lines. And how did he do it? With music, primarily, and we know the power of music to evoke feeling without offering tedious justifications. Music was sometimes used in past ages as a palliative for mad people. Probably the most famous patient was Philip v of Spain, who suffered from melancholy depression. Every night for ten years (1736–46) the famous *castrato* singer Farinelli sang the same four songs to the king: we know what they were: he sang them rather more than 3600 times. He saved the king's reason and he received a fee of 50,000 francs a year. Any of you who have pleasing voices might reflect on this story.

But to return to the case of Ophelia. Was this genius unaided by science, or did Shakespeare know anything specific about madness? I think he knew a good deal of what we might now call the clinical aspect of insanity, because a great deal more was known about madness in his time than we sometimes realize. One of the greatest books on madness that has ever been written in any age was the work of a man who was thirty-nine when Shakespeare died.The book is *The Anatomy of Melancholy* and its author was Robert Burton, an Oxford scholar; it first appeared in 1621, and it ran through five editions in the author's lifetime. Shakespeare, who died in 1616, could not have read it, but if its contents were in the air, so to speak, he might have been aware of much that Burton describes. Sir William Osler called this book 'the greatest work on medicine ever written by a layman'. Sir William meant that as praise, but I think the book is not the work of a layman; it is the work of a clergyman who was himself seriously afflicted with what he called melancholy, and what we might nowadays call neurosis; 'I write of melancholy,' he says, 'by being busy to avoid melancholy'; as a neurotic Burton was no amateur; he knew what he was talking about. There is strong suspicion that he died by hanging himself, but I do not see how that could be, for he is buried in the Cathedral at Oxford and I cannot conceive that the Dean and Chapter would permit a suicide to be buried there, especially with a rather showy monument which displays, among other information, the astrological chart of Burton's nativity. I mention the matter of suicide simply to show that Burton was the kind of man about whom such a thing could be said; he was a melancholy man, and everybody knew it.

I am sure that some of you know Burton's book, but I should be surprised if all of you had read it. What has he to say about melancholy? It would be easier to tell you what he does not say about it. The book is long, but none of its admirers—in which number I count myself—think it too long. I first met it when I was twenty, and I read it through; since that time I do not think a year has passed in which I have not reread some substantial portion of it. In the true sense of the word it is a delightful book. Not because it is quaint—though certainly it seems quaint when first one encounters it. Not because it is a repository of all sorts of queer information, obscure belief, and remote classical reference—though some of its charm lies there. Not because it affords us the trashy pleasure of laughing at some unquestionably exploded and absurd ideas—though there are plenty of these. No, the delight of *The Anatomy of Melancholy* lies in its splendidly humane scholarship and penetrating wisdom, which make it a book that is a friend for a lifetime. When I read it now I am not the student who read it when he was twenty, nor am I the man who read it when he was engaged in the often melancholy work of editing a daily newspaper. I have read it married and unmarried: I have read it when childless, when a father, and when a grandfather, and it has shown something new and valuable to me in these and all my other conditions of life. If I am lucky I shall read it as a very old man, and I am sure I shall find things in it then which elude me now.

But I am growing enthusiastic, and I can see you becoming restless, as you long to be through with me, and rush out to the bookshops to acquire this phoenix among books for yourself. If you do not know it already, be careful, I beg you. Your first acquaintance with the book may be like biting a peach and breaking a tooth on the stone. For one thing, it is a long book. For another, when you open it, you will find that it is crammed with quotations in Latin. And you will find the rhythm of it somewhat unfamiliar, for Burton writes headlong, as if he wanted to cram all he could into a single sentence; he roars, he ejaculates, sometimes he seems to stutter. So don't rush at Burton; creep up on him slowly. I told you I read the book through when first I bought it, but I am a book-glutton, and can read anything. You may find that the book has a powerful effect on your vocabulary, and that instead of describing your patients in the proper modern scientific terms, you fall into Burtonese and tell them or their relatives that they are the veriest hare-brains, dizzards, and creatures of wit most dry and adust; if they resent this (as they most certainly will) you may condemn their scurrile and malicious obloquies, flouts, and calumnies, and scorn them as railers and detractors. Because, you see, one of the charms of Burton is that he never uses one word when five or six will do, and his words are of a Jacobean directness and splendour. Like everybody else worth knowing, Burton takes a little getting used to. But once you have fallen under his spell, you are his forever.

Am I recommending mere quaintness, or has he anything to say to the modern psychiatrist—or, as he would say, mad-doctor? Yes, he has everything to say to you. Read him with care and you will find the basic ideas of Freud and Jung set before you in seventeenth-century terms. You will find recipes for drug therapy. The *Anatomy* is divided into three principal partitions, each of which is, in its turn, divided into sections, members, and subsections. The first part deals with the causes and symptoms of melancholy; part two tells of the cure of melancholy; part three deals particularly with love melancholy and religious melancholy. There is much in the book which is at present unfashionable, and about which we may fittingly be reminded. For instance, Burton pays detailed attention to jealousy as a cause of melancholy. Jealousy is much out of fashion; we do not hear it mentioned as a factor in professional life, or the world of business, or as an element in politics. Where is the modern critic, either in the arts or in the sciences, who will admit that jealousy plays any part in his judgements? Is this because jealousy has suddenly and mysteriously disappeared from our world? Is it, of all sins, the one we have conquered and banished? I do not think so. But when did you last hear jealousy mentioned as the mainspring of any mean action, or plot, or public or private attack? Read Burton on jealousy, and be refreshed.

Indeed, read Burton on almost anything. Dr. Samuel Johnson said that this was the only book that ever took him out of bed two hours sooner than he intended to rise. Sir William Osler, who was a good bookman as well as a good doctor, delighted in Burton. So, if you do not know him already, let me introduce you to this great master of your healing art. Let me offer a word of advice, however: if you are not thoroughly proficient in Latin, begin with the Everyman edition, which has translations of all the Latin passages included in the text. It makes the going very much easier.

I introduced Burton because he was for thirty-nine years of his life a contemporary of Shakespeare. There is no evidence that they knew each other, but the writer of *King Lear* would have been much at home with the writer of *The Anatomy of Melancholy*, and as they both understood jealousy to the uttermost depths of that powerful and destructive passion I am sure that they could have exchanged fruitful opinions about it.

I leave Burton only because I want to talk for a few minutes about the frequency with which we meet with scenes of madness in the theatre. The dramatists of an earlier day saw madmen in the streets—the Bethlehem-men, as they were called, because they were in a sense out-patients of the Hospital of St. Mary of Bethlehem in London, commonly called Bedlam. They wandered about in search of charity, and it is to the credit of mankind that they seem to have found it. Indeed, they were often accorded a special indulgence because it has for centuries, and in many lands, been a belief among simple people that madmen speak truth. It was as truth-speakers that Bedlamites often appeared in the drama of the seventeenth and eighteenth centuries. But the dramatists knew something that has always been acknowledged, though never trumpeted abroad, among the medical profession. That was that gross insanity among the poor and unfortunate becomes neurosis, or oddity, or eccentricity among those who are more fortunately placed in society. To be poor, and mad, is utter misery: to be mad, but to have well-to-do friends or family, is still misery, but it is not usually so gross in its manifestations. If you want to know what the eighteenth century thought of moneyed madness, look at Congreve's comedy *Love for Love*, in which young Valentine Legend pretends to be mad, because he is unlucky in love, and unlucky in money, as well. His disguise of madness makes it possible for him to speak truth as no man in his right mind would dare to do.

That is a comedy. But there is much madness in the tragedy of this era, as well. One of the greatest unjustly neglected tragedies in English is Otway's *Venice Preserv'd*, written in 1682 — forty-two years after Burton died. It is neglected now, I think, because during the Victorian era it was not fully understood. It is essentially a tragedy of homosexual love, in which a man stakes his whole life, including the wife whom he dearly loves, in order to prove himself to a male friend as a worthy partner in a conspiracy to overthrow a government. The woman, whose name is Belvidera, suffers horribly in this dreadful predicament, and at the end of the play she loses her reason; in the final desperately affecting scene we see her torn between the ghosts of her husband and the man whose esteem he values even above her affection. It is great tragedy, and its greatness owes much to the sufferings of its author, who spent a part of his life in the most painful subjection to a woman whom he loved to the pitch of madness, and who did not love him. I do not need to tell such an audience as this what that sort of love implies—a love which is in fact a bondage to an ideal that has nothing to do with the woman upon whom it is projected. The drama of the inner life is not something that has been discovered within the past century, as some people appear to think, and the complexities of homosexuality did not appear on the world stage at the end of the reign of Queen Victoria.

The tragedy of the seventeenth and eighteenth centuries abounds in mad scenes, and where there is tragedy there will also be comedy. The greatest comic mad scene in English drama, in my opinion, is in Sheridan's farce *The Critic*. The heroine, Tilburina, is crossed in love—precisely like my cousin, whom you will remember—and as the author observes, she comes in stark mad in white satin. A friend says, 'Why in white satin?', to which the author replies, very properly, 'O Lord, sir, when a heroine goes mad she always goes into white satin!' And Tilburina has her great mad speech, which was one of the things a leading actress demanded of a leading part. Here it is—

> The wind whistles—the moon rises—see,
> They have killed my squirrel in his cage!
> Is this a grasshopper!—Ha! no, it is my
> Whiskerandos—you shall not keep him—
> I know you have him in your pocket—
> An oyster may be crossed in love! Who says
> A whale's a bird?—Ha, did you call, my love?
> —He's here! He's here!—He's everywhere!
> Ah me! He's nowhere!

And the author inquires, with satisfaction, 'There, did you ever see anybody madder than that? You observe how she mangled the meter?' To which his friend replies, 'Yes, egad, it was the first thing made me suspect she was out of her senses.' There were many serious mad scenes in eighteenth-century plays that were not very different from that one. But by the end of the eighteenth century we had seen the end of the exploitation of madness for comic effect; during the nineteenth century it was regarded much more solemnly— which is not the same thing as taking it quite seriously.

The nineteenth century was pre-eminently an era of Romance in drama, poetry, and the novel, and the approach of the age to madness was deeply romantic. The squalor and destructiveness of lunacy were overlooked. Romance was itself often equated with madness, and a characteristic attitude is that of Matthew Gregory Lewis, who describes Romance as a 'fair enchantress'; one seeks her among

> …graves new-opened, or midst dungeons damp,
> Drear forests, ruin'd aisles and haunted towers,
> Forlorn she roves, and raves away the hours!

A very pretty picture, but it suggests a woman not so much mad as delightfully and self-indulgently melancholy. The figure of the beautiful lunatic—always female and young—is a common one in all romantic works. Where it arose, I cannot tell you, but it seems contrary to the experience of those who know most about the insane, and who do not find that insanity is a beautifier—is, indeed, quite the opposite. But now and again during the nineteenth century common sense and common observation assert themselves, as they do in Charlotte Brontë's *Jane Eyre*. The description of the mad Mrs. Rochester in that book is not glamourized, and the horrible moment when the heroine wakes from sleep and finds the madwoman looking down at her, about to set fire to the bed-curtains, is brilliantly described, but in well-controlled terms.

I should like, however, to direct your attention to a nineteenth-century writer whose name may be strange to many of you. Indeed, I find it is strange to all but inveterate book-gluttons like myself. His name is Henry Cockton, and he was not a very good writer; my amateur diagnosis of him, from reading several of his books, is that he was even more paranoid than authors generally are. His books abound in plots, schemes, treachery, and double-dealing, all on a strictly domestic scale. His heroes and heroines are rather disagreeable people, though he obviously wants us to like them. One of them is a tedious practical joker, whose name is Valentine Vox, and as you might guess, he is a ventriloquist, and uses his gift to make a thorough nuisance of himself. But it is not the jokes of *Valentine Vox the Ventriloquist* that interest us now, but the subplot of the story, which is about a man named Grimwood Goodman, whose relatives imprison him in a private lunatic asylum in order to get control of his money.

Would you believe that possible? It was quite possible in 1840, when the book appeared. In those days anybody in England could be committed to a private asylum if two medical practitioners certified him insane. Medical practitioners might mean apothecaries, and it was not even necessary for both of them to see the patient at the same time. The means by which Mr. Goodman is spirited away seem farcical, but they were founded on fact; two medical men visited him, tormented him with questions as to whether or not he claimed kinship with Queen Victoria, and drove the irascible man to such a pitch of rage that he ordered them out of his house; very soon afterward he was picked up in the street by two toughs, and whisked away to Dr. Holdem's private asylum, certified insane and violent by the two doctors who had provoked him. Dr. Holdem is a splendid character, described as having 'a fiend-like smile'—an invaluable possession for any psychiatrist, as I am sure you will admit. Once inside, how was Goodman to get out? The attendants included bruisers who took care of any complaints from patients and any attempts at escape. There were officials, also medical men, who were called Commissioners in Lunacy, whose task it was to visit such private asylums periodically, and inspect them. But when the Commissioners were expected Dr. Holdem had Mr. Goodman strapped down, and one of his assistants tickled the poor man's feet while the Doctor repeatedly asked him whether or not he had received a letter from the Emperor—no mention of which Emperor —recently. At last, to be released from torture, Goodman admitted to receiving such a letter, and when the Commissioners arrived, Dr. Holdem displayed poor Goodman to them, with the information that he had said that he had received a letter from the Emperor the day before. Perfectly simple, and quite horrible. Quite true, what is more, for the painstaking Cockton declared publicly that every outrage he described in his book he could swear had happened at a private asylum within forty miles of London. The book, though no great work of art, was instrumental in bringing about some reform of this abuse, though private asylums were a scandal in England for a long time afterward.

Valentine Vox contains a beautiful lunatic, by the way. She is kept in a special part of the madhouse, which is described as a 'den', and from which Goodman hears 'harsh screams and bitter imprecations'. So dreadful are these that he supposes the inmate of the den must be a raving maniac 'whose former life had been spent among the vilest and most degraded'. Not at all. Her case resembles Ophelia's. She is 'a fair girl, whose skin was as pure as alabaster, and whose hair hung luxuriantly down her back in flaxen ringlets'. Nevertheless, she was 'running round, shouting, screaming and uttering the most dreadful imprecations that ever proceeded from the lips of the most vicious of her sex'. It emerges that this girl has been locked up in the madhouse because she is an heiress who is a nuisance to her relatives. But what is perhaps most interesting about her to such an audience as this is contained in this very brief exchange between Goodman and one of the keepers. 'The character of her disease,' he says, 'is I suppose, very dreadful?' And the keeper replies: 'No: there ain't much the matter with her; she only wants a husband.' The theory of the sexual origin of neurosis was not so original with Sigmund Freud as we may have been led to believe. Indeed, he learned of it from J. M. Charcot, and as Cockton implies, it was part of the mythology of madness many decades earlier.

Not all nineteenth-century asylums were as dreadful as this. Bernard Shaw had an uncle who ended his days in an asylum, where the young Shaw and his father sometimes visited him. Upon these occasions he would not speak, or show any sign of recognition, until they were about to leave. Then he would take up his flute—for music was his great solace—and play *Home, Sweet Home*. A typically Irish story. But it demonstrates the fact that Shaw's uncle was contented and well-cared-for where he was, and perhaps had lost his taste for family life.

I do not want to weary you with detailed information about books in which insane people occur; my purpose, indeed, is simply to throw out a few hints as to books you might like to read if you are curious to discover what literary people have thought about madness. There is one modern novel which you should certainly not neglect, if your curiosity reaches so far. It is *The Ordeal of Gilbert Pinfold* by the late Evelyn Waugh. It appeared in 1957, and it is a classic of its kind. What gives it unusual interest is that it describes experiences which the author himself underwent during a period of stress in his life, and these are described with an economy and eloquence which I dare say are uncommon among the case histories your profession requires you to read. People of great talent have sometimes been mad, but only rarely have they written about it.

In 1954 Waugh was in bad shape, and in search of better health he went on a voyage to the Mediterranean and Ceylon. He had suffered disquieting symptoms, and on board ship they became worse. He heard voices in the night, calling his name, and jeering at him; he became aware of plots against his peace and even against his life; he suspected that the cables he sent home from the ship were being delayed by the radio officer, and circulated among the passengers for their amusement. His predicament is funny, and it is also horrible, because we know that Waugh underwent this confusion himself. His reason was not in good order, and his troubles were aggravated by the fact that he was taking massive doses of several sorts of medicine. He was taking some very strong pills for his rheumatism, and because he could not sleep he was taking a mixture of bromide and chloral; as it was ineffective he doubled and trebled his dosage. To quiet the nagging of his nerves he drank large quantities of port, gin, and brandy. More—he drank far more crème de menthe than most of us could possibly choke down, because he liked it. Let me repeat that these terrible dosings were not the cause of his doubtful sanity; they were little frills and arabesques which he added to it. The miracle is that he was able to write such a brilliant book as *Pinfold*, which I do not think has ever been equalled as a description of a man whose reason remains active, although the information on which it is acting is delusory. If you have not read it, read it. I do not suppose that you get many patients like Evelyn Waugh, but it can do you no harm to recognize the possibility.

I cannot pretend that I have done more than touch lightly on some of the high spots in the immense range of literature which deals with insanity. I have not spoken of writers who were acknowledged to be insane but whose work was of rare beauty—such poets as Christopher Smart in the eighteenth century, whose *A Song to David* I commend to you; and John Clare in the nineteenth century, whose poem *Written in Northampton County Asylum* is of a terrible pathos. I have not mentioned Thomas De Quincey's *Confessions of an English Opium Eater*, which is one of the great literary accounts of an addiction persisted in to the point of madness. I have said nothing of William Blake, a very great visionary poet who seemed mad to many of his contemporaries. I have purposely said nothing about my own novels, in which quite a lot of madness and borderline madness occurs, and occurs in a way which particularly interests me—that is, madness as, just possibly, a means of perceiving another sort of being from which something of great value may be learned. My most recent work is a trilogy in which a madwoman is one of the central characters because, although she is demonstrably insane, her insanity releases trains of thought and feeling in other people which are immensely fruitful. This is the way an author may look at unreason. I know it cannot be your way, but I think it has its purpose, for anything that coaxes us out of the beaten paths of thinking and feeling has value, and also presents us with great dangers.

I hope, however, that I have persuaded some of you that your work is not solely clinical, but has links with the world of art. A neurosis, as Dr. Freud often reminds us, is a form of creation—not the best kind, or an especially attractive kind, but undoubtedly one kind. And I hope that I have persuaded some of you that you are not the only people who look long and hard at insanity. Writers do so, too. Very often they think of it in relation to their own work. Thomas Mann, especially, wrote brilliantly about the relationship of art to madness, and of art to criminality. This is a direction in which several writers have tried to follow him. Of course some of them are silly and trivial, but not all. As Jung once said, the writer may see out of the corner of his eye what the grave clinician misses. And if I have trodden on anybody's toes, or seemed to intrude, as a layman, where I should have kept my distance, I can only say what Robert Burton says in the *Anatomy*: *Nemo aliquid recognoscat, nos mentimur omnia*. That is to say, let no one take these things to himself, they are all but fiction.

Five:
Masks of Satan

The Devil's
Burning Throne

THE FOUR LECTURES *that follow were the result of an invitation from Trinity College, Toronto, to give their Larkin-Stuart Lectures in November 1976. The problem of Evil in Literature had engaged me for some years, and I knew from personal experience that to make Evil palpable and acceptable in fiction was not simply a matter of inventing horrors and displaying them through the agency of characters who had been labelled as bad. Why bad? and who determines what badness is? I do not pretend that I met and defeated the problem, but I think I gave it a tussle, in terms of what public lectures may do.*

IT IS NOT UNCOMMON for the lecturer on such occasions as this to say that he approaches his task with a sense of his own inadequacy, and I ask your forgiveness for such a common-place. However, in my case it is not meant as a ritual cringe, but as a statement of truth. If I had known what I was getting into when I accepted the invitation of your Provost to be this year's lecturer in this distinguished series, I would have had the common sense to decline. But you know how persuasive the Provost is, and it was only after I had accepted and set about the task of preparing my lectures that I realized that I had bitten off more than I could ever hope to chew. As I recall our conversation he put it to me like this: 'Won't you come to Trinity in the autumn and talk about anything you like; the only condition is that whatever your subject may be, you should give it a mildly theological flavour.' I agreed, and he said, 'What do you suppose you might like to talk about?' As I had, for about five years, been busy with some writing which made me think a good deal about what Evil is, and how it works, and even where it comes from, I said, 'How would it be if I talked about ideas of Evil as they appear in literature?' 'Just the thing,' said he, 'and you'll have no difficulty in popping in a little theology here and there.' Light-heartedly I agreed to pop in any amount of theology, and we turned our conversation to other things.

Now the day of reckoning has arrived, and you cannot imagine what troubles I have had in the interval. I am not going to tell you about them; other people's troubles are the dullest sort of topic. But I realized as soon as I set to work that I would have to set some limits to my subject, so I decided that I would confine it to the literature of the nineteenth and twentieth centuries. I decided that I would say nothing about poetry. As for theology, I soon recognized with horror that I did not know enough about it.

Theology, like politics, is a subject on which every human creature, male and female, has some sort of opinion. Real theologians, however, are subtle fellows who very properly scorn amateur intruders into what they call the Queen of Sciences. I know that there are theologians among you, ready to explain the difference between a Principality and a Throne, and all the intricacies of Prevenient Grace. What I say will probably seem like baby-talk to them, but perhaps they will not be displeased that someone who is not professionally one of their number is nevertheless concerned about some of the problems that are their special concern.

Do I hear you say: If you don't know anything about your subject, what are you wasting our time for? But you see, I do know something about the literature of the nineteenth and twentieth centuries, and I do know something about the way in which Evil has been depicted and defined in it by writers who, like myself, are not theologians but who are seriously concerned by the problem of Evil. They look at it from a point of view which is not that of the theologians, but of the recorders, the analysts, the synthesizers of human experience. Their concern is principally to describe life, to experience human problems and to feel deeply, though not always sympathetically, about them. They are fascinated by Evil, in the true sense of that much misused word 'fascination', and in the main they agree with Thomas Hardy that

> *If way to the better there be*
> *It exacts a full look at the worst.*

But the full look at the worst may not leave the looker able to define the principle behind what he has seen. What is Evil? Can it be conquered or avoided? Where does it come from? Why is it so often more attractive than Good? Some writers have tried to answer these questions, and it is the answers they have given that I want to discuss with you in these lectures. The answers may not satisfy theologians, because the answers are not usually expressed in terms of philosophical clarity, and they are in every case tainted, or infected, or whatever word you want to use to say that they are coloured by the intense personal feeling of the literary artist.

Nevertheless, these literary answers have satisfied, or partly satisfied, millions of people whom theology does not reach. Theology is a discipline and it must retain a scholarly calm. Literature is not a discipline, but an art, and when it is calm it is easily overlooked. It is the heated, sometimes rowdy approach of literature to the problem of Evil that is my theme.

How do I propose to approach it? In the first of these lectures I want to talk about Melodrama. That is tonight's lecture, and its title is *The Devil's Burning Throne*. A luridly melodramatic title, is it not, quite in the nineteenth-century melodramatic mode? It comes from that supreme melodramatist Shakespeare. It is in *Measure for Measure* that he makes the Duke say

> —*let the Devil*
> *Be sometime honoured for his burning throne.*

And in the drama of the century past the Devil was given his full meed of respect, as I hope to show in a few minutes.

My second lecture, tomorrow night, is called *Phantasmagoria and Dream Grotto*; the phrase is from Carlyle, and it is also highly melodramatic, as was Carlyle's approach to history.

Under that general heading I want to talk about the nineteenth-century novel, with a good deal of emphasis, but not exclusive emphasis, on the work of Charles Dickens.

My third lecture will be called *Gleams and Glooms*. Whose phrase is that? It comes from Henry James, that great master of the ghost story and the uncanny story, and it is about ghost stories and uncanny stories I shall speak then. I offer no excuse for doing so. Ghost stories, as a *genre*, are somewhat neglected by literary critics, partly because so many of them are bad, but partly also, I think, because they tempt critics into quagmires and morasses in which critics fear to tread. The ghost story is above all things a story of feeling, and critics, for reasons we need not examine, are not particularly happy with feeling on this level. Tragedy—ah, with tragedy they are perfectly content, because you can discuss tragedy without becoming personally involved. But the ghost story is not tragedy; its light is moonlight, and there is an old belief that too much moonlight may make you mad. Critics, who prize their reason above all else, are understandably shy of it.

My final lecture is called *Thunder Without Rain*; that is T. S. Eliot's phrase. In it I shall talk about the novel of the twentieth century which seems to us so often to be rooted in the horror of life without any mitigation of whatever may be evoked of despair. Threat without blessing—that is, thunder without rain. Why are so many modern literary artists despairing? With some, of course, it is a fashionable pose. But what makes it fashionable? Why do so many readers hunger for this Dead Sea fruit? With our finest literary artists, however, it is far beyond any question of fashion: it is deep concern with the plight of man, to which there seems no solution. But I must confide to you that I am an optimist—not an idiot optimist, I hope, not a shallow-minded Pollyanna—and I think there is a solution, and in my final lecture I shall attempt to persuade you that it is an answer of a kind, though I dare not pretend that it is a complete answer.

There you are. That is what I am going to do, and I shall turn at once to the matter of Melodrama.

The word is often used now in a condescending manner, to suggest a bygone vulgar form of theatre art in which violent appeals to the emotions and sensational incidents were used to body forth a simple-minded morality. There are plenty of people—some of you may be of this class—to whom the word melodrama suggests a story about an innocent village maiden whose virtue is assailed by an evil squire, and who is rescued in the nick of time by her sailor-lover, whose nature is all courage, goodness, and devotion. Certainly there were melodramas of that sort, but they make up only a modest part of the whole melodramatic theatre. Similarly there are people who suppose that melodrama was always coarsely and vulgarly acted, and appealed only to humble and simple people. And there are many who cherish a few phrases from popular melodrama, such as 'Once aboard the lugger, and the girl is mine!' or 'Rags are royal raiment when worn for virtue's sake'; they suppose that all melodramatic writing was on that level. Consider this: melodrama was the most powerful and wide-spread dramatic mode of the nineteenth century, and it included all kinds of theatre except comedies and farces. Shakespeare, as the nineteenth century knew him, was a melodramatic writer. If you had gone to *The Merchant of Venice* a century ago, you would have seen a play about the thwarting of a bloody-minded villain seeking revenge on his tormentors, and everything in the play that diverted your attention from that theme—including the whole of the lyrically comic Fifth Act—would have been omitted. So also with *Hamlet*, in which virtually everything that makes the King, the Queen, and Laertes psychologically interesting was cut, to throw into prominence the character of Hamlet, who was represented as a poetical young man, too good for the surroundings in which he found himself.

Let us not be patronizing about this approach to Shakespeare. Nowadays we see productions of *A Midsummer Night's Dream* in which extraordinary pains are taken to show that all rulers and courtiers are rotten, that all people of humble station and limited education are good, and that fairies are malicious and sometimes dirty goblins.

We see *The Merchant of Venice* performed in a style which suggests that a principal theme is the struggle for Bassanio between Portia and his homosexual friend Antonio. We see *The Merry Wives of Windsor* with a corrupt aristocrat, Falstaff, at odds with some middle-class social climbers. Every age gets the Shakespeare it wants, and if the nineteenth century seemed to want it sweet and hot, our age seems to want it sour and cold. Melodrama dominated the stage of the nineteenth century, and brought everything to a pitch of passion that was sometimes irrational: our time, with its psychological and sociological bias, reduces whatever it can to psychology and sociology. We may say that, within certain limits, there is a correct and classical way to perform the music of Mozart or Beethoven, but we have not yet reached any agreement about a correct classical way in which to act Shakespeare and we put the stamp of our age upon him, however resistant his plays may be to that process.

The stamp of the nineteenth century was melodramatic. Emotion, the hottest and most violent that could be evoked, was what the public wanted. Why was it so?

In the nineteenth century in both Britain and the United States, hundreds of thousands of people moved from farms and villages to big cities, and changed from rural work to industrial work. These multitudes of uprooted people became aware of social inequality in a way that had not affected them before. More than that: they became aware of human inequality of the sort which is not subject to remedy by legislation and taxation in quite a new way. They found that some people were cleverer than others, more inventive and industrious than others, more adaptable than others and—it must be said and it is relevant to our main theme—luckier than others. It was no longer a world in which

> God bless the Squire and his relations
> And keep us in our proper stations

was a possible prayer. It was a world of new opportunities, where a factory-hand might see a man born in the same village as himself rise to extraordinary wealth and influence, and send his sons to Eton; understandably the unsuccessful man wondered what had gone wrong with the scheme of things. His strong back and biddable nature, which were all the capital he had, brought him less in town than it had in the country, and in town he had no Squire, who might be an easy-going gentleman with a kindly wife, who would feel an obligation toward him and perhaps take pity on his misfortunes, when they came.

What about this man's womenfolk? If they were lucky, they might escape factory work, and get into domestic service. And what was that? Very often it was slavery and wretchedness, psychological dwarfism and spiritual deformity. Frequently it was sexual exploitation. Maidservants in a badly conducted household were fair game for the footmen, who were great idle fellows with an inordinate opinion of themselves, of the kind made familiar to us in the writings of Thackeray. Sometimes also the girls were fair game for the sons of the household, or the master. And when a girl became pregnant, she lost her place, for who wants a pregnant housemaid, or her tedious bastard when it is born? So it was the street for her, and immediately the street became what Victorians called 'the streets'. It is an extraordinary fact that there were vastly more prostitutes in the great cities of the world in the nineteenth century than there are today. What then? Prostitution is not a calling which suits all those who take it up. One girl in a hundred might make a marriage of some sort; one girl in a thousand might do well at her trade; most ended up as prematurely old thieves, or prostitutes of the lowest grade, descriptively known as 'tuppenny uprights'—as distinguished, one assumes, from the 'grand horizontals'.

The respectable female servant might marry a footman and keep a pub; that was success. Or she might shrivel in service, only one in hundreds having the luck to be settled in a good place with a kind mistress. In either case, sexual denial was obligatory.

What has this to do with melodrama? Much indeed, for the theatre was the popular entertainment of the time, filling the place now occupied by the films and television, and providing the most acceptable night out for people who might not be able to read, and to whom a supper at an oyster bar, followed by five or six hours in a popular theatre, was bliss, and spiritual refreshment, and a glimpse of the world as they wished it to be, and as perhaps they believed it really was, if only a few things could be set right.

What was it like, a night out in one of these nineteenth-century theatres that played so important a part in the inner life—and I must emphasize that it was the inner life that these robust entertainments nourished—of the city-dwellers of that time? We know from a great amount of evidence how popular they were, and how faithful a local audience might be to a neighbourhood theatre. Because we must not think of London, let us say, in 1827, as having a 'theatrical district' like the present West End. Officially the theatrical life of London was very much what it had been in 1660, when Charles II was restored to his throne, and very quickly licensed the building of two theatres, Covent Garden and Drury Lane. Until 1843 these two theatres were the only 'legitimate' playhouses in London; there were others, of course, but they laboured under certain legal disadvantages: they might not present the plays of Shakespeare or indeed any of the classical repertoire, and they were officially regarded as music-halls. To escape legal trouble, they had to provide some music at every performance, and the result was a series of productions of Shakespeare into which quite a lot of music was interpolated, making them for legal purposes, melodramas. For our purpose the most interesting development was that a new style of play, which combined music and drama, and was called 'melodrama', came into being. At first the melodramas were performed in mime, with musical accompaniment, but very soon this gave way to a type of play in which there were plenty of songs, and a considerable amount of musical accompaniment from an orchestra which supported and heightened the dramatic impact of the plot. Any of you who have seen silent films with a musical accompaniment know how effective such drama can be. Even today, considerable numbers of film-goers are almost unaware of the music that accompanies what they see, even though the musical scores are of a high degree of sophistication, and are sometimes music of a high order. Anybody who has seen *Scott of the Antarctic* (1948) with music by the late Vaughan Williams knows how splendidly the music enlarged the emotional quality of the film.

There were many melodrama theatres; in 1827 there were twelve of them, and by 1880 the number had grown to fifty-two. Actors who played at Covent Garden and Drury Lane were not above taking a profitable engagement at a melodrama house, several of which were across the Thames, on the Surrey side of the water. Edmund Kean often played on the Surrey side, and one of the theatres in which he did so is still in existence and some of you doubtless have visited it, for until very recently it was the home of the National Theatre. But in Kean's day it was known as the Royal Coburg, and after the accession of Queen Victoria, in 1837, it became the Royal Victoria, and subsequently the Old Vic. When you are in that beautiful old auditorium you see, despite substantial changes, what the size and general appearance of an early-nineteenth-century theatre was.

What would you have seen if you had gone to the Coburg or one of the other melodrama theatres in, let us say, 1827? That would depend somewhat on your place in society; if you were poor, and sat in the Gallery, you would have been on hand not later than half past five in the evening, because the Gallery door opened between then and six o'clock. When the doors opened, you rushed in a pelting, shoving, eager mob up the stone stairs and snatched the best seats you could get in a cramped, steep gallery, equipped with hard, backless benches. The elderly and infirm were often crushed, squeezed, and pummelled unless they were so lucky as to go with young friends, who used them as battering-rams in the scramble up the very long stairs. But once you were in your place, there you stayed, because if you left it unguarded somebody would snatch it. However, you had providently brought a basket with you, and throughout the long evening you refreshed yourself with bottled beer and porter, sausages and fruit, and anything else that pleased your fancy. If you were so infirm as to need a retiring-room between six and midnight, you had to clamber over other people to the door, and make your way outside to a convenient alley, because the theatres made no provision for such needs.

If you were more affluent, you sat on the ground floor of the theatre, in the Pit. Competition here was not so strenuous, and you did not need to go so early, though you still sat on a backless bench. You might arrive any time up to eight o'clock, if you did not mind missing part of the entertainment. But you knew that at nine o'clock the Pit would be opened for half-price, and a horde of young men—City clerks, young lawyers, medical students, and the like—would come rushing in at that time and might jostle you uncomfortably, because they were a notoriously rude part of the audience.

If you had money, you sat in a box on a chair, because boxes surrounded the auditorium in two tiers, separating the Pit from the Gallery. You came when you pleased, and sat in comparative comfort. You left early. You were fashionably dressed, and a good deal of fan-waving and flirting was usual among box-holders.

You may see what it was like in a delightful drawing by the great George Cruikshank, which is called 'Pit, Boxes and Gallery', which was published in 1836. The Pit: solid people, not in their first youth, some with their hats on and some bare-headed. Children are to be seen, but pretty girls are few. The Boxes: lots of pretty girls, with their parents, and the kind of young men who habitually sucked the knobs of their walking-sticks; there is a great show of bosom and wealth, and because cloakrooms were rare, many gentlemen are wearing their hats. It is observable that nobody in the Pit seems to be eating, but in the boxes there are what look like elegant little packets of sweets. The Gallery: everybody wears a hat, a man who looks like a coal-heaver is waving his cudgel at the stage, a woman with a black eye seems to be wooing a stolidly indifferent man, and a chimney-sweep is peeling an apple and dropping the peelings into the boxes. We know from countless records that anyone in the Gallery who recognized a friend in the Pit gained his attention either by shouting or, if that failed, by spitting deftly on his hat.

If you can't find the Cruikshank drawing, you doubtless have access to an edition of Dickens that contains the original illustrations. Look in *The Old Curiosity Shop*, at the picture called 'At Astley's'; it is opposite page 376 in the Penguin edition; it shows you the gallery at one of the favourite melodrama theatres of that time—which was 1840—where one of the characters in the book—the boy Kit—is giving his mother and his little brother Jacob, and his girl Barbara, and her mother, and a baby, a night at the theatre. They have been lucky and strong; they are in the front row; the two older ladies have hung their bonnets over the rail, and the baby is sucking an orange; Barbara's mother has a basket containing oranges and apples, and we know that Kit hit a man on the head with a handkerchief filled with apples as they were coming up the stairs because he was 'scrowdging' his mother. Behind this happy group are women drinking porter, a man smoking a pipe, a man eating something out of his hat, and a man flourishing a cudgel. Cudgels seem to have been a common part of the dress of the humbler population.

What did they see, this happy family party? 'Then the play itself! The horses which little Jacob believed from the first to be alive, and the ladies and gentlemen of whose reality he could by no means be persuaded, having never seen or heard anything at all like them—the firing, which made Barbara wink—the forlorn lady, who made her cry—the tyrant who made her tremble—the man who sang a song with the lady's-maid and danced the chorus, who made her laugh—the pony who reared up on his hind legs when he saw the murderer, and wouldn't hear of walking on all-fours again until he was taken into custody—the clown who ventured on such familiarities with the military man in boots—the lady who jumped over the nine-and-twenty ribbons and came down safe on the horse's back—everything was delightful, splendid and surprising! Little Jacob applauded till his hands were sore; Kit cried "an-kor" at the end of everything, the three-act piece included; and Barbara's mother beat her umbrella on the floor, in her ecstasies, until it was nearly worn down to the gingham.'

These were long theatre evenings, for the hardy. They began with a full-length comedy, which played from six until half past seven or so; then followed the melodrama, which was the main fare of the evening; but when it was over there might be an extravaganza, or a harlequinade, or something light and fanciful with lots of music and dancing in it, and the curtain came down for the last time at about midnight. A big night out, for Kit and his party.

I find that modern students are often puzzled by the fact that so few melodramas are plays of protest—cries for the redress of wrongs. The answer to that, as to all such questions, is complex, but there is one important aspect of it that is simple: the masses in the nineteenth century did not think of themselves as masses, or mobs, or unions, or pressure groups, but as individuals. Melodramas are about individuals—single people who suffer wrongs and at last either get the better of their enemies in this world, or triumph over their enemies by going to an assured reward in the next world. There are melodramas about strikes, and about mutinies in the army or navy, but the hero is always well-defined, and he is a single man; if there is any sociological assumption behind such plays, it is that if the hero triumphs, all his lesser comrades will triumph with him, but to a lesser degree. It is important also that the wrongs he suffers are not solely or even primarily economic; they are wrongs to his self-esteem. He has been unjustly deprived of his job, or his superior officer has beaten him without cause, or—and this is psychologically significant—his superior has seduced or attempted to seduce his wife or his sweetheart.

In the world of melodrama, the wife or the sweetheart is not an autonomous human being; she is very plainly a psychological appendage of the hero. She is the Vessel of his Honour, or in a term used by anthropologists, she is the External Image of His Soul. A wrong to her is the most grievous wrong he can sustain and if it is not avenged, he has lost his soul, and he is no longer a man. Absurd? I don't think so. Read your morning paper any Monday in the year, and you will probably find a report of two or three fights over the weekend, sometimes ending in murder, because somebody in this city has seduced or attempted to seduce the External Soul of somebody who cannot bear it, and behaves very much like a character in melodrama. That is to say, he takes matters into his own hands and seeks redress on the personal level.

It is this intensely personal quality of melodrama that concerns us in our discussion of Evil and the way it is represented in literary art. The path I mean to take in discussing this theme may be familiar to some of you, and if that is so I beg your pardon for labouring matters which you may consider obvious. I must explain my grounds, because I know that there will be many of you to whom the ideas I set forth are unfamiliar, and certainly at the beginning unacceptable.

To put my initial proposal as clearly as possible, I am convinced that the essential character of much literature— poetry, the novel, and drama—is that of the dream. I have said 'much literature' though I really mean 'all literature', but if

I say that I shall not have time to make any convincing argument as to how—for instance—the novels of E. M. Forster are dreamlike. But if you will permit me to employ some shorthand to put forward my belief, here it is:

The dream-world is the area of human experience in which the Conscious Mind and the Unconscious Mind meet and the elements of the dream come from both realms in varying proportions.

Literature—poetry, novel, and drama—is a product of its creator that draws upon conscious experience and reflection, but important elements in it come from the Unconscious realm.

The reader, or the playgoer, is powerfully affected by the elements of the poem, the novel, or the play that arise from the writer's Unconscious, and anyone who is at all sensitive to literature is sensitive to this dream-like aspect which speaks to the dreamer in himself, and the more powerful this dream-like aspect is the more powerfully it will affect him.

The application of this way of looking at literature to drama is special, because in the theatre an audience, large or small, encounters the play at one time, and in so far as the play they encounter is a dream, they may be said to dream it together. Among primitive peoples the great dreams of the race are common property, and are thought to contain great lessons and great riches of spirit for all the tribe. The great dreams of our tribe may be said to be the epics of Homer, the Greek tragedies, the Bible, the plays of Shakespeare, the novels of Cervantes and Dickens, a mass of poetry, and much, much more. But in the theatre we dream together, and the sense of community gives special power to our dream.

You see at once the bias of my mind and my approach to literature. It is certainly not the only approach, but I think it is a fruitful approach, and particularly appropriate to a study of Ideas of Evil in Literature. Of course it is a psychological approach, and that may put some of you against it because so much that is advanced as being of psychological orientation is repugnant to you. Well, let me go on and narrow my psychological focus, perhaps with the effect of clearing the hall: I attempt to consider literature in accordance with the psychological thinking of the late Carl Gustav Jung.

Let me tell you a story which may quiet some of your misgivings. Not long before his death, which took place in 1961, a young interviewer, not very well versed in any psychological thinking and certainly not in that of Jung, gained an interview with the old Doctor, and they talked for a considerable time. At last the young man, somewhat baffled, but fascinated, said: 'Dr. Jung, do you realize that we have talked for an hour, and in all that time you have not said anything that wasn't complete common sense?' Jung was celebrated for his very loud laugh, and on this occasion he almost brought down the roof. When he could speak he said, 'And what had you supposed that psychology was?' Jungianism is not a system of dogma, and it is no enemy to common sense. It does, however, try to persuade common sense to venture into paths which are not commonly explored, though they are not new, and many people before Jung called attention to them.

One of these paths is the dream-path. From Biblical times and doubtless before then, mankind has had a feeling that dreams have a significance, but dream-interpretation was always regarded with suspicion for the excellent reason that if you tell someone your dream you put yourself, to some extent, into his hands: you have given him a secret about yourself. It was at the very beginning of this century, in 1900, that the pioneer of psycho-analysis, Sigmund Freud, published his remarkable book *The Interpretation of Dreams*, in which he attempted to give scientific relevance to the age-old, dubious art. Freudian dream-interpretation has been a powerful instrument in psycho-analysis as Freud conceived it, but his method is chiefly useful in dealing with the dreams of neurotics and sometimes of psychotics. It was left to his great pupil, Jung, to take heed of the fact that most people are not neurotic or psychotic, and to look at dreams as universal human experience. And universal not simply in terms of people now living, but allied to the dreams of the past, which were dreamed by people long dead, but in their essential human experience very much like ourselves. At the risk of labouring what is already known to many of you, I must point out that both Freud and Jung were empirical in their scientific method: what they asserted they derived from experience of their patients—in Freud's case neurotic patients, but in Jung's case very frequently people in good mental health who wished to enlarge the realm of their understanding.

One of the things Jung emphasized, and you will quickly see its relevance both to melodrama and to our larger theme, was that in a dream all the elements—all the characters, including the evil ones, the terrifying monsters, and the benign spirits, and even including the landscape of the dream, or its stage-setting—were aspects of the psyche of the dreamer. He was indeed an observer of his inner theatre, in which the full company of actors, the scene-designer, the director, and the author were included in himself.

Now, back to melodrama. Who are the invariable characters, the people without whom a melodrama cannot be constructed? Everybody knows the answer. They are the Hero, the Heroine, the Hero's Friend (usually a comic character, but none the less faithful and ingenious for all that), and the Villain. There were others, of course. The Heroine is usually equipped with a Faithful Friend of her own, who is her confidante and comforter; there may be a Mysterious Stranger, who bears a fateful secret; there may be Elderly Parents, who are tyrants or perhaps pitiful and deserving victims of ill-fortune. But without a Hero, a Heroine, a Friend, and a Villain you cannot have a melodrama.

Have these people dream counterparts? Indeed they have and I must describe them baldly, for we have not time to talk of the thousands of dreams, docketed and filed by analysts, in which they show their infinite variety. The Hero is the dreamer's self as he conceives of himself in his innermost heart, and in melodrama he is the Great-Hearted Sailor, or Soldier, the Wronged Sufferer, the man at the very centre of his life-drama. The Heroine is the figure sometimes called in medieval morality plays Lady Soul, and she is the treasure protected by the Hero and threatened by external forces. The Friend is, quite simply, the Friend who sometimes appears in dreams as a dog or—in the case of Dick Whittington—a cat, who will befriend the Hero under all circumstances and make his interests his own. And the Villain—who is he? He looks so utterly unlike the Hero; he seeks to drag the Hero down into disgrace and even to death. He is more than merely ill-luck, which has a quality of impersonality; the Villain is whole-souledly determined to destroy the Hero and destroy Lady Soul in the process. The Villain is Contrary Destiny, summing up in himself all that the Villain, and Lady Soul, and the Friend know to be hateful, inimical, and remorseless. But if our argument has any worth at all, can we doubt that the Villain is also a portion of the Hero's composition—a rejected and despised portion, a portion which is recognized in consciousness only on the rarest occasions, but a psychological fact none the less? The tension and fascination of melodrama lies here; the Villain is inescapable, because he is very, very near.

Of course melodramas are optimistic plays, in which the Villain is worsted. If he is not worsted, spiritually if not physically, our melodrama draws very close to tragedy.

What are the characteristics of the Villain? He is very often someone of a station and fortune above that of the Hero, and he has power in the world that seems extraordinary in anyone. Frequently he is witty and he is invariably eloquent, whereas the Hero, though often a great talker, is quick to declare himself a simple, downright chap with no rhetorical airs about him. The Villain is a thorough-going crook, who sticks at nothing to gain his ends. His ends are dishonourable, but almost always productive of pleasure—he covets the fortune, he lusts after the body of Lady Soul, and he eats and drinks uncommonly well: he is, if we permit ourselves a flying psychological leap—the Hero with the lid off. He is what the Hero would be if the Hero were not one of Nature's Noblemen, heavily laden with principle, greatness of heart, and —yes, it must be said—an invincible self-esteem. But as he appears in the play, he is Evil Incarnate.

To talk to you about melodrama without giving some examples of melodramatic rhetoric would be inexcusable, for it is by rhetoric that melodrama lives. But the subject demands a lecture to itself, and I can do no more than hint at the power of language that distinguishes the best of these plays. Very often the drama of the nineteenth century is condemned as of no literary value. That is not quite true. It is rarely poetic, and it is rarely philosophical, but it is vivid and racy and memorable. Those of us whose parents were born before the First World War may recall them as quoting often from melodramas, usually with humorous intent. But who quotes from a modern play, humorously or otherwise? I recall elders who, in moments of stress—not extreme stress, but when, for instance, the car broke down—would utter that poignant cry of William Danvers from *The Silver King*—'Oh, God! put back Thy Universe, and give me Yesterday!' But example is worth any amount of description. Listen to this brief scene from *Black-Eyed Susan*, one of the most popular of melodramas. The sailor hero, William, has returned from a voyage, and his dear wife Susan has not greeted him. He hails a former friend, a countryman named Ploughshare, who says

PLOUGHSHARE: What—William! William that married Susan!
WILLIAM: Avast there! hang it—that name, spoke by another, has brought the salt water up; I can feel one tear standing in either eye, like a marine at each gangway; but come, let's send them below. (*Wipes his eyes*.) Now, don't pay away your line till I pipe. I have been three years at sea; all that time I have heard but once from Susan—she has been to me a mainstay in all weathers. I have been piped up, roused from my hammock, dreaming of her—for the cold black middle watch. I have walked the deck, the surf beating in my face, but Susan was at my side, and I did not feel it. I have been reefing on the yards, in cold and darkness, when I could hardly see the hand of my next messmate—but Susan's eyes were on me, and there was light. I have heard the boatswain pipe to quarters—a voice in my heart whispered 'Susan' and I strode like a lion. The first broadside was given—shipmates whose words were hardly off their lips, lay torn and mangled about me—their groans were in my ears, and their blood hot on my face—I whispered 'Susan'. It was a word that seemed to turn the balls aside, and keep me safe. When land was cried at the mast-head, I seized the glass—my

shipmates saw England—I, I could see but Susan! I
leap upon the beach; my shipmates find hands to grasp
and lips to press—I find not Susan's.

Ploughshare breaks it to this loving sailor that Susan is in great
trouble, because her cruel landlord, who is also her uncle, has
driven her from her cottage. William cries:

I see it! Damn it, I'll overhaul him—I'll bring him on
his beam ends. Heave a-head shipmate! Now for my
dear Susan, and no quarter for her uncle.

But worse than financial trouble afflicts Susan. William's
superior officer, Captain Crosstree, has cast a roving eye on
her, and he says

The wife of a sailor! wife of a common seaman! why,
she's fit for an admiral. I know it is wrong, but I will see
her—and come what may I must and will possess her.

Of course not all melodrama dealt with humble life,
and not every Hero was a lover. So restricted a drama would
not have drawn audiences that included many people of middle age, of education and position in the world. What they
wanted were plays about an idealized version of themselves.
One of the most successful in this realm was Edward
Bulwer-Lytton's *Richelieu*, which first appeared in 1839, and
held the stage for ninety years. It is a romantic piece about the
great Cardinal and the courtiers who plot against him; one of
their schemes is to secure his beautiful niece as a mistress of the
King. Is there anyone here, except myself, I wonder, who
suffered as a youth from hearing his elders quote these words
at him:

In the lexicon of youth, which Fate reserves
For a bright manhood, there is no such word
As—FAIL.

That was from Richelieu, spoken to his adoring Page,

François. It was this same François who, at a critical moment, brings the Cardinal his sword, which he can no longer wield, and the old man says:

> You see, a child could
> Slay Richelieu now.

The admiring youth says:

> But now, at your command
> Are other weapons, my good Lord.

Richelieu replies—picking up his pen—

> True, this!
> Beneath the rule of men entirely great
> The pen is mightier than the sword. Behold
> The arch-enchanter's wand: itself a nothing,
> But taking sorcery from the master-hand
> To paralyse the Caesars—and to strike
> The loud earth breathless! Take away the sword,
> States can be saved without it.

Now that is good stage rhetoric, and our great-grandfathers responded to it, just as they did to Richelieu's final words, as the play ends:

> No—let us own it—there is One above who
> Sways the harmonious mystery of the world
> Ev'n better than prime ministers!

What about Villains? Let me quote to you a speech by a favourite Villain of mine from *The Vampire, or the Bride of the Isles*; the date is 1820. The speaker appears to the other characters in the play to be the noble Ruthven, Earl of Marsden, but we know that he is also a Vampire, and that he is going to take some very disagreeable freedoms with his fiancée, Lady Margaret, who is daughter of Ronald, the Baron of the Isles. Ruthven explains himself thus:

> Demon as I am, that walk the earth to slaughter and
> devour, the little of heart that remains within this

wizard frame,sustained alone by human blood,shrinks from the appalling act of planting misery in the bosom of this veteran chieftain.Still must the fearful sacrifice be made, and suddenly, for the approaching night will find my wretched frame exhausted, and darkness, worse than death, annihilation is my lot! Margaret, unhappy maid, thou art my destined prey! Thy blood must feed a Vampire's life, and prove the food of his disgusting banquet.

You see that Ruthven is in the grip of Remorse, an ailment from which Villains occasionally suffer, but from which they always make a quick recovery.

Villains enjoyed a very special sort of popularity, because in spite of their detestable morals a great part of every audience felt a sneaking sympathy and measure of envy toward them—because they spoke what was, for every decent person, the unspeakable, and almost managed to achieve the unthinkable.

Have we solved our problem, then? Is Evil no more than uninhibited, self-seeking Man? No, that answer will not do because the world of melodrama, though a large and vivid world, is still too limited to serve as a mirror of life in general, or even of a sufficiently large part of life. Melodrama is a form of art in which the Hero—that is to say, every observer of the play—stands right in the middle of the action and everything relates to him; melodrama casts a wide net, and tells us something that is relevant to our study of the forms of Evil, but there is much yet to be explored.

Nevertheless, melodrama offers its audiences one of the sweetest rewards that art has to give, and that is Poetic Justice. It ministers to that furtively acknowledged feeling in us all that we have, in some respects at least, had a raw deal, that inferior people have triumphed where we have been cheated, and that our true worth—our Finest Self—has not been sufficiently appreciated. To the working classes of the nineteenth century, and to many above that level, melodrama was, in Isaiah's words, 'as when a hungry man dreameth, and behold, he eateth.' Vicariously he received his due, he was recognized for what he was. And indeed it is still so.

For melodrama lives, splendidly and to immense applause, on the opera stage, and to a very great extent in ballet, as well. True, music has supplanted language as the principal means of expression, but melodrama is not tied to language, and music expresses emotion with a fullness and directness that only the language of great literary artists can rival. *Rigoletto*, *Pagliacci*, *The Flying Dutchman*, *La Bohème*, *The Magic Flute*, *Peter Grimes*, *Tosca*, all of Verdi, and a substantial portion of Wagner—this is the world of melodrama as we have it today, and who doubts its power? And in it—particularly in somewhat naive opera, like Gounod's *Faust*—we see Evil set forth as the Contrary Destiny, the Opponent, and the Villain, as one in whom 'every imagination of the thoughts of his heart is only evil continually.'

It may be that you wonder why I have chosen to begin this discussion of Evil in Literature with an examination of the roots of melodrama. Perhaps you are reminded of the story of the traveller in Ireland who stopped a native on a country road and asked him if he were going in the right direction for Ballyragget; 'Ballyragget, is it?' said the Irishman, much amazed; 'sure, if I wanted to get there I wouldn't start from here at all.' But it seems to me that melodrama is a very good place to start, because it shows clearly one or two things that are less obvious in more complex literary works. First, it shows us Evil as a requirement—indeed, a necessity—for a plot that will hold our attention and provoke our concern. Without Evil there is no tension, and without tension there is no drama. One of the things that makes the usual descriptions of Heaven so repulsive is that it is shown as a place utterly wanting in tension. Similarly, Hell is unbearable to contemplate because it is imagined as a place of unrelenting and agonizing tension. Our conception of human life is of a varying degree of tension between opposites. In melodrama this tension of opposites is displayed in a manner that is simplified, but not therefore falsified. In its simplified form it is a reflection, not of the surface of life, but of its underlying structure, and thus it satisfies us as a form of art. And thus, also, it resembles our dreams—those dreams that arise from a realm within us not otherwise attainable, and understandable only from these symbolic messages. The modern forms of melodrama of which

I have spoken—ballet and opera—are nearer to dreams than to photographic realism.

If these works of art are essentially dreams, whose Evil is this? It is our own. But is it all the Evil that exists? Is Evil entirely subjective? Has it no external reality? That is a question we must examine in the lectures that follow.

Phantasmagoria
and Dream Grotto

THE TRANSITION FROM our subject of last night—the melodrama theatre of the nineteenth century—to our theme for this evening—the novel in the nineteenth century—is by no means a complex or difficult one. It is the manner of the novel, rather than its matter, which is unlike the nineteenth-century play. The drama was so wanting in the qualities that literary critics value that it presented criticism then, and presents it still, with a state of affairs that critics find deeply disturbing: the drama of the nineteenth century was naked proof that drama is not necessarily a branch of literature, and that a vivid and satisfying drama and a lively theatre can exist almost without literary values.

Only literary critics, however, would be either surprised or disquieted. When we look at the long history of human culture we find that three elements are of great antiquity; they are Prophecy, the Epic, and Drama. Although language is the medium in which they express themselves, and sometimes express themselves magnificently, the subtlety of what we generally call literature is not necessary to them. Of the three, Prophecy and the Epic are somewhat in eclipse at present, but Drama has flourished for several centuries and flourishes still, and it undeniably flourished in the nineteenth century. I suggested that much of its strength lies in its quality of dreamlikeness; a drama is a dream which we dream as one of a group. The Novel, which reached great peaks of achievement in the nineteenth century, has dreamlike qualities as well, but as we encounter it alone, and interpret it much more personally than we interpret a play, it partakes more powerfully of purely literary qualities and appeals in a different way. I will not suggest that it is a better way, for any such judgement is so hedged around by exceptions and qualifications that it is really valueless.

What lies behind the Novel and the Drama, however, is somebody's desire to impart feeling and a measure of thought that is of great importance to him. The novel may be a medium for thought, and be valued chiefly for that reason, but woe betide the play which relies on thought before all else. When too much is said, and too little is done, a play will not last long. It was this plain fact that made *Hamlet* and *Othello* great favourites with nineteenth-century audiences, who thought of them as melodramas, and were unconcerned with the fact that they are also great poems. Whereas Byron's *Marino Faliero*—the only one of his plays to be presented in his lifetime—did not please at all, because Byron was first a poet and secondarily a dramatist. It is interesting, though not relevant to our purpose, that when he had died, and practical men of the theatre had hacked and re-shaped his plays, he had a lively, posthumous theatre success. Byron, however, would not have liked what happened to such a play, for instance, as his *Werner*, when Macready had made it acceptable to a nineteenth-century public. Indeed, I should not be surprised to see Byron have a new life as a playwright in our own day, for theatre audiences have changed greatly in their character; the people who simply want action and sensation now go to the films and the television for it; not very long ago Byron's play *Cain*, which I personally admire very much, and think a splendid melodrama of the soul, had a strikingly successful production, in the most modern manner, in Switzerland. Perhaps Byron the dramatist was ahead of his time.

In talking about the nineteenth-century novel I shall have a good deal to say about Charles Dickens, because he suits my theme, and I have spent much time over many years reading his books, and reading them again, and thinking about them. One of the things that has worked against Dickens' reputation, until recent years, is that he is so easily and immediately comprehensible, on a simple level. We have all met those people who make no pretension to literary taste but who like 'a good read' and who exult, somewhat embarrassingly, over Dickens. I say their enthusiasm is embarrassing, because the things they like about him are so obvious and reveal so slight a depth of penetration.

They seem to care so little for his plots, and are so sentimental about his characters; they repeat over and over the assertion (which is open to debate) that he was a great social reformer, and that he loved the common people; what he actually said, or implied, about society and people generally, they have missed. But oh! how they exult in his inordinate and grotesque characterization! They do not examine or discuss; they simply name names. 'Mrs. Gamp!' they cry, and look at you with a gloating enthusiasm which invites you to join them in a huge laugh about Sairey Gamp. Of course Mrs. Gamp is a very great comic creation, but she is also a criticism of society, and of humanity which, if you think about her, makes your flesh creep. Or they go into ecstasy about Mr. Pickwick, regardless of the fact that for the greater part of a very long book Mr. Pickwick is a fool who, like another great creation, Bertie Wooster, is saved from disaster by his valet, who is a cheerful cynic. Pickwick is endearing, as so many fools are, but he is also an acidulated portrait of what a private fortune, linked with intellectual pretension, may do to a man. These sentimentalists love the Dickensian villains; Uriah Heep and Fagin are as dear to them as the obviously good people, though Dickens makes it clear to any careful reader that Heeps and Fagins are caterpillars of society.

Much of this unthinking enthusiasm arises from the fact that its possessors have read some Dickens when they were very young, and have understood him as very young people may. But it has long been a contention of mine that if you truly value a book you should read it when you are the age the author was when he wrote it. If he is a great author, you may well read him again at a much later time. I am older now than

Dickens was when he died, and I am still reading his novels, and still find in them things I missed the first few times, and things that no very young reader could possibly hope to comprehend.

It is characteristic of the people who speak of Dickens with unthinking adoration that they do not like his later books as well as his earlier ones, and may not really have read them at all. I have, in my lifetime, had the disappointing experience of addressing several Dickens societies, and have done so assuming that the members had at least read all of his major works. This was naive of me. They had read little and that poorly. But although I may be naive in my tendency to over-estimate the extent of other people's reading, and the acuity of their comprehension, I can learn something when it is thrust right under my nose. And what I learned from these Dickens enthusiasts was of value; I discerned that it was not Dickens' books they loved, but Dickens' World as it appeared to them, and that one of the characteristics that makes Charles Dickens a great writer—a writer perhaps second only to Shakespeare in English—is that he brought forth from within himself a world complete in itself, into which other people can penetrate— even if they do not venture very far—and which seems as real as the world of everyday, and in some respects vastly more attractive. How many writers can do that?

There are several, and I cannot hope to give you anything approaching a complete list, because there are vast tracts of literature that are unknown to me. (Let me say, parenthetically, that I was once naive enough to believe those people who give the impression that they have read everything; they haven't, and they are faking, sometimes very cleverly, but faking none the less.) But who are the writers who have created worlds of their own, with laws that seem to apply to their own characters in ways that are improbable in real life, and weather, and architecture, and turns of fate that are supreme within their books, but not applicable elsewhere? Tolstoy was such a writer. Dostoevsky, who declared himself to be Dickens' pupil, and who wrote what he thought were Dickensian novels, but aren't, was such a writer. Marcel Proust was one of this special category of great novelists. It is a small and awe-inspiring group to which many writers of extraordinary powers do not belong. There are borderline cases, some of whom are favourites of mine. One among them is Anthony Trollope, who has certainly never yet received his full due, although he attracts many admirers. The people who love Trollope because he seems so calm, so much at ease in Zion in the world of Victorian politics and the Victorian church, are usually people who have read the Palliser novels or the Barchester novels, in search of a special quality of well-bred nullity, relieved by intrigue. That is all they seek and all they find. A very popular writer of our time, Mrs. Angela Thirkell, based a substantial reputation on her development of this tiny corner of Trollope, slightly enlivened with some of the lime-juice of her own personality. But Trollope the stern judge of society, who wrote *The Way We Live Now*, and *The Eustace Diamonds*, and *Orley Farm*, has eluded such readers, and the world we find in these and several others among his great output, is the Victorian world with its skin off, and the Trollopian world is a disquieting place, when you really explore it. I never cease to be surprised that Victorian fathers and the fussy Puritans who controlled Victorian circulating libraries allowed Trollope to fall into the hands of innocent young women; a girl with her head screwed on straight could learn more about the kid-glove evil of the world—about selfishness, money-madness, sexual manipulation, and cold-hearted social climbing—from Trollope than from any other Victorian, and it was all presented with a manner which seemed to say: This is how it is; what do you make of it? There is extraordinary understanding of Evil in Trollope.

The Evil, however, is presented in a manner that robs it of much of its sting. All the Seven Deadly Sins are paraded in this long series of novels, and they are all condemned. Condemned not as a moralist condemns, but as an artist condemns. But Trollope's kingdom is unquestionably a Kingdom of This World. If his people are evil, they either get away with it or they don't; their lives may be blighted by it, but they are frequently so worldly and stupid that the life they get is as good as any they can conceive. They know no sanction but the sanction of man. It is an irreligious world.

Trollope irreligious, you may say? How then, did he write so much about churchmen? Read him and see. His churchmen are not bad men, and one assumes that they are not irreligious men, but religion is not the first concern of their lives: personal ambition, or learning, or politics, or society are the affairs to which we see them giving their best efforts. Do they ever pray? Oh, indeed, they do. In my opinion the finest chapter Trollope ever wrote is the first of *Barchester Towers*. The Bishop of Barchester is dying; his son, the archdeacon, sits by his bedside and reflects that if the death comes before the fall of the ministry in London he himself is likely to be the new bishop, because he is of the right political party. Time presses. Does he wish his father dead? Ashamed of himself, he kneels by the old man's bedside and prays: prays that his father may live? No, he prays that his own sins may be forgiven. Then his father does die. What does Trollope say?

> The archdeacon's mind had already travelled from the death chamber to the closet of the prime minister. He had brought himself to pray for his father's life, but now that that life was done, minutes were too precious to be lost. It was now useless to dally with the fact of the bishop's death—useless to lose perhaps everything for pretence of a foolish sentiment.

This is the perfection of a certain sort of novelist's art. Did you observe that the archdeacon prayed for forgiveness for his contemplation of his father's death; nowhere are we told that he prayed for the continuance of his father's life; yet when his father was dead, that was what he remembered himself as doing. Do we judge him severely? I can imagine a young reader doing so, and setting down Archdeacon Grantly as a hypocrite. But would any reader over thirty-five be able to do so?

Why do I say that Trollope is irreligious? I use the word in a particular sense: I mean that his people live in the light of this world, and do not refer their actions to any judgement that is not that of the law or their Victorian society.

What then do I mean by a religious novelist? Somebody who writes as if his characters were responsible to law and society but, *above all else*, to a divine ruling power, and were in danger also of falling under the sway of the constant and implacable enemy of that power. In short, a novelist who is conscious of God and the Devil.

Such an attitude is capable of producing the greatest art, and also the most trashy, sentimental, and tendentious art. To make things easier, let us look at painting; religious belief can produce Van Eyck's *Adoration of the Lamb* and the ceiling of the Sistine Chapel, and it can also produce all the silly statues and crude pictures of the Sacred Heart and of Guardian Angels that one sees in the *bondieuserie* shops. In the novel it may give you *War and Peace* or *The Brothers Karamazov*, or *Uncle Tom's Cabin* or *Oliver Twist*, or whole libraries of pious rubbish. It may give you a book for boys like Dean Farrar's *Eric, or Little by Little*, the name of which always raises a laugh, especially from people who have not read it; but I read it last year, and it is a book of considerable power with a highly developed idea of Evil as part of the machinery behind it.

What a religious attitude will not give you is a shrewd, worldly-wise novel by Trollope or Thackeray. Do not for an instant suppose that I underrate their art. It is the restriction on their range of feeling and apprehension I refer to. Where will you find the art of the novelist so brilliantly employed as in the final words of Chapter 32 of *Vanity Fair*; it is the chapter that refers to the Battle of Waterloo, at which, Thackeray tells us, both nations served 'the Devil's code of honour.' This is how it ends:

> No more firing was heard at Brussels—the pursuit rolled miles away. Darkness came on the field and city; and Amelia was praying for George, who was lying on his face, dead, with a bullet through his heart.

Pathetic? Yes. Moving? Yes. The work of a novelist deeply imbued with religious feeling? No. Thackeray has made us too much aware that he thinks Amelia a charming simpleton, and George a commonplace, vain young man, for us to feel anything other than the compassion that human folly and human limitation call forth. That is a noble feeling, certainly, but it is a cool feeling—as cool as, for instance, Thackeray's depiction in the same great novel of his villain, Lord Steyne, who is not a villain at all, but merely a man of privilege and wealth, who does not see why he should not have anything money can buy—including other men's wives. Thackeray is often called a cynic; if he was one, he was a cynic with a very tender heart. But a religious novelist he was not.

The novelists whose Kingdom is of This World may be artists of subtlety and depth of perception, and they often touch our hearts (if I may be permitted to speak of such an indecency to a modern audience). But they do not sound the deepest or the highest strings. Those are reserved for the writers whose own gamut of feeling extends both above and below the Kingdom of This World.

A subtle and profound artist in the greater realm—yet for all that not the subtlest or most profound—is George Eliot. She brings her people and her themes under the sway of a divine ruling power and its opposite, though she is a good deal weaker on the Devil than she is on God. This makes her curiously modern, and of late years her reputation has soared immensely. Now, as I told you when we began these lectures, I am no theologian, and I do not know how to put my beliefs about these things into theological or philosophical terms. So let me say crudely that I do not believe very much in the God of somebody who hasn't a first-class Devil as well. We have all seen during the past fifty years what happens to God when you try to pretend there is no Devil; God develops rheumatoid arthritis and senile dementia and rumours of his death are heard everywhere, including some of the very advanced church groups. Justice is vitiated by compassion, and compassion melts into a sticky sentimentality. And as the invitations are being issued to God's funeral, the Devil is laughing so hard that he can hardly cope with his extraordinary flow of business.

Am I a vile Nestorian? Am I a hateful Manichee? It seems very likely. But let me assure you that I became so by reading English and other literatures, and trying to make up my mind which works of art within them were of the highest quality. Art, I am utterly convinced, is one of the principal roads by which we find our way to such knowledge of this world and the Universe to which it belongs as may be possible to us. If art makes me a Nestorian, a Manichee, a dualist, and probably a Gnostic—so be it. I shall present myself in the world to come carrying those credit cards, and will have to take whatever accommodation is coming to me.

Let us look for a few minutes at what is probably George Eliot's best-known novel, *The Mill on the Floss*. What is it about? In a sense it is about the love of a brother and a sister which ends with the death of both. It is set in the English countryside, and the village of St. Ogg's, where it takes place, has usually been identified as Gainsborough, in Lincolnshire, so that the Floss must be the river Trent. The period is the first thirty years of the nineteenth century. What kind of place was it? The author tells us:

> Observing these people narrowly, even when the iron hand of misfortune has shaken them from their un- questioning hold on the world, one sees little trace of religion, still less of a distinctively Christian creed. Their belief in the Unseen, so far as it manifests itself at all, seems to be rather of a pagan kind.

Yet conventional Christianity is as much a part of their ac- cepted world as the weather, and the author tells us we should not be surprised when Tulliver the Miller, having suffered a terrible wrong from his enemy, Lawyer Wakem, records his curse and his wish that evil may befall him on the fly-leaf of his Bible. We are assured by the author, 'Mr. Tulliver did not want spiritual consolation—he wanted to shake off the degradation of debt, and to have his revenge.' Revenge is certainly un- Christian but it is not un-human; the Devil is very fond of it, and has coated it in an undeniable sweetness.

Evil, as it exists in this story, is shown as want of human kindness, of having succumbed to the heartlessness of a con- ventional provincial society and the cult of success, of *having*, of possessions. When Miller Tulliver is brought low his relatives, the Gleggs and the Pullets, are as hard as nails; they cannot relinquish any of their wealth to save him from disgrace, and they are crabbed about helping his wife, sister to the women of these two families, to save the linen and china on which she sets great store. With this slavery to possessions goes pride. The Miller speaks of life as a ladder, and assures his son that 'you'll maybe see the day when Wakem and his son'll be a round or two below you.' Tom Tulliver, the hero, is described as 'proud as Lucifer'; he is untouched by religion, and his education, which his father was determined he should have, is worthless. What does the author say? 'Tom, like every one of us, was imprisoned within the limits of his own nature, and his education had simply glided over him, leaving a slight deposit of polish.' And so, when Tom thinks his sister Maggie has run off with a man to whom she is not married he has no kindly thought toward her at all. We are told, 'Would the news be that she was married—or what? Probably that she was not married: Tom's mind was set to the expectation of the worst that could happen—not death, but disgrace.'

This is certainly a world where the Devil is at work. George Eliot mentions him. When Maggie is a child one of the book she reads is Daniel Defoe's *History of the Devil*; her father bought it in a job-lot at a sale. Maggie explains to a guest: 'the devil takes the shape of wicked men, and walks about and sets people doing wicked things, and he's oftener in the shape of a bad man than any other because, you know, if people saw he was the devil, and he roared at 'em, they'd run away, and he couldn't make 'em do what he pleased.' But when Maggie meets the Devil, he has taken the pallid disguise of a heartless womanizer, and rather a fool. Her real Devil, I suspect, is her brother Tom. Surprising, but then, as Miller Tulliver says, 'this is a puzzling world, and Old Harry's got a finger in it.'

The world in which these people live is not an evil world; there is a great deal of conventional probity and sense of business honour. But it is a mean world, where people rarely lift their heads above provincial concerns. Maggie Tulliver does so, and much of her unhappy fate has its origin in her impulse to go beyond what is permitted by the society to which she belongs. Little people, little concerns, paganism without any of the freedom which sentimental people think goes with paganism; this is a world where almost everyone ignores the beauty of nature which surrounds St. Ogg's and gives it whatever dignity it possesses.

But it most decidedly is not a world in which everyone is without feeling. Maggie Tulliver is dominated by feeling; we can see how she comes by it, for her father is a man of deep passion, even though the outlet of that passion is restricted; her pudding of a mother feels little and understands less. George Eliot is particularly adept at drawing portraits of female fools and she has small pity for them. The fact that

Mrs. Tulliver had once been a pretty, desirable girl cuts no ice with this writer, as it might do with a male author. A fool is a fool is a fool, and George Eliot is one of the writers in English who, though without rancour, never forgets it.

The edition of *The Mill on the Floss* which is most generally available to students is that which has an introduction by Walter Allen. Everything he says demands respect, but I cannot myself agree with his notion that at the end of the book Maggie has 'refused sexual passion'. Maggie dies when she and her brother Tom are swept away in a flood on the Floss, and drown locked in each other's arms. It seems to me that this is the direction in which Maggie has been heading since the beginning of the book, and this is a love-death. Tom is her strongest attachment. I do not imply any trivial incestuous element in the novel; incest is, after all, a form of love, and it may therefore be noble or ignoble. It need not be the sort of thing that gets simple and usually rather stupid people into the police courts. Maggie has sought sexual fulfilment with two men, neither of whom was the right man for her, because there was only one right man in her life, and it was her brother Tom. Tom, unhappily, is a selfish egotist who takes Maggie for granted, as a responsibility, a chattel. Her death with him, when they are symbolically overwhelmed by the river which has been one of the dominant elements in their lives, is, I think, meant to be a happy ending, though it is not happiness as conventional and sentimental novels provide it. Not happiness, perhaps, but fulfilment, is what we find here, and fulfilment may be vastly greater, and less obviously pleasurable, than happiness.

Mr. Allen does not think so. He writes of 'the distressing sentimentality of the last paragraphs of the novel'. I don't agree. Sentimentality is a flaw in a work of art, certainly, but the word is often thrown at great and overpowering works of art that embarrass critics who live, emotionally, in St. Ogg's, though intellectually they have journeyed south as far as Cambridge. The ending of *The Mill on the Floss* moves me to tears, though I am not an easy weeper. It is not the immediate pathos of the death of Maggie and Tom that thus affects me: it is rather that a genuine completion of a human involvement has been attained, but attained only through Death. A happiness beyond mere delight has been experienced—a happiness as blasting and destroying as an encounter with the gods.

To my mind, this is anything but sentimental. People who prate of sentimentality are very often people who hate being made to feel, and who hate anything that cannot be intellectually manipulated. But the purgation through pity and terror which is said to be the effect of tragedy is not the only kind of purgation that art can bring. The tempest in the heart that great novels can evoke is rarely tragic in the strict sense, but it is an arousal of feelings of wonder at the strangeness of life, and desolation at the implacability of life, and dread of the capriciousness of life which for a few minutes overwhelms all our calculations and certainties and leaves us naked in a turmoil from which cleverness cannot save us. Sentimentality is sometimes used by critics as a term to rebuke artists who seek to sound this terrifying note; if the artist fails, he is probably merely sentimental, but if he succeeds, the critic would be wise to slink back into his kennel and whimper till the storm passes. The critic knows that something great has been attempted, and that the chaos it brings is deeply disturbing to the heart. If it is a St. Ogg's heart—and St. Ogg's is a very large parish indeed—the critic will mock and rebuke.

No great novelist has been so bethumped with mockery and rebuke for his sentimentality as Charles Dickens. And of course he was often sentimental, because that is what sentiment becomes when it is pumped up, and does not arise naturally from a situation. Now I fully agree with the critical dictum that a man should be judged on his best work, rather than on his lesser achievements, and if I were to follow that path I should talk to you about *Great Expectations*, *Bleak House*, and *Our Mutual Friend*—the creations of Dickens' artistic maturity. But because I am talking to you about Evil as it asserts itself in books I shall talk instead about two of Dickens' novels that are most often reproached with sentimentality—*Oliver Twist* and *The Old Curiosity Shop*. Have you read them recently? I have—or rather I have not long ago completed the most recent of several rereadings. In them the barometer needle waggles distractingly between Sentiment and Sentimentality. But they are also written in the clear light of heaven and the lurid light of hell, and are therefore much to our purpose. Let us take a look at them.

First, however, let me speak once again about the structure of these lectures. Are you wondering why I gave one of our hours, last night, to a consideration of melodrama? I said, did I not, that melodrama was the prevailing weather of art during the nineteenth century, and attempted to persuade you that the melodramatic way of life is a good and a revealing way—just as good and revealing as the gifts of the artist who employs it. In the theatre the artists were not very good, but they met the needs of playgoers, not all of whom were critically sophisticated. In the novel, the artists were some of the best who have ever written in English. One of them of whom we have just spoken, George Eliot, is rarely called melodramatic, because the word is still so often tinged with contempt, but *The Mill on the Floss* in my opinion is highly melodramatic; if you agree with me that melodrama may well mean a way of dealing with artistic material that reveals the wonder and caprice of life, as well as its undeniable tragedy, you will agree with me about that book. Melodrama is art in which not an implacable and malign Fate dominates the life of man, but art in which Good and Evil contend, and in which the dividing line between Good and Evil may often be blurred, and in which Good may often be the winner.

Did I say that in melodrama the Humble Friend is a character to be reckoned with, and that the Humble Friend may often be an animal, as it often is in fairy-tale? In *The Mill on the Floss* there are three of these animal friends, and I have never seen any comment on them by a critic. One is Maggie's dog, Yap, who is all that Maggie is herself, but with the freedom of an animal. Devoted, emotional, sadly undisciplined, Yap is very much Maggie's dog. Then consider the dog who is the pet of the girl who is the belle of St. Ogg's, Lucy Deane; this is Minny, a lap-spaniel in poorish health because it eats too many sweets, a sensitive, cosseted creature and a perfect fool, like its mistress. It is of interest that Maggie's dog is a male, and thus his folly is very different from that of Minny, who is very much a female—a silly bitch. And lastly there is Bob Jakin's dog, Mumps, a clever, common dog who is full of animal sagacity;

his master says of him, 'Lors, it's a fine thing to hev a dumb brute fond on you; it'll stick to you, and make no jaw.' Bob tells Mumps to be a friend to Maggie, and Mumps does his best, but he comes too late.

Dickens was far too astute a melodramatist to neglect the Animal Friend, and *Oliver Twist* shows us a splendid example of the kind in Bill Sykes' dog. This was 'a white, shaggy dog, with his face scratched and torn in twenty different places', a skulking dog which his master kicks so savagely that it is driven right across the room. What are we to make of this creature? Except for the harlot Nancy, it is the only creature in the world that is attached to Sykes. But Sykes is a character familiar in melodrama, and perhaps some of us have met him in daily life: he is the Damned Man, bent on his own destruction. In the end he murders Nancy in a scene of terrible brutality, and then he is on the run. Because everybody knows that Bill Sykes is always accompanied by a white dog, disguise is impossible, so he determines to kill the dog—determines, so to say, to be rid of the last redeeming bit of good that is in him. The dog won't stay to be killed; it runs away. But it comes back again; it cannot bear to be without Sykes, so it searches all the places in which he might hide until it comes to the foul thieves' hangout on Jacob's Island. When at last Sykes tries to escape by leaping from the roof, and is hanged in his own rope, the dog leaps to join him, and is dashed to death in the stony ditch beneath.

There is melodrama indeed! In all of Dickens the conflict of Good and Evil is presented vividly, and for some readers, too vividly. Their taste is too refined for these naked, hair-raising expositions of Nestorian dualism: or, to put it another way, they lack stomach for the gaudier aspects of the Eternal Struggle. But Bill Sykes is by no means the most shocking depiction of Evil in *Oliver Twist*. That, surely is Fagin, the receiver of stolen goods and the corrupter of children. Of late it has become a fashion in the criticism of Dickens to seek for evidence of homosexual elements in the relation of Fagin to his crew of pickpockets. Is it important? Only if you think that sexual corruption is the worst sort of corruption. I stick to the opinion that what Fagin manifestly does is the worst that such a creature could do: he makes evil appear to be good, and throws over it such a mantle of humorous charm, and makes himself appear to be such a gentle, unworldly, genial old soul, that Oliver becomes a thief to please this dear old gentleman, rather than through any brutal compulsion. Isn't that how Maggie Tulliver saw the Devil? There is a wonderful portrait of Fagin at the end of the book, when he is in the hands of the police, and clings to them as if they were his friends, because if they once divert their attention from him, the angry crowd will destroy him. If you find Bill Sykes and his dog crude melodramatic workmanship, what do you make of this splendid depiction of the ambiguity of Evil, which we find in Fagin?

How well did Dickens understand Evil? He was fascinated by it all his life and when we read of his visits to wretched slums and thieves' dens, as a guest of the police in the days of his fame, we must also bear in mind the child who lived alone in London when his parents were imprisoned in the Marshalsea for debt. We must remember the boy in the blacking-factory, employed in pasting labels on packets of shoe-polish. This time in Dickens' life was so horrible to him that it was many years before he could confide the secret of it even to his closest friends. Some people think this was because of shame that he, the famous, feted author, should once have been so low in the social scale. I think better of Dickens than that. I think it was because what he saw then, with the clear eyes of a child, was so horrible that it burnt itself forever into his nature, and he could not be rid of it, except through the art that was his. Human degradation: yes. Ignorance and Want: you recall how the Spirit of Christmas Present shows these to Scrooge, in the guise of two horrible children, in whom the terror of the future is implicit. But also Crime, and Dickens is not one of those who tells us that Crime arises only from Ignorance and Want, though they are its friends; it is an element of humanity with autonomous power of its own. It is Evil, though it is not the whole of Evil.

Dickens explores Evil in a way that no other literary artist of anything like comparable stature does, because he contrasts it constantly with Good. The Evil of Pride we find in the casual seducer Steerforth in *David Copperfield*. And in that same book we find another sort of Pride in the extraordinary character of Mrs. Gummidge, that lone, lorn creetur with whom everything went contrairy; Mrs. Gummidge seeks and embraces quite unnecessary misfortunes in order to throw herself into prominence and exploit the kindness of others. Pride is, among other things, egotism.

All of the Seven Deadly Sins are constantly on parade in Dickens. Pride is extensively dealt with, and to those I have mentioned I should like to add perhaps his masterpiece in this realm—Mr. Dombey. Envy? Lots of it, with Uriah Heep at the head of the list. Wrath? We have talked of Bill Sykes, and we think of Mr. Murdstone, whose cruelty to people for their own good is so impressively described in *David Copperfield*. Lechery? You'll find plenty of it in Uriah Heep and in Mr. Carker, in *Dombey*. (Whether Lechery, which might be defined as sexual desire untouched by affection, is still a sin or not is a matter of dispute; there are those today who prefer to call it an alternative life-style.) Avarice? Scrooge is the obvious example, but the finest portrait of this quality in Dickens, to my mind, is that of Jonas Chuzzlewit. Sloth? Very subtly handled, in Mrs. Jellyby, whose pity is all for the unfortunate of distant lands, but she is bored by her own wretched children. And what of Harold Skimpole, that superb portrait of a particular sort of artist who thinks the world owes him a living? Gluttony? We think at once of the Fat Boy in *Pickwick*, but he is a pathological case. In what novel of Dickens' do you not find people exulting and gloating over food and drink? Think of the gormandizing at Dingley Dell, after the Pickwickians went for that twenty-five-mile walk. Think of the pints of sherry, hot and cold, that everybody drinks apparently without feeling in the least tipsy. Think of Old Krook, the marine-stores dealer in *Bleak House*, who drinks for years until at last he bursts into flames and perishes of Spontaneous Combustion, in one of Dickens' most lurid scenes. Oh, yes; plenty of Gluttony.

Apart from these sins, so carefully defined in the Middle Ages, Dickens is superb in his depiction of a sin very prevalent in the Victorian era, and a profuse growth in modern democracies. I mean Hypocrisy. How well and in what a variety of tints he paints it! The full-length portraits, of course, are represented by Seth Pecksniff and Chadband. But how many hypocrites there are who are merely sketched, but sketched with a master-hand; like Mr. Spenlow, in *Copperfield*, who was all compliance himself, but dared not take action for fear of his invisible, and perhaps even imaginary, partner, Mr. Jorkins.

All of these sins, of course, are aspects of Evil, and bring about not only obvious and palpable Evil, but also that unbounded, grey unhappiness, that arthritis of the spirit, which we might call everyday or bread-and-butter evil. How did Dickens know so much about it? Well, he was a very keen observer, but that quality alone makes a detective, not a novelist. Not only could he see what was under his nose (which only a limited number of people can do) but he could find a response to it in himself. He was, as only the greatest artists are, continually in communication with what psychiatrists call his Unconscious, and not simply his personal Unconscious, but that vast Collective Unconscious which glues the race together. Goethe once said that he knew of no crime of which he could not imagine himself capable, and if Dickens had been as cool a customer as Goethe, he could have said the same. But Dickens was not a cool customer. He was, in fact, a ripsnorting, raging, egotistical cad, and if he had not also been a supremely great writer he would have been intolerable. What he was is the price of what he could do. Thackeray, who was also a great writer, couldn't do it because Thackeray, by birth and instinct, was a gentleman, and he always handles Evil with tongs. Dickens didn't: he lived it.

I mean that. He sweated and toiled and wept over his writing, and in his later years he killed himself by giving public readings in which the intensity of his emotion was far too great for a man already ill to sustain. His favourite reading was the Murder of Nancy, from *Oliver Twist*; it was melodramatic acting of the most extraordinary—though not the highest—kind. I say 'not the highest' because acting is an art, and the actor works to excite and move his audiences, while remaining in control of himself. Otherwise, a week of playing Othello or Lear might kill him. But Dickens lived his readings, and paid the terrible price. This is not imagination; his doctor begged him to drop the Murder from his repertory. But the Murder was not the only killer. Dickens' normal pulse was 72, but when he read the Death of Paul Dombey it was never below 82, and might rise above 100. On Friday, January 21, 1870, when he read the Murder, his pulse was 90 when he began, and rose to

112. On February 15 of the same year, he confided to his manager, 'I shall tear myself to pieces,' and when he spoke his pulse was already 90, and when he came off the stage it was 124. If this was not self-destruction, what was it? It was, among other things, an acting out of Evil that brought audiences to their feet in applause. It was a fainting era, and lots of people fainted. Dickens' reading of the Murder was a stupendous feat of making external and actual something which had existed as an artistic creation. The story of the Dickens readings—there were, in all, 444 of them—is a fascinating psychological study. But there is one aspect of them that interests me in a ghoulish fashion, and that is that Dickens never read anything from *The Old Curiosity Shop*. He never, in public, brought himself face to face with Daniel Quilp.

There will be those among you who have not read *The Old Curiosity Shop*. Students nowadays are often warned off it; it is not 'essential Dickens'. I say you can't know Dickens without it; it is the essence of at least a large portion of Dickens. The story is simple in outline. The proprietor of the Old Curiosity Shop is an old man named Trent, who falls a victim to gambling mania; he rationalizes his obsession by pretending that he gambles only to secure a fortune and future safety for his granddaughter, Nell. He is an unlucky gambler, and the dupe of cheats, so he is in continual need of money and borrows it from a money-lender named Quilp, a filthy, cruel, lecherous, and demonic dwarf. When ruin comes the old man and the child flee from London and wander in poverty through England, pursued by the dwarf, and also by Nell's brother, who is convinced that possession of the child will bring him the money he is sure the old man still has. At last the wanderers are taken in by a kind village schoolmaster, but Nell is exhausted by her travels and her anxiety about her grandfather, and she dies. A very good plot, apt for melodrama, which Dickens bountifully supplies.

It is the character of Little Nell that gets under the skin of those who detest the book, and in especial they resent Dickens' description of her death. His contemporaries thought it magnificent. The great actor Macready, when he read it, was too stunned to weep; Carlyle, not a notably easy audience, was overcome by it; Landor, Washington Irving, and many other people of distinguished taste thought it superb. Everybody knows the story of how a crowd assembled on the dock in New York harbour, when the monthly installment of the story was due aboard ship, shouting across the water to know if Nelly were really dead or not. But our refined age does not like it; our generation is described by George Santayana, a brilliant critic of Dickens, as aesthetically snobbish, and desirous of 'a mincing art'. And indeed there may be something wrong with us; we hate to have our feelings touched.

Aldous Huxley, a notable novelist in his chosen realm, loathed *The Old Curiosity Shop* and wrote scathingly about it in his interesting but unsound essay *Vulgarity in Literature*. He shows us, in his own novel *Point Counter Point* how he thinks the death of a child may be described without vulgarity. And indeed it is very finely done. But can you recall the name of the child? If you can, did you much like the child when he was alive? He was a nice little boy, but no more. Little Nell was a very different creature, and the inspiration for her came from a very different place. Huxley's mind was broad but his spirit was not deep; he simply could not comprehend what Dickens was doing.

Little Nell was one of Dickens' earliest Good Women. There were to be many of them, and even to an enthusiast like myself they are trying. They are, in the true melodramatic style, embodied goodness. Why are the good people in books so rarely appealing? I shall try to say something about that in a later lecture. We must confine ourselves here to some consideration of Little Nell; the worst I can say of her is that I cannot imagine any man hoping that Little Nell had lived and grown up in order that he might marry her. But somebody did want Nell, not perhaps for marriage, but for sexual enjoyment of the most alarmingly sadistic kind. That man was Daniel Quilp, the dwarf usurer.

Quilp had a wife, a very pretty one, who was frightened out of her wits by him. Dickens had to walk carefully in his descriptions of their married life, because the sensibilities of his age were very tender about sexual things. But we get the message, and when we read that Mrs. Quilp had to sit up all night waiting for his return, and then make his breakfast, and then watch him as 'he ate hard eggs, shell and all, devoured gigantic prawns with their heads and tails on, chewed tobacco and water-cresses at the same time with extraordinary greediness, drank boiling tea without winking, bit his fork and spoon till they bent again, and in short performed so many horrifying and uncommon acts that the women were nearly frightened out of their wits,' we can dimly guess at the sort of thing that went on when the curtains of the connubial bed were drawn. Where, and how often, do you suppose pretty Mrs. Quilp was bitten and bruised?

All the great nineteenth-century novelists found their way around the prudery of their time, and they send us signals which we must be alert to receive. When Quilp says: 'Be a good girl, Nelly, a very good girl, and see if one of these days you don't come to be Mrs. Quilp of Tower Hill,' we know that he could easily get rid of Mrs. Quilp Number One. The first Mrs. Quilp, the pretty Mrs. Quilp, might just happen to die, you see. It is like Richard III's wooing of Lady Anne beside the coffin of Henry VI. There is a scene of terror in which Quilp has seized the Old Curiosity Shop for debt, and has romped and exulted on Nell's pretty bed; and a later scene, when Nell has to creep into her old bedroom to steal a key, and finds Quilp sleeping in her bed, his head lolling upside down over the edge of the mattress, and his eyes open, but with only the yellow whites showing.

Quilp is a masterly and daemonic creation. Where did he come from? Out of the depths of Charles Dickens, where every novelist's characters come from. If the waters in those depths are shallow, or heavily chlorinated, or else simply stagnant, the characters are not particularly arresting. But the imagination of Charles Dickens contained wells of very dark water indeed, and they were of a terrifying depth, lit by strange lights. It is because of them that I have attached Carlyle's phrase 'Phantasmagoria and Dream Grotto' to this lecture. But if Quilp came from the depths, where did Nelly come from—'chubby, rosy, cosy little Nell', as Quilp calls her? From the same grottoes, but the light is different. We know something about Charles Dickens that throws quite a lot of light on Nell and most of his other idealized women. When he was young and impressionable, he encountered a charming family—all lucky young men encounter at least one such family—that possessed charming daughters. He married the wrong one. He married Kate. But the one he later wished he had married came to live with him and his wife, and died not long afterward. He wrote her epitaph, and here it is:

Mary Scott Hogarth
died 7th May 1837
young, beautiful and good,
God in his mercy
numbered her with his angels
at the early age of
seventeen

It is the idealized image of Mary we meet again and again in Dickens. He learned much about women, and his earliest love, Maria Beadnell, is hilariously but rather cruelly caricatured as she appeared in middle age, in the character of Flora Finching in *Little Dorrit*. But the angelic form of Mary Hogarth never deserted him until, perhaps, he found it again in the mistress of his last years, Ellen Ternan. For Dickens a woman of the highest order was always that figure from melodrama Lady Soul.

I have never seen a criticism of *The Old Curiosity Shop* that called attention to the fact that it contains two remarkable death scenes. That of Little Nell is famous; though prolonged, I do not find it over-written in terms of the book as a whole. It is long, and Death is sometimes long; it is pathetic, and if we do not find the death of a child pathetic, we should ask ourselves why. Oscar Wilde once said that anyone who could read of the death of Little Nell without laughing must have a heart of stone; it is a good enough wisecrack, but it springs from that limitation of sensibility that was the flaw in Wilde's own art; Dickens gushed, but Wilde trickled, and only the most strenuous pumping could force the trickle to look like a fountain. I am surprised that Wilde did not observe the contrasted death scenes in the book to which I now direct your attention.

Quilp dies, too. He is on the run, and he takes a false step on the rotten wharf where he lives, falls into the filthy river, and is drowned. Read it. The passage is quite a short one, but it is in Dickens' finest Caravaggio style. Artistic control and emotional scope are finely linked here. Next time somebody speaks to you of the death of Little Nell, ask them if they have compared it with the death of Daniel Quilp. For linked they are: Good and Evil quit the scene very near together.

We know who Nell was. Who was Quilp? Dickens loved acting out his characters in private life, and he used to do Quilp to frighten his mother-in-law, who was not a favourite of his. He found Quilp where he found all the rest of his characters, in the strange land where his Conscious and Unconscious met and united, in the land of Phantasmagoria and Dream Grotto.

Our time is at an end. Do not go away supposing that because I have told you that in my opinion Charles Dickens drew upon his own depths of potential but unacted Evil for Quilp and the rest of his villains, I intend to fob you off with the old conclusion that Evil is simply an unredeemed portion of the human spirit or, to be even more theological, simply an absence of good, a *privatio boni*. That is not what I think at all. But to arrive at my conclusion I must next make a dive into an area not often considered by literary critics; next time I shall talk about tales of the uncanny, of ghosts, of what Henry James called Gleams and Glooms.

Gleams and Glooms

Some of the oldest stories we have are ghost stories; mankind never seems to tire of them. They have been neglected by critics, because critics, as we all know, are wonderfully wide-awake fellows, alert to the sources, the promptings, the mainsprings of works of literary art; they love to take the clock apart and demonstrate what makes it tick. With a ghost story we know without telling what makes it tick; it is a recognition of the supernatural—what Carlyle called 'the Unseen World or the No-World'—and this source of inspiration is not readily accessible to the sort of knowledge critics usually possess. Though they deal with works of art, they approach them as rationalists, and rationalism and the supernatural are cat and dog. If we look for common sense on the matter we cannot do better than to turn to that monument of common sense, Dr. Johnson, and his words are well known. He said: 'It is wonderful that five thousand years have now elapsed since the creation of the world, and it is still undecided whether or not there has ever been an instance of the spirit of any person appearing after death. All argument is against it, but all belief is for it.'

When Johnson discussed the matter with his friends, of course people spoke up who had seen ghosts. Cave, whom the Doctor thought 'an honest man and a man of sense', had seen one. Oliver Goldsmith's brother, who was a clergyman, had seen a ghost. And it is much the same today; if the question of ghosts comes up in conversation, it must be a very dull group indeed in which somebody does not come forward with a tale, or a fragment, that seems to support the belief that there are such things as spirits of the dead which do, under appropriate circumstances, show themselves to some people, though not to everybody, and certainly not on demand. The possession of a ghost is thought to confer prestige on the owner of the house to which it belongs. For many years in my youth I lived in an old house in Kingston that had a ghost; it was of an elderly doctor who was reputed to have drowned his troublesome daughter in the bath. Several people had seen it. I confess that I was not of their number, but I knew two ladies of unimpeachable veracity who saw him—one at four o'clock in the afternoon, and because the ghost wore evening dress, she supposed him to be a servant. The other, who did not know the first lady, saw him some years later. I myself saw a ghost in that house, at a subsequent time, no less than twice in the same night, and I sat up the rest of the night because I had a very strong premonition that if I saw it a third time, it would be the worse for me. But it was not the ghost of Dr. Betts, who had such a short way with tedious daughters, and I do not propose to tell you who it was. So you see, in the dispute as to the reality of ghosts, I am not of the sceptical party, though I hope I am not foolishly credulous, either.

Nor was Shakespeare sceptical. He has given us some of the most famous ghosts in literary history. Caesar's ghost appears to Brutus. Hamlet's father appears to his son, with what is undoubtedly the commonest of ghostly messages: Revenge my death. *Macbeth* is a very great play of the supernatural, and although I have seen that play many times I have never seen it really well done, because I have never seen it directed by anyone who truly believed in the supernatural. Theatrical directors, like critics, seem unable to accept the fact that Shakespeare believed in ghosts, but I am strongly of the opinion that he did, and as I admire Shakespeare more than I admire his critics, I think he knew what he was writing about. As did Homer, and Vergil, and some writers whom I propose to discuss very soon, whose insight into life is that of creators, rather than critics. To be a creator is to be in touch, sometimes in uncomfortably close touch, with what psychiatrists call the Unconscious—and not always one's personal Unconscious, but the vast, troubled Unconscious of mankind.

Let us look at a characteristic ghost story. I take my example from the period of literature which concerns us in these lectures, the nineteenth and twentieth centuries, and from a writer who was not an artist in fiction, but a famous writer of guide books and biographies. His name was Augustus Hare, and his dates were 1834 to 1903; he was a well-known figure in good English society, for a time tutor to the Crown Prince of Sweden, and author of an autobiography that fills six volumes. There are many people who dislike Hare; they say he was shockingly indiscreet; that is why I like him very much. The indiscretion of yesterday is the rich feeding of today. Hare delighted in tales of ghosts and uncanny happenings, and his autobiography is full of them, and each one is attributed to somebody—usually somebody very well known—who told him the tale. I recommend his life to you as bedside reading and agreeable browsing. Here is a simple, short story from the riches he provides:

> Lady Georgiana Grey told me a curious story of some friends of hers: Lady Pennyman and her daughters took a house at Lille. The day after they arrived they went to order some things from a warehouse in the town, and gave their address. 'What,' said the man, 'are you living there, ma'am? Did I not misunderstand you?'—'Yes,' said Lady Pennyman, 'that is where I live. Is there anything against the place?'
>
> 'Oh dear, no, ma'am,' said the warehouseman; 'only the house has been for a long time without being let, because they say it's haunted.' Going home, Lady Pennyman laughed to her daughters, and said, 'Well, we shall see if the ghost will frighten *us* away.'
>
> But the next morning Lady Pennyman's maid came to her and said, 'If you please, ma'am, Mrs.

Crowder and me must change our rooms. We can't remain where we are, ma'am; it's quite impossible. The ghost, he makes such a noise over our heads, we can get no sleep at all.'—'Well, you can change your rooms,' said Lady Pennyman; 'but what is there over your room where you sleep? I will go and see,' and she found a very long gallery, quite empty except for a huge iron cage, in which it was evident some human being had been confined.

A few days after, a friend, a lady living in Lille, came to dine with them. She was a very strong-minded person, and when she heard of the servants' alarm, she said, 'Oh, Lady Pennyman, do let me sleep in that room; I shall not be frightened, and if I sleep there, perhaps the ghost will be laid.' So she sent away her carriage and stayed; but the next morning she came down quite pale and haggard, and said certainly she had seen the figure of a young man in a dressing-gown standing opposite her bed, and yet the door was locked, and there could have been no real person there. A few days afterward, toward evening, Lady Pennyman said to her daughter, 'Bessie, just go up and fetch the shawl which I left in my room.' Bessie went, and came down saying that as she went up she saw the figure of a young man in a dressing-gown standing on the flight of stairs opposite to her.

One more attempt at explanation was made. A sailor son, just come from sea, was put to sleep in the room. When he came down in the morning, he was quite angry, and said, 'What did you think I was going to be up to, mother, that you had me watched? Why did you send that fellow in the dressing-gown to look after me?' The next day the Pennymans left the house.

There you have it, a classical ghost story, or a part of one, for nobody troubled to find out what the ghost wanted or why it appeared. But we can make a guess: it was by no means uncommon in the eighteenth and nineteenth centuries to lock up a troublesome relative—a madman, or a monster—in the attics. It is not so uncommon nowadays as it ought to be, as careful reading of the daily papers will assure you. The ghost obviously wanted to be given justice—to be understood. It wanted somebody to know that it had not been mad, or wholly mad, and that it had been cheated out of whatever its proper fortune in life happened to be. That is what ghosts are: they are the dead who cannot rest because their story on this earth has not been told. There is a wrong to be righted, and often what is sought is vengeance. And thus, you see, ghosts are linked with that idea of Poetic Justice which we discussed in connection with nineteenth-century melodrama; they are a manifestation of the deeply rooted notion that somehow and somewhere, every living creature should have his due, and if he cannot get it before death he may return to demand it after death.

How do ghosts fit into our discussion of forms of evil as they make their appearance in literature? Ghosts are generally regarded as evil things, or if not evil, uncanny and apt to bring ill-luck to those who see them. There are a few ghost stories which attempt to offer us a benevolent ghost; I remember one in which the ghost was a mother who returned to earth to brood tearfully over the cradle of her little one. As a ghost she was a failure. It is the Senecan ghost, with its terrible cry of 'Revenge!', that makes us glance over our shoulders in apprehension. We know that the Lord has claimed vengeance as His own, presumably because mankind is so ready to assume the God-like prerogative, in the name of justice. The ghost is prompting someone to an act which is contrary to religion, an act linked to the age-old yearning for poetic justice. Revengeful ghosts arouse that sneaking belief in the supernatural that lingers among people who have no use for religion. Religion may include the uncanny and the evil, but its emphasis is on the redemptive and doctrinal aspect of belief. The people who have lost religion, or who have simply grown up as religious illiterates—a very common class today—have lost their sense of the beneficent part religion plays in life, but they have not shaken off their primitive fears. They dimly guess at an area of being which is not readily approached, and which is certainly not good; this is the haunt of Evil, the Devil's Kingdom. Christianity has not for many decades paid much attention to this realm or its Dark Master. Hebraism, in its orthodox form, has not been so ready to abandon the Devil or his many agents, and in this respect I think the Jews are wiser than we. How their belief lives, and what extraordinary forms it takes, are readily and enjoyably discovered in the works of one of the greatest writers living today, Isaac Bashevis Singer, most of whose brilliant stories are available in English translations from the Yiddish.

Do I hear you say that orthodox Jews are stuck in the eighteenth century? And that we have advanced beyond their curious compound of peasant credulity and infinitely complex scholarship? If that is your belief, take a look at what the movie houses offer in this city, at any time of the year, and answer honestly what you think *Rosemary's Baby*, and *The Exorcist*, and *The Omen*, and *The Devil Within Her* are all about? They are enormously popular exercises in the age-old cheat of having your cake and eating it too. They give their audiences a faint sense of having encountered something profound, of having peeped into an abyss, of having dallied with evil, without having really been obliged to accept the reality of evil. They are poisoned sweetmeats, these films, but they satisfy a longing in the public heart for some approach to an essential human problem: What is Evil and how does it manifest itself in the world? The evil these trumpery films offer is feeble, because the people who put the films together are not sincere in what they are doing; they are a pack of Dickensian Fat Boys who want to make our flesh creep. But when there is nothing better, the hungry public appeases its appetite with what it can get.

Let us look at the history of the ghost story, and some of its ablest practitioners, during the period with which these lectures are concerned. In doing so I expect I shall mention some names that will be unfamiliar to most of you. They are the names of writers of great quality and high attainment, but not of the greatest quality or the highest attainment, and for this reason they are seldom mentioned in universities. We must not blame the universities, who are expected to teach something that looks like the body of English literature in three or four years to students who often come to the university without any substantial acquaintance with literature on any level. They have to be force-fed, like Strasbourg geese, if they are to put on any intellectual flesh at all; unfortunately, like

Strasbourg geese, they often develop pathological symptoms in the process. They must hit the high spots, and gobble the best that has been thought and said as fast as they can; they have no time for lesser figures in literature. But when they have left the university, they surely have time to read for pleasure and for enlargement of the spirit; they have time to read what they like, rather than what they must. It is to be hoped that they will read some authors who are neither among the certifiably great, nor among the certifiably fashionable. Only people with no taste shun reading which is not in the highest taste; the true reader has favourites whose faults and deficiencies are obvious, but whose virtues are highly individual and uncommon.

A writer in our realm for whom the universities have some indulgence is Edgar Allan Poe, and he is often referred to as a master of the uncanny and the horrible. Indeed, he was so, but I do not think that he was as great a master as several others whose names I shall mention shortly. Poe never, so far as I know, wrote a classical ghost story, though he wrote many familiar tales of premature burial, of murder and vengeance, of terror and the macabre. He wrote them in a manner which I myself do not like; it is a style of nervous excitability that is never far from hysteria. Behind all of Poe's writing lurks a sense of grievance, of having had a raw deal, of being a lost child in a hostile world, which is amply justified by the story of his life. But though we may pity him, we do not have to like his work. The admiration that he received in France, which still persists, has done much to sustain his reputation in American literature. But is he really the wonder-worker in his realm that we are told he is? I put the question but I do not offer an answer; I content myself with asking you to compare his work with that of Mervyn Peake, a writer born in 1911 and not long dead, whose trilogy of *Titus Groan*, *Gormenghast*, and *Titus Alone* possesses qualities of sustained macabre fantasy, of poetic expression, and of sheer creative power which I do not think Poe can rival. Peake achieves the real poet's feat of creating a world with its own laws, its own nature, and even its own weather—a world in which the reader lives as he reads, and which he never forgets, and this is achievement indeed.

If you object that it is improper to compare two writers

who are separated by more than a century, let me mention a contemporary of Poe's, who seems to me to be, in his best vein, fully Poe's equal. That is the Irish writer of uncanny stories, Joseph Sheridan LeFanu (1814-73). Like Poe, he was an oddity. (Indeed the writers of ghosts stories are often oddities: Poe was a neurotic, Peake a sadly afflicted invalid, and LeFanu a man whose life was darkened by a domestic tragedy of the sort we should now put in the psychoanalytic category, but which was in the nineteenth century thought to be chiefly religious.) LeFanu had flirted with the ideas of Swedenborg, whose *Caelestia Arcana* has crept into a remarkable number of ghost stories. But what concerns us here is that LeFanu was successful in creating an atmosphere of evil in his books and short stories which can only have been possible to a man who believed in evil, not as an intellectual concept, but as a living reality. Many of his admirers recommend *Carmilla*, which is a tale of vampirism complicated by what we should now recognize as Lesbianism, but which the nineteenth century saw as passionate friendship. This story was plundered later in the century by another Irishman, Bram Stoker, who wrote *Dracula*; Stoker was good on creating sensation, but lacked the higher qualities of an author, and we shall not return to him. I am an admirer of LeFanu, and I greatly prefer his novel *Uncle Silas* to his short stories. He was a novelist of fine attainment; his characterization, and the skill with which he moves, slowly and teasingly, to his denouement, are masterly. The threat that hangs over his heroine, Maude Ruthyn, is finely suggested and sustained. Indeed we are astonished that, in the end, Maude pulls through. As we read we recall Poe's dictum that the most poetical topic in the world is the death of a beautiful woman. But Maude does not die, and the clouds of evil that surround her are dispelled.

LeFanu is remarkable among writers of this genre because so many of his stories are about women. Many writers assume that the supernatural, as a serious matter, is necessarily a masculine business. Not LeFanu; he makes us fear for threatened women, and the fear we feel is not a simple worry that some simpleton may lose her virginity, but that a human creature may lose its soul. LeFanu, by the way, suffered all his life from a recurrent nightmare that he was trapped in a falling house, from which he was rescued in the nick of time; when he died, his physician commented, perceptively, that the house had fallen at last. I mention that because I think it gives a hint of the quality of LeFanu's mind.

It seems odd that the greatest of nineteenth-century writers of fiction was not at his best in the ghostly mode. Charles Dickens was a man who, when he was off his guard, had extraordinary intimations of the Unseen World or the No-World, but as a general thing he liked to pose as a hard-headed rationalist. When we read in *The Old Curiosity Shop* that magnificent passage in which the animal showman makes a dog that has disgraced itself grind out the tune of the Old Hundredth on the barrel-organ, while the showmen talk about what becomes of old giants, we know that we are in the pres-ence of a great and uncanny imagination. But when Dickens faces the Unknown head-on, he becomes jokey and the wine grows thin. In *A Christmas Carol* he leads off with a splendid ghost, that of Jacob Marley, the tight-fisted man of business, who in his ghostly state is condemned to drag a terrible chain of ledgers and cash-boxes; but the story degenerates to a disap-pointing denouement, where we are told that the spirits that visited Scrooge had their origin in a bottle. I think we may say we know better; they originated in a great imagination which, in this area, mistrusted itself. Dickens might write to a friend about his determination to make the public 'writhe and stagger in their shoes' with a horror story, but his vision of Evil is clearest when he explores the depravity of the living.

The desire to joke about ghosts is very common. One of the most popular jokers of this sort was the Reverend Richard Harris Barham, who, under the name of Thomas Ingoldsby, wrote that extraordinary series of ghostly pieces called *The Ingoldsby Legends*. From the early portion of the nineteenth century until about 1914 it seemed that people could not get enough of these tales, and they appeared in eighty-eight editions. But now the *Legends* seem to be forgot-ten, save for 'The Jackdaw of Rheims', which is neither the best nor the most characteristic. I suggest that you hunt them up and look at them afresh, because they provide two kinds of pleasure: they are good ghost stories and they are brilliant light verse—for all but a very few of the legends are in verse form, and Barham was a master of the tripping measure and the unexpected rhyme.

Barham died in 1845, and as a clergyman—he was a Canon of St. Paul's—he was in the midst of the religious ferment of his time, much of which was concentrated in what was called the Oxford Movement, a call for a return to pre-Reformation usages in the Church of England, and a revulsion against both the easy-going ways of the Church in the eighteenth century and the increase of liberalism and rationalism in the nineteenth. The Oxford Movement tried to arouse the English people to the emotional power and the aesthetic beauty of religion. Barham was not of the Oxford party, but he seems to have been fascinated by its awakened sense of the splendours of the religious life, and especially the example and influence of the saints.

He wrote many of his legends about saints, and in them he makes fun of saints, and Popes, and Cardinals, and all the apparatus of the pre-Reformation Church, as a conservative Anglican clergyman of his time might see them. His ideas are historically absurd, his approach to any sort of Catholicism is uncharitably ignorant, and his idea of the spiritual life is flawed by a jocose vulgarity. But he has two things on his side: first, he is very funny and not infrequently witty, and second, he has a fine imagination, even if its flights are hampered by a huge Anglican ball-and-chain on his left leg. What is more, he understood terror and evil, and they often assert themselves when he is doing his excellent best to be amusing.

Allow me the indulgence of a personal reminiscence. When I was a small boy my father used to read to me before bedtime on Sunday nights, and one of his star performances was 'Nell Cook!! A Legend of the Dark Entry' from the *Legends*. I didn't understand all of it, and when my father thought he was amusing me he was frightening the wits out of me. The tale is of Canterbury Cathedral in its pre-Reformation days; a highly placed cleric of that establishment, who lives in the Dark Entry, has brought a beautiful lady, whom he calls his niece, to live with him and they have a high old time. Now the Canon has a servant, a pretty girl called—well, this is what Barham says:

Although within the Priory the fare was scant and thin
The Canon's house it stood without;—he kept good
    cheer within;
Unto the best he prest each guest with free and jovial
    look,
And Ellen Bean ruled his *cuisine*. He called her 'Nelly
    Cook'.

For soups and stews and choice *ragouts*, Nell Cook was
    famous still;
She'd make them even of old shoes, she had such
    wondrous skill;
Her manchets fine were quite divine, her cakes were
    nicely brown'd,
Her boiled and roast, they were the boast of all the
    Precinct round.

And Nelly was a comely lass, but calm and staid her air,
And earthward bent her modest look—yet she was
    passing fair;
And though her gown was russet brown, their heads
    grave people shook;
—They all agreed no Clerk had need of such a pretty
    Cook.

One night Nelly puts the firetongs in the gay lady's
bed, and there they remain, undisturbed and without any
complaint from anyone for some time. So where has the lady
been sleeping? The merriment goes on. A passage which—for
no reason I can understand—struck me with dread was that
which described the niece's musical performances:

And fine upon the Virginals is that gay lady's touch,
And sweet her voice unto the lute, you'll scarce hear
    any such;
But is it 'O Sanctissima!' she sings in dulcet tone?
Or 'Angels ever bright and fair'? Ah no,—it's 'Bobbing
    Joan'!

So Nell Cook makes a huge warden pie for the happy couple, in which she puts poison, and they both die. The Canons of the Cathedral, faithful to their order, bury Nell alive under the pavement of the Dark Entry, with nothing but the remains of the pie to comfort her. And so Nell becomes a ghost.

I did not understand the mainspring of the plot. I did not know that the niece was not a niece, or that there was anything odd about the sleeping arrangements, because to me sleep meant sleep, and nothing else. I believed that Nell was a cook and no more. But I half-understood her jealousy. The spirit of evil that the tripping verses conveyed struck upon my childish heart like the blows of a coffin-maker's hammer, and I think my critical instinct was right, even though it was immature and ill-informed. And since then I have become increasingly aware of the splendid mixture of wit and terror that lurks in the *Legends*.

A few years ago I was shown over Canterbury Cathedral by Dr. Burgon Bickersteth, whom some of you know. When we came to the Dark Entry all the dread of childhood arose in me and I understood as never before what another nineteenth-century versifier meant when he spoke of the moment when

> . . . *the pain that is all but a pleasure will change*
> *For the pleasure that's all but pain.*

Dr. Bickersteth was much engaged with the real history of the Dark Entry, but all my thoughts were for the Canon, and the merry lady, and for Nell Cook, below the flagstones, with her evil pie.

By that time, you see, I knew a great deal more about the *Legends* and about their author. Barham is described in the *Life* written by his son as the good father and family man, the good clergyman who rose to be a Priest of the Household to the Royal Family, and the genial, good fellow who knew all the wits of London, and combined clerical decency with a great deal of roistering conviviality. The reality, which has fairly recently emerged, is decidedly different. Barham was the child, not of his father's wife, but of his father's cook; his childhood was darkened by a powerful sense of not being what he seemed; a coach-accident ruined one of his arms; he was early separated from his beloved sister Sarah, another illegitimate child, and his childhood in Canterbury and later life at the family manor of Tappington Everard was lonely; the peasant tales of the Romney Marsh were almost daily fare when he was living there. His married life was by no means an idyll, and he suffered the deaths of six of his children before he died himself, of something that sounds very much like melancholia, called then 'a decline'.

When we look at the *Legends* again we see that the jolly tales of the saints are not so predominant as a casual glance might suggest; it is the ghost stories of the Romney Marshes that take the foremost place, and the sensibility of a man who was outwardly merry, but whose childhood had been sad, gives the *Legends* their characteristic nervous grotesquerie.

I am not, of course, indulging in the silly game of suggesting that Barham wrote *The Ingoldsby Legends*, or that Poe wrote his tales of terror, because they had wretched experiences in childhood; if an unhappy childhood were all that is needed to make a genius, or a man of talent, the world would be crowded with such people. Between the experience and the creation something intervenes that we cannot explain, and though the experience may do something to shape the creation it does not cause it. However, we may go so far as to say that unhappiness in very early life brings with it a premature recognition of the double-sidedness of human nature and of life in general, and that a large number of our writers of ghost stories, about whose early experiences we have undisputable information, had unenviable childhoods. Even when they seem to have had normally pacific childhoods, these writers of ghost stories are themselves queer fish.

Consider one of the best of the group, the late Montague Rhodes James, born in 1862, who lived until 1932, and was famous both as a Provost of King's College, Cambridge, and as Provost of Eton. He was not just your normal little boy. His first work was *Short Sketches of the Principal Northern Saints, Volume I, Illustrated*, which he wrote—and illustrated—at the age of seven! He grew up to become a great medievalist and antiquary, a great humorist and mimic, and a splendid writer of ghost stories, with which he used to amuse his Eton and Cambridge friends. I commend them to you as among the best of the genre. He is a daring writer, for he makes no concessions to the public, and indeed one of his best stories, *The Treasure of Abbot Thomas* begins with fifteen lines of rather dense Latin, of which no translation is offered. But even more daring is his refusal to offer any explanation of any of his ghosts; they simply exist, and he makes us believe in their existence, giving no quarter to the anti-ghost party. He was, of course, a clergyman, and repeated reading of his work suggests to me that he regarded the dangerous and terrifying side of the supernatural as the shadow of its redemptive side. Many writers about ghosts seem to be dualists in their hearts, even when they are orthodox in their professions.

Dualism has rarely had such a thorough and successful presentation as in *The Strange Case of Dr. Jekyll and Mr. Hyde*, written by Robert Louis Stevenson in 1886. Everybody knows the story: the admired philanthropist Dr. Jekyll experiments with what would, in our day, be called 'mood-changing drugs' and turns himself into the diabolical Mr. Hyde. If we read with our eyes open, we know that the evil of Hyde is the unlived life of the exemplary Jekyll, released and given its head by the drug. It is a famous thriller. But the same theme, of the unlived life, the inadmissible portion of a personality, is explored with vastly greater subtlety by Joseph Conrad in two of his most celebrated tales, *The Secret Sharer* and *Heart of Darkness*; Conrad had a penetration not given to Stevenson, and in *The Secret Sharer* we see that the supposedly evil part of a character is not without its attraction and sympathetic spirit; the evil is as much a consequence of suppression, of having been disowned, as it is inherently wicked and unacceptable. This is the ambiguity of evil, a subject that few writers have been able to convey; but the ambiguity of evil, when we consider it, gives us a different conception of that much-maligned and grossly caricatured metaphysical power whom we speak of as the Devil.

This same theme is apparent, though it is never quite brought into focus, by a writer who seems now to have been forgotten, though once he had a considerable vogue. He was Arthur Machen, a Welshman, born in 1863, who died in 1947. He wrote magnificently during a period when style was greatly valued for its own sake, and I sometimes think that this was his undoing. If someone had said: 'Come on, Machen, chuck the crepuscular mists and unspeakable horrors, and give us a sharp, clear horror,' he would have left a greater name. The titles of his books, *Far Off Things*, *Things Near and Far*, *The Three Impostors*, *The Great God Pan*, and *The Hill of Dreams*, suggest the kind of writer he was—one capable of what John Masefield called 'beautiful and terrible stories' but inclined to a wooziness which was at one time supposed to be Celtic by people who know little about the Celts. Machen is apt to lead us up to a splendid mystery, and then to sheer off, declaring it to be too dreadful for description. This leaves it to our imagination; but of course we don't want our own imaginations, with which we are too tediously familiar; we want the imagination of an author with a turn for the horrible.

Of course, some of the best writers of uncanny tales have done precisely this, but they wield a greater magic wand than was given to Arthur Machen. At the very top of the list we must place Henry James, whose tales of horror, and haunting, and the uncanny, seem to me to make him the great genius in this department of literature. He is so important a figure in the world of the novel generally, that his authority in the world of terror and evil is sometimes forgotten.

His most famous tale is, of course, *The Turn of the Screw*, and here he does precisely what I have blamed poor Machen for doing: he leaves the final explanation up to us, if there is to be a final explanation. Was the governess in that story a little mad? Was she unsettled by a suppressed and dangerous affection for her employer? How did the ghosts of Peter Quint and his female accessory debauch the children Miles and Flora? There is a strong whiff of sexual corruption hanging over the story, but do we accept sexual corruption as the ultimate in evil? The story presents us with a net of questions that we are left to answer from the hints we have been given, and the interpretation we put on what we are plainly told. It is an undoubted masterpiece.

For my taste, however, it is not James's greatest work in this realm. For me that is *The Beast in the Jungle*. There are people who read it without any feeling that it belongs among James's ghostly tales, though this is not the opinion of the great Jamesian Leon Edel, who included it in his collection that bears that name. Do you recall it? It is about a man called John Marcher who confides to his friend May Bartram that he had, from the very earliest time, had a sense of being kept for something rare and strange, possibly prodigious and terrible, that was to happen to him. They are friends for a lifetime, and the great thing never happens, until, when she is dying, she tells him what it is: it is the recognition of the unlived life; he has had from her all that a man can have from a woman, except love. Not that she was not ready to give it, but because his sense of his own isolation and his egotism prevented him from knowing that, and taking what was there to be taken. She dies, and it is some time after her death before he understands the truth of what she has said. He is a man who has allowed egotism to devour him and isolate him from life, and that is the strange and terrible thing that he has been waiting for. When he understood, we are told, the very tears in his eyes seemed to freeze. Such a précis as this does violence to a great work of art, but as a tale of the horrible and the uncanny, masked as a sober account of a man's life, I do not think it has an equal. The ghost that haunts John Marcher—the ghost of the unlived life, and the love he was too self-delighted to see—is a dreadful ghost indeed.

Such tales as these are a long way from the simple ghosts we find recorded in the pages of Augustus Hare's autobiography. Are they to be taken, therefore, as marks of a greater sophistication in public taste? I should not say so; they mark a change, rather than an advancement, though I realize that there might well be dispute on that point. It is of interest in terms of our central theme—the depiction of evil in literature—that the appetite for tales of the uncanny persisted into the twentieth century and that literary artists who were both gifted and strongly aware of fashionable trends took pains to satisfy the demand. One of the most successful was Sir James Barrie. His play *Dear Brutus*, which made its appearance in 1917, has a theme that is reminiscent of Henry James, for it is a play about unlived lives. A curious host, named Lob, invites a group of people to visit his house on Midsummer Eve; they enter an enchanted wood where they are given a second chance at life—a chance to avoid the mistakes they made the first time. And do they do so? With one pathetic exception, they do not. It is in Barrie's familiar bittersweet manner; never has there been a dramatist so adept at making audiences swallow the sugar-coated pill. His play *Mary Rose* is another adventure into the uncanny, about a girl who visits a curious island in the Hebrides, and vanishes for several years. Its first audiences thought it very pretty to begin with, then they found it distasteful, for it said clearly that the unseen and the unchancy stands very close to us, and we never know when it may assert itself even in our own well-managed and somewhat commonplace lives. People do not like to be told that the uncanny is as near to you as the coat you wear. To the end of his life Barrie pondered the theme of the unlived life, and in 1931, when he was not far from his death, he wrote one of the masterpieces of the uncanny, his short novel *Farewell, Miss Julie Logan*. It is a brilliant story of a delusion which may, on the other hand, have been a haunting; a young Presbyterian minister, something of a bigot, falls in love with a beautiful girl and rejects her when he discovers that she is a Papist. His difficulty is that nobody else sees the girl. I commend it to you as the work of a master who is at present out of fashion.

Perhaps the concept of the 'unlived life' calls for some expansion. It is not suggested that we should all obey every prompting of our desires, though it is healthy for us to give full attention to those desires which we will not fulfil, but which sometimes arise to plague us. We must be aware of the darker side of our natures. We must know what lurks in the shadows. Goethe said that he had never heard of a crime which he could not imagine himself committing, under appropriate circumstances; that is the sort of self-knowledge we should seek. But the 'unlived life' is something different: it is very often the life that has been put aside in order to serve the demands of a career, or an idea of one's place in the world, or simply—as in the case of the hero of Henry James's story—to serve one's own comfort and egotism. Very often it is love that is sacrificed in this way, but it may also be adventure, or a concern with the arts, or friendship, or simply a greater freedom of action: these unlived elements revenge themselves and sometimes they do it with compounded interest.

We all know the saying that preachers' children are the worst harum-scarums, but do we ever look to see what ghosts of the parsonage they are laying by their rowdy behaviour? The banker's boy who becomes the school thief is bodying forth a repressed part of his father's concern for money. The young people who make a cult of promiscuous sex may be doing what their elders were afraid to do but longed to do. The druggies and the layabouts are living out the unlived life of too scrupulously moral and work-ridden families.

This does not mean that these disreputable people are in the right, or that their elders are to blame for their bad behaviour. What is demonstrated is simply the principle of *enantiodromia*, which is the tendency of things to run into their opposites if they are exaggerated. Excessive self-love becomes no love at all; extreme prudence ends up by spoiling the ship for a ha'p'orth of tar; a rejection of all that is coarsely vital in life brings a shrivelling of sensibility. As a very eminent psychiatrist once said to me: 'We attract what we fear.' What we fear is the portion of life that remains unlived. Our task, if we seek spiritual wholeness, is to be sure that what has been rejected is not, therefore, forgotten, and its possibility wiped out.

The more recent years of the twentieth century have not lacked their distinguished practitioners of the ghost story. We have not time to look at them all, but I suppose that many of you are familiar with the stories written by Raold Dahl, which are elegant, frequently funny, and always somewhat cruel in theme. One of the few successful novels in this genre is the work of Sylvia Townsend-Warner, a writer who has never, in my opinion, been sufficiently recognized; it is called *Lolly Willowes*, written in 1925, and it is about a woman who, without wishing to do so, becomes a witch. Miss Townsend-Warner, who is now eighty-three, still occasionally publishes tales of the other world in the *New Yorker*, a magazine not usually associated with this sort of fiction. And of course in our own time the remarkable Alphonsus Joseph-Mary Augustus Montagu Summers has published his highly Catholic ghost stories, as well as his better-known and controversial works of scholarship, many of which relate to ghost literature and the Gothic novel. When I was at Oxford it was common to see Father Summers taking his afternoon walk, dressed in the soutane and shovel hat of a European priest, accompanied either by his secretary (a pale young man dressed entirely in black), or by a large black dog. You never saw him with both secretary *and* dog, and it was rumoured that this was for the best of reasons; Father Summers was said not merely to be a scholar of the supernatural, but an adept in its horrid mysteries.

Nor can I complete even such a hop-skip-and-jump as this through the uncanny literature of our time without mentioning what I consider one of the finest ghost stories of recent years; it is 'The Portobello Road' by the very popular novelist Muriel Spark.

Upon the whole, the ghost stories of the twentieth century have taken a psychological turn; the ghost, or the possession, or whatever the uncanny element in the story may be, is represented as having its origin not in Hell, but in the psyche. The difference seems often to be one merely of terminology. The twentieth century has seen the psyche become a scientific reality, and the world has embraced it with a whoop and a holler. What is strange is that so many people—possibly a majority—suppose that the psyche must be a region of terrors and a breeding-ground of unhappiness. As the word 'psyche' means, after all, Soul, one wonders what has happened; the Soul in the old days had a better reputation. Indeed, for many people, Soul is the most embarrassing of the four-letter words. I want to talk about that, because it is very near the root of our central discussion, and gives some evidence about the nature and origin of evil.

This century has seen one of the great intellectual revolutions of the last two thousand years—a revolution at least as far-reaching in its consequences as the Renaissance. For convenience, let us call it the Freudian Revolution, because the theories and explorations of Sigmund Freud are central to it.

What is perhaps the most revolutionary of Freud's books, *The Interpretation of Dreams*, appeared in 1900; it was not very well received, and sold slowly; it was not translated into English until 1913. Indeed, it was not until the twenties that it was read widely, and of course it, and his two volumes of *Introductory Lectures on Psycho-Analysis*, and all his subsequent works, were attacked and derided, as much by members of his own profession as by others. But Freud was fond of saying that his desire was to disturb the sleep of the world, and the world found itself unable to resist the force of what he had to say. The import of his teaching is familiar to us all: in brief, it is that the conscious part of the mind is only a part, and not always the dominant part, of the whole mind, and that many of our troubles have their origins in those areas which lie below the surface, and which declare themselves in dreams, or often in undesirable symptoms of one sort and another, or in madness. The supernatural world, to Freud and his followers, was an illusion arising from the Unconscious. More than that: the whole structure of religion, including belief in God, was an illusion, persisting from the early period of man's development, and something that man must set aside if man hoped ever to attain full freedom and self-determination.

The argument, set out in his brilliant essay *The Future of an Illusion*, is that God is an obsessional neurosis of which mankind must be cured. Freud says: 'Religion consists of certain dogmas, assertions about facts or conditions of...reality, which tell one something that one has not oneself discovered, and which claim that one should give them credence.' Now one might be prepared to agree with all of that except the important word 'consists'; if religion were nothing more than what Freud says it is, one wonders if it would have lasted so long, and in such a variety of forms. But in that word 'consists' we find a basic Freudian attitude; the cast of his mind is strongly reductive, and whatever came under the inspection of that remarkable mind emerged notably smaller and less impressive than what it had been before.

Do not think, I beg you, that I am deriding Freud. I am strongly conscious of what he has done for mankind; he is one of the greatest liberators of the human mind in our history. He roused the world from its sleep, and he swept away a great amount of troublesome and decaying rubbish that had been under our feet. He was a man of probity and a man of genius. But he was still a man, and subject to error, and as with other men whatever he said took its colour and its dimensions from his own extraordinary but none the less finite mode of perception. And the prevailing mode of Freud's mind was reductive.

To him, with his nineteenth-century scientific training, that was what science meant. But one wonders sometimes — wonders timidly and tentatively — how well Freud knew himself. How clearly did he understand that he was not only a genius and a scientist, but also a spell-binder, and a controversialist of enviable wit and elegance of style? Like all such people, he can slip things past you that you do not notice; he can persuade you to accept his arguments because they are so well marshalled that you do not see what has been left out—or if you do see it, you are ashamed to mention it, because Freud has made it seem inconsequential. Freud did not believe in God. Very well; perhaps God as the nineteenth century knew Him was an illusion—or nine-tenths an illusion. But Freud did believe, with his whole heart and soul, in Science, and it never seems to have occurred to him to question that structure of causality and proof which is called Science. It is notorious that if you give a theologian an inch, he will have you bound and gagged in fifteen minutes, unable to voice a doubt. But scientists are just such monsters of dialectic; admit a few assertions which you have to accept on faith, and in no time they have put you to silence and shame. What does Freud say in *The Future of an Illusion*: 'Science is no illusion. But it would be an illusion to suppose that we could get anywhere else what it cannot give us.' There you are; with that sentence, if you accept it, bang go all the insights of art and literature.

Or do they? Do they really go bang? For some people, it seems, they do. But not for me. It was on this point that I finally had to make up my mind about my allegiance to Freud, whose writings I perused with fascination and great benefit to myself for many years in my younger days. But it just wouldn't do. Art and literature were the things that sustained me in this life, and as time went on I became convinced of the existence of another dimension of life without which I could not live as a free and courageous being; if people wanted to call it God, the term had no evil echo for me, and indeed the weight of tradition behind it seemed to me to be an argument in its favour. If foolish people want to define a silly God, and then declare that he does not exist, I am not interested in their game. Defining God has always seemed to me a pompous and self-defeating exercise. I am content that God should encompass me: I do not think it likely that I shall encompass Him. Where God is concerned, I am the object, not the subject.

I am not, I assure you, indulging in this personal confession for its own sake, but because I think my experience of the Freudian Revolution was a powerful one. I took it seriously. But at last the time came when I could accept its reductive, vainglorious, scientific outlook no more, and fortunately I was able to turn my attention to the work of Freud's great pupil C. G. Jung. Jung had broken with Freud, after a period of discipleship, because he could not swallow the dogmatic atheism, the science-worship, and the trick of looking at the whole world through the wrong end of the binoculars. The Freudians have suggested that Jung, who was the son of a Lutheran pastor, could not accept atheism because of loyalty to his father—and to Freudians loyalty to a father is pretty dubious conduct. But they were wrong. Jung's father had lost his faith; that was part of his personal tragedy. Jung's insistence on God as, at the least, a psychological fact, and at the best as a transcendent authority manifesting itself in man through the activity of the psyche, was the result of his work with his patients. Jung was an empiricist, and thus far he too was a scientist. For Jung, God was a fact for which evidence existed in the mind of man—which is not to say that God is nothing more than that: for Freud, God was an imposture upon the mind of man. The rights and wrongs of this matter are not for us to pursue here. What concerns us is that Freudian teachings, half-understood and freely adapted, have had immeasurable effect on the popular thinking of our time, and have strongly influenced our ideas about good and evil.

Freud banished for many people the belief that a transcendent authority exists to which mankind is accountable for its actions. We see the consequences all about us. Many dogmatically supported rigidities of thought, and some manifest cruelties, have lost their authority under the Freudian attack. But inevitably the common acceptance of ideas of right and wrong has suffered, as well. Extraordinary horrors and indecencies are now regarded, not as simply evil, but as a consequence of some inequity in society, or in nature, for which we are all, in very vague terms, thought to be responsible, and against which, therefore, we should not seek redress. The supposed death of God has loaded us all with a new kind of guilt. If a policeman is killed in attempting to apprehend a homicidal robber, the emphasis is likely to be on what has made the robber anti-social, rather than on the fact that the police-.

man, and his immediate family, have suffered an irreparable loss. We are all, somehow, thought to be responsible for the robber. His personal responsibility has almost vanished. Any notion that the homicidal robber may be the instrument of a force of Evil which is rather more than his personal psychological disturbance is rarely discussed, and the anti-God party does not want it to be discussed. The wallow of sentimentalism that attended the recent abandonment of capital punishment in Canada was typical of the kind of thinking that springs from half-baked Freudian morality. Under the Freudian flag, the Devil has gained a good deal of ground, which was not, of course, what Freud intended. But great revolutions are never achieved without some unforeseen losses, and terrible outbursts of sentimentality which is, as I have said elsewhere, the philosophy of boobs.

The Jungian point of view has not gained much ground because it is not so readily susceptible to popular simplification as is its Freudian counterpart. The Jungians assert the existence of God, but they have also sought to re-examine some beliefs which were long ago discarded by Christian orthodoxy. They have some good words for the Gnostics —who are hateful to orthodoxy. They have asserted that the alchemists were not wholly fools—which is detestable to modern science. And they suggest that the Devil is not a joke, and that he may be encompassed in the being of God, which gets up the dander of all those modern clergy who want a God, but can't bear the notion of a Devil. Of course I am putting these things in very simple terms, because I must. These are not our primary concerns here, and we must get back at once to the question of ghost stories and their continued popularity in an age when the benign aspect of the supernatural has been banished from popular thinking.

In brief, I think the explanation is this: the rejection of God as a transcendent authority does not, for most people, settle all the problems that come under the general term of the supernatural. It does not settle the problem of Evil, which most people decline to associate with their concept of God, and which they most decidedly do not reject when they reject the idea of God. The Freudian Revolution has dismissed, for those under its influence, the all-wise, all-loving Father; it has done nothing to rid them of the Devil, or the burden of guilt and fear that might suitably be considered as the Devil's realm. It seems to be characteristic of the human mind to allow itself to be robbed of what is beneficent, but to regard what is maleficent as an inalienable burden.

I have emphasized that many people who reject God have a sneaking acceptance of the supernatural. The Freudian Revolution offers them little comfort. In the matter of ghosts, for instance, of which we have been speaking, it would be acceptable Freudian argument to say that a ghost is a constellation of a fear, or a neurosis, which has its origin in the personal unconscious. But what about the ghosts, of whom there are so many, who appear to more than one person, and who—like the ghost I spoke of in my home in Kingston—appear to people of honest mind, who have no expectation of seeing any such thing, and who have not collaborated on a story to deceive others. On the face of it, it looks as if the supernatural had a genesis other than somebody's disordered psyche. Ghost stories approach, usually by some oblique path, an area of which we have only an oblique perception, but which seems to have some relevance to the world we inhabit.

Ghost stories are also an approach, often tentative and hesitant, to a question which most people put to themselves at some time, and it is: What happens to me when I die?

It is a question that strikes very deep. We all know people who declare with bravado that they expect oblivion in death—that they hope for it and indeed refuse to consider any other possibility. If their attitude were widespread, why would there be the inveterate belief in ghosts, and the ready market for stories about them? I think most people, when they are not putting up a show, have other ideas—and indeed there are few civilizations so crude that they have no notion of a life after death. We all know that we were not nowhere before we were born; scientists will give us, in concrete terms, their notion of where we were—or where a part of us was. Are we to conclude that all that long chain of being ceases when what we call ourselves ceases to be present in the guise we now wear? Such an answer would not, I think, appeal to a scientist—and we know that the concept of what science is and what its limits are has changed radically since the time when Freud made his bold claim that science holds all we may know or expect from life. Ghost stories are very often attempts to answer our question, ranging from the crude concept of the spirit that cannot rest until its wrongs are avenged on earth, to such subtle concepts as that of Henry James—though even that is still rooted in the idea of unfinished business.

The Freudian Revolution stops short of being a really satisfactory explanation of anything except certain sorts of mental illness. Saying that God is dead is like saying that there is no Santa Claus; the jolly old man with the white beard may vanish, but the gifts are under the Christmas tree just the same. All that has happened is that the child who thinks it has discovered a great secret no longer feels that it need be good in order to receive its gifts; Santa has gone, but parental love is just where it always was.

In life, however, the gifts, or the circumstances of life, are not always delightful; there are many surprises of a devastating character in store for us as we unwrap the parcels that contain the things that make up a life. If that is the case in the life we know—and it is—what makes us think that the life we do not know, the life that insists on asserting itself in our persistent belief in ghosts, is a blissful oblivion? Ghost stories, and the universal fondness for them, are indirect evidence of our vastly deeper concern.

Tomorrow we conclude these lectures, and in the last of the series I shall attempt to answer some of the questions that have been raised already, or if I cannot answer them I shall try to suggest lines of speculation that may lead toward answers. But I shall attempt to give some hints about the nature of Evil as it shows itself in the literature of our own day, the literature of the Freudian Age. And because it dwells so much on damnation, without any prospect of blessing, I have called it by T. S. Eliot's phrase, Thunder Without Rain.

Thunder Without Rain

I<small>N THIS</small>, the last lecture in this series, I want to talk about the novel in this century, attempting some assessment of its attitude toward Evil, and its ways of depicting Evil. The theme is much too large for the time we have, and therefore I warn you at the beginning that I shall speak only of a few novelists, not always the best-known, as any attempt to include the many famous writers of our era would demand another method of approach, and might result in nothing better than a rich confusion. Even as matters stand I must pick and choose in a manner which is certainly arbitrary, but which I hope will make it possible to touch some of the high spots. The title of the lecture is Thunder Without Rain; the phrase is T. S. Eliot's, and signifies threat from the heavens, without any blessing to soften its severity.

Those among you who are accustomed to keeping up with the modern novel are aware of the atmosphere of Existentialist gloom, of malice against mankind, of the concentration on misfortune, and the delight in gallows-humour, that characterizes so much of the work of even the most talented of our writers. There are no gods, they seem to say, but there is a Lurking Something that acts against mankind, to render his works futile. The people in these novels rarely love, but if they do their love is complex and productive of pain and disillusionment. They lust a great deal, but without gusto; they copulate compulsively, but without joy and often with pain. They are ill at ease in their world. Only very rarely do they grow old, and age brings no wisdom. If they die, they die without hope or resignation. They are ridden with guilt. They seek what they call Identity, by which they frequently mean some reconciliation with what is least admirable in themselves. Of course my description involves a measure of caricature, but not a great deal of it. The Evil they put forward as a pervasive element in life is that very old sin which used to be called Wanhope, and later Despair. A medieval name for it was Acedia, and it was attributed to monotony of life. This seems to me to be psychologically very perceptive, and I have ventured to wonder whether our modern proneness to this plague is not attributable, at least in part, to the monotony of life that afflicts so many people. Has there ever, I wonder, been a period of history when so many people worked so hard, at such dull tasks, in order to maintain a quality of life which is better than anything the majority of mankind could have enjoyed in the past, but which is bought at the cost of unremitting work, economic complexity, lifelong burdens of debt, and an hysterical craving for more and costlier physical objects of a kind that can never requite the toil and servitude it takes to acquire them. In the midst of our heaped-up abundance of things made of metal and wires and plastic, we starve for the bread of the spirit. As I argued yesterday, the Freudian Revolution has changed our ideas about the spirit, and for many people it has killed the spirit as a source of enrichment, leaving only what breeds guilt and dread. Guilt and dread are what we find in the most up-to-date exercises in the age-old art of story-telling, where they are cloaked as revelations of the inner life of man.

Let me repeat what I said yesterday: we must not blame Sigmund Freud for this. He said he came to rouse the world from its sleep, and to some extent he did so. But most of mankind are slow to wake, and find themselves now not awakened, but roused only to a terrifying, unrefreshed Katzenjammer—a hang-over from the indulgences of the past.

As it is mirrored in fiction, this awakening did not come in a hurry. Let us take a few minutes to look at some of the most popular fiction of the first half of this century. This is not, I am convinced, a waste of our time. I have great faith in popular art as a clue to what people desire, and as a picture of the world as they wish it were. We can find this evidence in the class of books called best-sellers.

What is a best-seller? Can we agree that it is a book that has sold over a million copies? They are of all sorts, and we should be foolish to deride a book because it has sold widely and given delight to great numbers of people. When people knock best-sellers I remember that Dickens and Tolstoy were best-sellers in their day, and are best-sellers still; beside their names we could place a score of other names, unquestionably meritorious. But I want to talk now of the best-seller as the lily of a day—the book which captures the enthusiasm of the reading world but which never becomes the theme of academics or sophisticates.

Let us begin with Edgar Rice Burroughs' extraordinary fantasy *Tarzan of the Apes*, which appeared first in 1912. Something in the neighbourhood of fifty million copies of these books—there are several of them—have been sold, in sixty languages. They are fantasy-books; their author was a man who was a failure in business, and wrote—in the beginning—to give rein to his stifled imagination. I don't have to tell you what they are about. The powerful ape-man, Tarzan, is in reality an English nobleman, Lord Greystoke, lost in the jungle as an infant and nurtured by kindly primates. He possesses simplicity of mind, nobility of spirit, and immense physical power. Let the Freudians explain his habit of swinging rapidly through the trees, howling with high spirits as 'levitation-fantasy'; of course it is. But it has been the spiritual nurture of many a poor brute whose family are apes only in a metaphorical sense, and it has released him from the shackles of the modern world in which, as several statesmen have loved to tell us, 'we never had it so good'.

Is Tarzan too coarse for you? Best-sellers can be very refined, if refinement is what you want. Have you read Florence L. Barclay's enormously popular novel *The Rosary* (1909)? It is about a fat woman who finds love. Of course she is never

called fat in the book, but we are told that the Hon. Jane
Champion is thirty years old, and 'of almost massive proportions'. She is so massive that nobody 'has ever apprehended her
wonder as a woman'. Where Tarzan howled, the Hon. Jane
sang, and what she sang was Ethelbert Nevin's richly evocative
ballad *The Rosary*. You remember it—

> *The hours I spent with thee, dear heart,*
> *Are as a string of pearls to me;*
> *I count them over, every one apart—*
>   *My rosary.*

That was what she sang in a voice described as 'low and vibrant
as the softest note of a 'cello'. She never knew she could sing
like that until she did so at a charity affair, and from then on
her romance blossomed, and a very fine fellow who is of artistic
temperament—he wears red socks with evening dress—
apprehends her wonder as a woman.

Not all the heroes and heroines of best-sellers were as
lucky as Lord Greystoke and the Hon. Jane. In 1921 the world
was enchanted with the misfortunes of Mark Sabre, hero of
A. S. M. Hutchison's best-seller *If Winter Comes*. Mark is that
popular character, known from Bible times, the Suffering
Servant. He says himself, in the rueful, slangy style that makes
him so likable, 'My sort's out to be kicked, and I wouldn't be any
other sort.' And kicked he certainly is. His wife snubs him
because he is friendly toward the servants, and finally she
deserts him; he is cheated by his business partners, because he
is so trusting and they, of course, are such crooks; in this sort of
book all real businessmen are crooked—success is in itself a
kind of dishonesty. He befriends a girl who is going to have an
illegitimate child, and of course everybody thinks it must be
his; but he stands by the girl, whose name is Effie, and whom
he thinks of as 'a jolly little sister', and at last he ends up in
court, where he is humiliated by a beastly prosecuting lawyer
who is not a gentleman and shows it by having a hump-back.
Mark is that darling of the literary symbol-seeker, a Christ
Figure, which always seems to mean an incompetent no-hoper.
It is of interest that the book appeared in the year that Freud's
early works first attained some popularity in the English-
speaking world. Freudians, I am sure, spotted Mark Sabre at

once as a masochist and a grievance-seeker, but there is enough of that spirit in all of us to ensure the success of a book. It is of some interest that the late Mackenzie King, not usually known as a literary critic, declared the book to be one of the greatest ever written. Which shows, if it shows anything, that a resolute winner can still be stirred to admiration by the tale of a resolute loser.

The loser as winner—this has always been a popular theme. The year after *If Winter Comes* there appeared another book which delighted the general reading public; it was *Tell England*; its author was Ernest Raymond. It was called by its publishers 'A Great Romance of Glorious Youth, in Two Episodes, School and War'. It is about a couple of clean-limbed, fine English lads, who discover something of the complexity of life in their schooldays, and then go to War, full of chivalrous determination, and die at Gallipoli. The title comes from a translation one of them did of the epitaph written to commemorate the Spartans who fell at Thermopylae:

Tell England, ye who pass this monument,
We died for her, and here we rest content.

I am not the man to jeer at it, because it moved me profoundly when I read it as a schoolboy, and though I think differently now, I know that one derides one's long-lost self at the cost of some self-respect. The book was one of the last flings of the chivalrous spirit that was so completely destroyed by the First World War. Chivalry was not wholly a good thing; in foolish people it had foolish consequences. But the world is the poorer for its passing, and I know I could not read *Tell England* now without mingling mirth with a painful sense of loss.

A book I could read now, and have indeed reread quite recently, is another best-seller that came before the Freudian Revolution had completed its work. It is *Precious Bane*, by Mary Webb (1926), which, after a somewhat slow start, was pushed into prominence by the enthusiasm of the then Prime Minister of England, Stanley Baldwin. Whatever you may think of Baldwin as a statesman, he was not a trivial literary critic, and unquestionably this book is of a special order of excellence. I mention it here to emphasize what I said earlier: a best-seller is not by definition a bad book. I must admit at once to a special interest; *Precious Bane* is a tale of the borderland between Shropshire and Wales, and that is country I know well, because my forebears lived there from the dawn of time. It is a country of extraordinary and subtle beauty, and the book conveys that quality as only a writer who was a poet could do it. It is a tale of the era of the Napoleonic Wars, and it is about love and avarice. Gideon Sarn is a young farmer who sacrifices everything to money; his sister Prue has almost abandoned hope of love because she has a hare-lip, which is not merely disfiguring but is a mark of a witch. But she finds love all the same, and as she writes in her diary, 'I took my crumb, and behold, it was the Lord's Supper.' It was this book that was chiefly responsible for Stella Gibbons' brilliant pseudo-Freudian parody of a whole school of books of rural life, *Cold Comfort Farm*, which appeared in 1932. As parodies go, it is in the front rank, but parodies never go very far. A parody is a compliment; nobody troubles to mock what nobody takes seriously.

Precious Bane is a novel of powerful, but artistically controlled, feeling. It came at a time when feeling was being severely frost-nipped by the chill blasts of the Freudian Revolution. A modern poet of high reputation and merit, Stevie Smith, has written, 'I suppose it was Aldous Huxley who is the watershed of feelings in novels. Before his time feelings were permissible. But he, not being able to express emotion, made a virtue of necessity and set up the half-man for hero, the little creature who itches and fidgets but cannot feel.'

This is somewhat unjust. Huxley's characters do feel; shame, embarrassment, frustration, rejection, ineffectuality—whatever is negative and life-diminishing—they feel all of these things, often very amusingly. They do not feel love, except when their love is to be mocked by the author. They are a cruel, heartless lot, but very funny. I speak of course of the early Huxley, of *Crome Yellow*, of *Antic Hay*, and of *Point Counter Point*. In middle age Huxley underwent a change not unfamiliar to psychologists, and became fascinated with those things which he had formerly derided, and wrote at length about religion and social justice and how to embrace the Perennial Philosophy. But as a philosopher and a magus he suffered from his earlier defect—he thought too much and felt too little, and what had made him a splendid comic novelist made him rather a bore as a world-saviour.

It would have taken more than Huxley to kill the novel of feeling. It lived on and lives still, for many of the admired novels of our day, with their everlasting whine about the meaninglessness of life, are obviously deeply felt. The best-seller that dealt in coarse, obvious feeling certainly did not die. At the time of Huxley's greatest popularity one of the huge successes in this realm was Vicki Baum's *Grand Hotel*, which has something for everybody. It has not aged well, but we can see what gave it power. First of all, the story of Herr Kringelein, the little clerk who is told that he has cancer of the stomach and cannot live long; he goes to the Grand Hotel to splurge his savings on a last fling, and in no time at all he opens his bedroom door to find a naked girl on the threshold. 'She staggered toward him, fell heavily...and the helpless collapse of the warm golden body filled him with a sweet enchanting terror.' One thing leads to another and after a blossoming of love—it blossoms in minutes in such novels as this—'he fell asleep blissfully in a blaze of gold that looked like Flämmchen's breast and was also a hill of broom in flower.' From then on he never looks back; he tells off his domineering boss (which is always a sure card) and leaves the hotel with a girl who is determined he shall not die. Against him we must balance his boss, who is rich but never mistakes a girl's breast for a hill of broom, and Baron Gaiger, the aristocratic burglar who is so sensual that he licks the petals of flowers for fun; and Madame Grusinskaya, the great ballerina, who wants to kill herself because she is frigid, until the Baron shows her that she has been under a misapprehension. And for sophistication, we have Dr. Otternschlag, the man with a face ruined by war, who sits in the foyer, and reflects that nothing ever happens, although we know that the Grand Hotel is a hotbed of passion and intrigue.

I have taken some time to speak of these books because they were once influential as well as popular. They were no more naive than many popular books of our day—consider *The Naked and the Dead*, or *Exodus*—but their naiveté was of a different order. The popular books of our time draw upon the resources of the Freudian Revolution; even when they attempt a great sweep of action, their tone is reductive. When I was an undergraduate a popular song began, 'Life is just a bowl of cherries'; campus wags altered it to 'Life is just a bowl of pits'. To the popular modern novelist, life is just a bowl of pits. But it is to writers more enduring and influential than they—the writers whom they imitate, at a distance and with greatly diminished talent—that we must look for the kind of evidence we are seeking about the appearance of Evil in modern fiction.

Where do we begin? The slow publication and slow acceptance of James Joyce's *Ulysses* suggests itself, and its date, 1922, is an attractive one. But it was many years before the full influence of *Ulysses* was felt, although many writers were quick to adopt the stream-of-consciousness technique of narration, and use it with varying degrees of success. But I would rather not talk of it here, first because it is a superbly comic novel and thousands who have acclaimed its novelty have missed its humour, and second because it is by no means a book wanting either in feeling or in a sense of a transcendent reality behind the world of appearances. I would prefer to speak instead of a great writer who has never, it seems to me, been given his due, and that is John Cowper Powys. Powys, who was born in 1872, lived until 1963, and wrote forty or more books of poetry, essays, and fiction. He daunts many readers because his novels are so long. *Owen Glendower* runs to 938 pages; *Wolf Solent* is 966 pages; the book that some critics consider his masterpiece, *A Glastonbury Romance*, numbers 1174 pages: nor are these pages which flick quickly under the reader's fingers—they demand concentration or something important will be missed. And what is important is not narrative, but feelings, infinitely varied and minutely described feelings.

What kind of feelings? It is here that Powys appears as an innovative and essentially modern novelist. He does not adopt new ways of writing prose, as Joyce does; nothing in the manner of his books will confuse you. But as an explorer of sensibility Powys is very much a novelty for his time, and a writer of such mastery that his work still has surprises for us. Sometimes he is said to be of the school of Thomas Hardy, because he writes about rural or village life in the area of Hardy's Wessex. I have not much patience with the tracing of schools and influences in the work of writers who are plainly able to stand on their own feet. It is true that Hardy is not a novelist of Christian feeling, but what of that? Powys is not a novelist of Christian feeling either, but he is no more like Hardy than he is like Huxley. It is worth noting, I think, that serious or tragic novelists are so often expected to write under the influence of some sort of religion, whereas comic novelists are not thought to have any such requirement. Such an attitude springs from the old, fallacious idea that joy and merriment are not religious feelings, whereas a miserable fate or a tragic life must carry with it some paraphernalia of the displeasure of God, or of the gods.

Powys does not exclude religion from his novels; they are full of parsons and church people, but the parsons have a range of feeling, and an attitude toward nature, that are not, in my observation, the outcome of any seminary training. Even in *A Glastonbury Romance*, where the mainspring of the plot is the presentation of a Passion Play in the old and numinous town of Glastonbury, conventional Christian feeling has little place, but pagan feeling, and the weight of legend and mythic history, are breath of the book's life. How does Powys make these things manifest to his readers? Because he does make them manifest to anyone who reads him sympathetically, and it is this intensity and immediacy of feeling that gives the books their value and importance. He does it through loving and evocative description of states of emotion.

In religion Powys was a sceptic; in psychological type he was a sensualist, and as a sensualist he was very much a sadist. His books contain extraordinary descriptions of pain, either directly felt or observed in others, and this pain is productive of heightened sensibility and of a special kind of joy. Perverse, would you say? Possibly so, but great art, as well.

Let us look at a book by Powys, and I propose to take one that is less popular than *A Glastonbury Romance*. I decide for *Wolf Solent*. The title is the hero's name, because Powys's characters have extraordinary names; the girl he marries is called Gerda Torp. Their love-scenes are described at considerable length, and a certain tedium may overcome even the most sympathetic reader as he works his way through them. Love-scenes are great tests of a novelist, and many of the greatest have solved the problem by merely hinting at them. After all, in a love-scene, it is what is understood that is important; what is said may be jejune or embarrassing. A Shakespeare may write great love-scenes, because his lovers have to convey their passion by words; in the more realistic world of the novel a talkative lover may prove unconvincing. Powys does not agree, and his love-scenes range from the transporting to the tedious. Apart from this, his descriptions of scenes and people are vivid. Consider what he says about a country squire: 'From one corner of his twitching mouth a trickle of saliva descended, towards which a small fly persistently darted.' That fly is almost Powys's signature; thousands of novelists make people drool, but only he makes them attract flies. Who is this unseemly squire? When he is tormenting the Vicar, who is a poor creature, Wolf knows, we are told that Wolf 'was tolerant enough of the various forms of normal and abnormal sensuality; but what at that instant he got a glimpse of, beneath this man's gentlemanly mask, was something different from viciousness. It was as if some abysmal ooze from the slime of that which underlies all evil had been projected to the surface.'

It is not easy to quote from Powys; the language seems strained and high-coloured. All his talk of perversities and acute states of sensibility is puzzling and almost without meaning when it is removed from context. But in the preface to *Wolf Solent* he makes a plain statement of what he calls 'the purpose and essence, the inmost meaning of this book,' and it is 'the necessity of opposites. Life and Death, Good and Evil, Matter and Spirit, Body and Soul, Reality and Appearance have to be joined together, have to be forced into one another, have to be proved dependent upon each other, while all solid entities have to dissolve....' The book demonstrates this proposition with remorseless intensity. What he has said is easy enough to accept; we nod as if it were a commonplace when we hear it. But as demonstrated in the novel it is something new in experience. Solent, his remarkable mother, his wife Gerda and her rustic family, his maniacal employer, and all the queer *dramatis personae* of this book attest to what Powys has said in a way that is unexampled even in the work of George Eliot. Without each other, they could not be themselves, and without the Reserved Sacrament in the Church, the evil of Lenty Pond would be as nothing. This novel is at the farthest extreme from *The Old Curiosity Shop* with its all-good Little Nell and its all-bad Mr. Quilp. It is a work of art in which the vice and virtue of the characters is interdependent, and where good and evil, though always in contention, will never fight to a lasting victory for one or the other. Is *Wolf Solent*, then, a greater work of art than the novel by Dickens? I am not here to award marks or establish ranks among novelists. Both are books directed at the ages in which they were written, and each partakes of the character of its age. *Wolf Solent* is a novel of a time when we have seen the need to establish some reconciliation among opposites, not by attempting to alter their nature, but by more clearly understanding their interdependence.

It is this seriousness of vision that divides Powys, as an author, from the vastly more popular Aldous Huxley. Brilliant as Huxley is, he is in the grip of the fashionable Wanhope of his time, and he seems at least in the earlier part of his career to have accepted wholly that immutability of cause-and-effect which, in these latter days, some of the most eminent scientists have begun to question. His later quest for transcendency, through Eastern mysticism, and Western mysticism, and finally through drugs, never fully convinces, because he seems to be in quest of Absolutes. Powys knew in his bones—which is perhaps the only place to begin with such knowledge—that there are no Absolutes, but rather an infinitely complex mingling of contrarieties—at least in so far as such things can be ascertained by the means we possess.

A strong recognition of the interdependency of human creatures and moral concepts need not always lead to a recognition of the sort of transcendent power in the universe that can be likened to the God of the Old or the New Testament. One of the most extraordinarily gifted novelists in the serious modern vein is Marcel Proust, whose great novel of social life is called *A la recherche du temps perdu* (*Remembrance of Things Past* in the English translation). To trace that novel through its long course is to be rewarded, at last, with an enduring, heightened sense of the interdependence of its characters, down to the least of them; no one could be quite what he or she is without the others, and no single character seems to have the powerful individuality that would raise him to unchallenged supremacy. This is, of course, because they are all in search of the same idea of what is good and enduring in life, and it is simply a rather limited personal satisfaction. Nobody wants to depart very far from the norm established by the society he worships; nobody wants to be a saint, or a devil, except as society understands these terms. Their kingdom is a kingdom of this world; their religion, where it exists, is an aspect of society. In consequence the book offers some careful studies of Acedia, of monotony, of boredom, of Wanhope. Even the Baron de Charlus, who is surely the finest portrait in fiction of a particular sort of sensualist, gets very little fun out of his wickedness; when, at the last, the author gives us a portrait of him, blasted by vice, being wheeled about in an invalid chair, raising his hat in a pathetic parody of his earlier, splendidly aristocratic and daemonic style, we wonder for a moment if Proust has not set up in business as a moralist. But we are quickly reassured on that point.

One of the questions this great novel raises in our minds is: What on earth did they all get out of it? What were they struggling for? Of course Madame Verdurin ends her career as the Duchesse de Guermantes, but by that time our concept of that splendour has shrunk to the dimensions of the shrivelled old schemer and society-harlot that she is. The supreme social position is no greater than she who has attained it, after Time has worked its reductive magic. Life is just a bowl of pits. But—and this is one of the many points—art is not a bowl of pits, and the art of this book fully justifies its reputation. It is as a work of art that it leaves us enlarged. Nor is it a book in which we cannot see the working of a transcendent power. In Proust the dominating, all-pervasive element is Time: the god here is Time, who devours all his childen, and we may decide that he is an evil god.

Proust's method is, however, wholly his own. His imitators cannot do what he has done. There have been several of them, but the one most in the public eye at present is the English writer Anthony Powell, whose long novel—there are twelve volumes—is called *The Music of Time*. It presents us with a prospect of English society, beginning with a group of schoolboys, one of whom is the narrator; the boys do not all last into their sixties, but some of them do, especially the egregious

Widmerpool, who is a splendid comic creation. We follow him from his inept schooldays through a career in which he achieves various kinds of power, in business, in the Army, and at last in government. But he seems never fully to hit the mark; there is an essential clownishness about him; even when his career is at its height he is involved in humiliations with which he cannot cope; he becomes a cuckold—and it takes a King Arthur to be a cuckold and maintain a high measure of dignity. Widmerpool is seen at the end as a deluded old ass engaged in that common pursuit of deluded old asses—he is trying to mix on terms of physical equality with his juniors, who despise him. As a picture of Widmerpool the long, long book is a fine creation, but as a portrait of society it lacks the certainty of Proust, and because Proust went before it along this path, we are aware from the beginning what the theme of the book must be: Life is just a bowl of pits.

Superior to Powell in this sort of creation is his friend Evelyn Waugh. Waugh's novels are, for the most part, short works, and they are of a special order of perfection. He is a fine stylist, though his style is unobtrusive. Yet, though they are brief and compressed, his works are not miniatures. Their strength and dimension arises from the coherence of the point of view from which they are written. Waugh was a moralist. His morality was always that of dogmatic Christianity, and early in his career it became the morality of the Church of Rome. It is not a morality that excludes any sort of human experience, or that imposes a sober attitude toward life, but it is a morality that insists that man should live, at all times, in awareness of a transcendent power from whom his life is derived and toward whom his life will return. An awareness of God, in short, which cannot protect a human creature from folly and sin, but which keeps him aware of a scale of things in which follies and sins must assume their proper place.

In Waugh's later work this awareness increases, until *The Loved One*, for instance, assumes almost the dimensions of a tract against superstition and triviality. *Brideshead Revisited*— which startled and disappointed those readers who had stupidly regarded Waugh as no more than a gifted funny man —contains a scene of deathbed penitence and acceptance of faith that aroused strong antagonism among people who

insisted that death was no more than a passage to oblivion—
a point of view we have already discussed at some length.
And his trilogy, *Officers and Gentlemen*, surveys the War of 1939-
45 as one man's struggle against a world being enclosed in
folly and sin, triviality and spiritual shoddiness, and is, in my
opinion, the most complete and poignant work of literary art
to be inspired by that conflict.

Waugh does not, as you will observe, partake of the
follies of the Freudian Revolution, and he draws his insights
from Catholic doctrine, rather than from the Freudian enlight-
enment. He most decidedly does not believe that life is a bowl
of pits, merely because that is what a great many people seek to
make it. It is the moral weight of his novels that raises them
above the level of those of Powell, of whom we have spoken,
and whose subject-matter is much the same as his. Waugh's
concept of Evil is a powerfully Catholic concept; the great Evil
is to forget God, or to turn one's face from Him.

Is it necessary, therefore, to be a Catholic, or an adher-
ent of Christian dogma, in order to depict life seriously—for
Waugh is always serious, though he is rarely solemn. No,
because one of the great novelists of this century, the late
Thomas Mann, achieves the same end, in a very different
manner, and with full acceptance of the Freudian
Revolution — or perhaps it would be wiser to say the
Psychoanalytical Revolution. I make that qualification because
on a famous occasion, when he was called upon to pay tribute
to Freud at a public dinner, he somewhat astonished the guest
of honour by including a very warm encomium upon the work
of Freud's rival and apostate pupil, Carl Jung. Mann was prone
to such failures of commonplace tact, as anyone who has
studied his life is aware. Mann writes in a manner inimitable by
anyone else; the density and prolixity of his novels would be
intolerable in a writer who did not also possess his extraordinary sweep and complexity of mind. It is unsatisfactory to call
this quality Teutonic, for it is not common among Teutons. It
is wholly his own. Mann was a philosopher, steeped in the
thought of Goethe and of Nietzsche, and yet his conclusions
are not those of either of his masters.

Think of *The Magic Mountain*, which I choose because I
assume that many of you will have read it. The concept is not

altogether unlike that of Vicki Baum's *Grand Hotel*, but the execution is of a very different order: a group of people are assembled in a tuberculosis sanatorium in Switzerland; they represent a wide variety of human attitudes, which they expound in an atmosphere of invalidish reasoning and invalidish living. These sick people present a paradigm of Europe and its civilization. They expound and haggle about life and death until we could bear no more if we were not certain that some conclusion is in prospect, and indeed it comes. The hero, Hans Castorp, who is not himself a gifted disputant, arrives at it in a time of isolation and stress, and here it is, in the words of the English translation: 'For the sake of goodness and love, man shall let death have no sovereignty over his thoughts.' It is, you see, a rejection of Wanhope, a statement of moral courage, a rejection of the notion that life is just a bowl of pits. Goodness and love are not, of course, put forward as simple-minded, Pollyanna concepts; the whole thrust of the book is to show their profundity and final worth.

Even more clearly, though with an intensification of Mann's accustomed denseness of argument and prolixity of expression, this concept of life as a noble thing is put forth in what is perhaps his most difficult novel, *Dr. Faustus*. I shall not assume that you have read it, for it is a book that has been known to damp the courage of even determined and serious readers. It is easy to see it as a political allegory, expressing in the form of human tragedy the tragedy of the German people, who asserted an arrogance of intellect which drew its inspiration from spiritually archaic and obsolete sources; this, says Mann, is 'the Devil's domain' and leads to ruin. But the story of the musician Adrian Leverkühn is decidedly more than that. Leverkühn is shown to us as born in 1885, in what Mann calls 'Luther's Germany', and his first love is theology; but he turns to music—a daemonic art—and finds that his powerful intellect is a gift he enjoys at the expense of the God-given creative spontaneity of natural genius. He becomes infected with syphilis; indeed, he seeks it; later he makes a bargain with the Devil—and it is interesting that the Devil is drawn to him by his proud intellectual powers, as a correlative of his infected body. He receives, in return for his soul, the assurance of twenty-four years of genius, with only one stipulation; during that time he may not love. He has his gift, and the Devil claims his price; Leverkühn goes mad and the last ten years of his life are spent in dotage. Power is bought at the price of complete humanity, and the downfall is of tragic dimension. Yes, it is a political allegory, but it is something more profound than that. Here again we have Evil depicted as the failure of Love, or to use the older word that has no merely romantic overtone, of loving-kindness.

In another statement, not in one of his novels, Mann sets forth the doctrine of the union of contraries, which I have spoken of in my remarks on John Cowper Powys. In the essay 'What I Believe' he speaks of 'the new humanity' in which he sees 'the union of darkness and light, feeling and mind, the primitive and the civilized, wisdom and the happy heart'. I do not want to oppress you with my own Jungian prejudices, but this sounds uncommonly like that Mystical Marriage of Opposites, resulting in wholeness, which Jung found in his investigation of the discarded writings of the Alchemists, and which he puts forward as the way of life in which the hope of mankind lies.

I warned you at the beginning of these lectures that I am no theologian; I have not even amateur qualification in that complex realm. But from what I have already said, or adduced from the writings of a number of novelists of high repute, it is clear to anyone that this union of opposites is something different from the dualism which Christian theologians have condemned. It may not be any less a heresy, but that is not for me to decide. Dualism is the continual opposition of Good and Evil, the war in heaven between God and the Devil, with the implication that at some time one of the opposed forces will emerge as undoubted victor—but without saying which it may be. The union of opposites of which these writers speak is something else; it is the merging of apparent opposites to produce a new and stronger spirit in man, because it is in the soul, or heart, or mind of man—in all three we may presume—that the struggle is carried on, and the eventual new element appears in the form of a wider sensibility, a greater wisdom, and an enlarged charity. But as you have immediately observed, this is to happen in individual men, and be manifested through them, and that is not what I have been hinting at through these lectures; I have been suggesting the existence of a power of good and a power of evil external to man, and working through him as an agency—a God, in fact, infinitely greater than man can conceive, and a Devil vastly more terrible than even the uttermost terrors of human evil. It is part of mankind's vanity to assume that all of Nature is merely a background against which he works out his destiny—the scenery for his drama. Religion, in some of its aspects, has encouraged this vanity, but I suggest that the idea is open to question.

This vanity on the part of mankind is not unreasonable. We are the only creatures, so far as we know, to achieve the intricate and extensive consciousness of self that makes us in so great a degree the masters of our lives. Unless we are greatly mistaken, there is no other creature on earth that begins to rival us in power of communication, of degree of interrelation and co-operation, and of abstract thought. But whether we are or are not the end toward which all evolution has been striving is open to doubt. Any assertion we may make that the forces we call, for brevity and convenience, God and the Devil are forces contained in ourselves, and without external being, is open to even greater doubt. Visionaries and philosophical thinkers like Powys and Mann appear to have doubts on this point, and writers who are professing Christians have no doubt about it at all.

Indeed, doubt as to whether science can answer all man's questions, and remove his God from him as if God were a tumour, is likely to crop up in unexpected places. Last night I gave you examples of the atheistic dogma of Sigmund Freud. Because I respect him so much, I am happy tonight to give you a sample of a later doubt. He wrote, in a lecture of 1933, 'If one regards oneself as a sceptic, it is a good plan to have occasional doubts about one's scepticism too. It may be that I too have a secret inclination toward the miraculous that goes half way to meet the creation of occult facts.' Not much of a chink in his armour, you may say. But consider whose armour it was, and how thick it was.

Our time is running short and I cannot detain you with a multitude of further examples. I should like to speak of two, however, both of whom have achieved eminence as writers, mingling critical appreciation with widespread popularity in the way that remarkable writers do.

The first is Graham Greene, who is sometimes called a Catholic novelist, though I think that too narrow a label. He is a Christian novelist, and Christian belief is at the heart of his best work. He has some tiresome characteristics; one of these is a fondness for losers as principal characters; sometimes as I read him I wonder if I have not picked up the wrong book, and have *If Winter Comes* in my hand, with its exaltation of the loser-hero. It is just as romantic, and just as wrong, to exalt trivial failure as it is to exalt trivial success. Greene's whisky-priests, struggling against booze and lechery, are interesting to read about, but in a life that has brought me into contact with a great many priests I have never met one who was in the least like them. Success is not always bought at the cost of the soul, and if the winners are always wrong, we must regard evolution as a gigantic swindle, because it is a long chronicle of victory. But when we have disposed of Greene's romanticism, we have still to face his theology, and what is it?

In a recent novel, *The Honorary Consul*—it appeared in 1973—he offers an unusually clear statement, and I shall quote it to you at some length. A priest who has sinned deeply, but has served his people nobly, is talking to a group of Argentine peasants, one of whom is the mother of his child, and a doctor. He says: 'I believe in the evil of God, but I believe in his goodness, too.... The God I believe in must be responsible for all the evil as well as for all the saints. He has to be a God made in our image with a night-side as well as a day-side.... I believe the time will come when the night-side will wither away...and we shall see only the daylight of the good God. You believe in evolution...and I believe God is suffering the same evolution that we are, but perhaps with more pain.' The doctor intervenes; in novels doctors are generally spokesmen for strict rationality, though how they come by this reputation puzzles me when I talk to those I know. The doctor says: 'Suppose the night-side of God swallows up the day-side altogether? Suppose it is the good side which withers away. If I believed what you believe, I would sometimes think that had happened already.' The priest has an answer: 'But I believe in Christ; I believe in the Cross and the Redemption. I believe that the day-side of God, in one moment of happy creation, produces perfect goodness, as a man might paint one perfect picture. God's good intention for once was completely fulfilled so that the night-side can never win more than a little victory here and there. With our help. Because the evolution of God depends on our evolution. Every evil act of ours strengthens his night-side, and every good one helps his day-side. We belong to him and he belongs to us. But now at last we can be sure where evolution will end one day—it will end in a goodness like Christ's. It is a terrible process all the same, and the God I believe in suffers as we suffer while he struggles against himself—against his evil side.... God when he is evil demands evil things; He can create monsters like Hitler; He destroys children and cities. But one day with our help He will be able to tear his evil mask off forever. How often the saints have worn an evil mask for a time, even Paul. God is joined to us in a sort of blood transfusion. His good blood runs in our veins, and our tainted blood runs through his.'

To me, at least, this sounds uncommonly like Bernard Shaw's theory of Creative Evolution. The notion that Shaw was an atheist dies hard, especially in people who have not troubled to read the works of his old age. A God who is bound to us, and whose redemption we assist and share in, is a Shavian concept which seems not to be repugnant to the declared Catholic Graham Greene.

The idea of complete perfection, even when it is an attribute of Christ himself, has been known to cause disquiet in some souls, who long for wholeness in the Redeemer of Mankind, and who see wholeness as including human attributes of which the Biblical Christ knows nothing. There has been a great fuss recently in England, because a Scandinavian film-maker has announced his intention of making a film there about Christ's sex-life. The terms in which the film is described are distasteful, and as several people have said, there would be an even greater outcry if such a film were projected about Mahomet, or Abraham. But so far as I have followed the controversy, nobody has yet suggested that this plan may have its root in the human desire for wholeness, and a wish for a Redeemer not so far removed from the common fate of man. Wholeness is not wholly admirable—or at least not in orthodox terms—and to be wholly admirable is, in the eyes of some truly sincere people, to be repellent. Of course, Christ rejected Satan when Satan tempted him. Whether his rejection included so powerful an element of humanity as the sexual urge is a question for better-equipped theologians than I.

The idea of a wholly good God, however, is by no means wanting in modern adherents, and one of them is a writer much admired and discussed in our time, Aleksandr Solzhenitsyn. In the famous broadcast he gave last April, he accused the modern world of a loss of courage and a loss of reason, and this was his comment on that state of affairs: 'There is a perfectly simple explanation...not the superficial one so fashionable in our day, according to which man himself is irreproachable, and everything is blamed on a badly or-ganized society. The explanation I have in mind is a purely human one. Once it was proclaimed and accepted that above man there is no Supreme Being, and that instead man is the crowning glory of the universe and the measure of all things, then man's needs and desires—and indeed his weaknesses —were taken to be the supreme imperatives of the universe.' He draws a humiliating conclusion: 'In the years which fol-lowed the world wide upheaval of 1917 that pragmatic philosophy on which present-day Europe was nourished, with its refusal to take moral decisions, has reached its logical con-clusion: since there are no higher spiritual forces *above* us and since I—Man with a capital M—am the crowning glory of the universe, then should anyone have to perish today let it be someone else, anybody but not I, not my precious self, nor those who are close to me.'

These are heroic words, uttered by a man who has hero-ically earned the right to utter them. They are strong meat for reflection, but we must not forget our theme, which is the appear-ance of Evil in literature, and a discussion of its manifestations.

Why does evil appear in literature at all? The question seems a foolish one at first utterance, but its answer is not simple. A book about wholly good people would be intolerably dull reading. We demand of literature a reflection of life, and life without some evil, or some falling-away from strict moral-ity of conduct, is unthinkable. As Graham Greene points out, even the saints knew evil, and Paul was the greater saint because he had been one of those who took part in the martyr-dom of Saint Stephen—and Paul was on the wrong side in that encounter. The Christian urge for nearly two thousand years has been toward a perfection that we profess to admire; but when we are off-guard, it is wholeness rather than perfection that we are interested in and the full development of human possibility is what we ask of literature.

That is what we have been talking about during these evenings. And we have met with the paradox that when there is a sharp dichotomy between good and evil in a novel—as, for instance, between Little Nell and Daniel Quilp in *The Old Curiosity Shop*—the evil character seems to enlist the superior creative powers of the writer, and therefore is more attractive than the good. Every writer of melodrama knew that without a good strong villain, his play was lost; the subtler novelists of the nineteenth century offered us villains who are very near to being monsters, in the case of Dickens, but we feel a truth in their enormities; in the ghost stories we talked about there was no doubt that a good ghost was worse than no ghost at all, and a ghost that could inspire terror with its cry of 'Revenge', or that could chill us by the nearness of its threat, as in the master-pieces of Henry James, was the ghost that won our terrified confidence. So often the good seems contrived, whereas the evil is vital and engrossing.

The solution, I think, lies in the fact that novels taken as complete works of art possess a wholeness that we respond to as a reflection of life. Little Nell is almost too good to be true; I say 'almost' advisedly, because good people are not as rare as cynics pretend. Daniel Quilp is almost too bad to be true—though some of us have met a Quilp here and there, and policemen and lawyers and judges can tell some strange tales. But Nell and Quilp together give us a heightened picture of life that produces the satisfaction of a genuine, if high-coloured, work of literary art. The gaudiness is immaterial; it is only people of ultra-refined taste who cannot stand these strong portraits. If, in the world of some literary artists, their good people seem pallid and feebly conceived, whereas their villains have the breath of robust life, it is surely because the creative energy that rises from the unconscious of the writer tends toward what is evil; he is wanting in the wholeness of spirit we have been discussing. He is not a bad man; he is a man who can evoke and transmute into art the evil in himself.

It is by putting Man in the highest position in the universe that we diminish the vigour and tension of literary art. Some works of undoubted artistic interest have certainly been produced under the influence of such a belief, and I mention the novels of Virginia Woolf as examples. But as time wears on, literary fashion changes, and the novels of Mrs. Woolf seem to have lost some of their gloss recently, whereas the novels of Arnold Bennett, whom she derided with the remorseless cruelty of a Bloomsbury wit, have shown themselves to have unexpected powers of endurance. To put it with the uttermost bluntness, the writers who are enclosed in a kingdom of this world do not have the big literary artillery, and when we have wearied of them, we are likely to turn again to the authors who, overtly or by implication, write as if man lived in the presence of a transcendent authority, and of an Adversary who sought to come between him and the light.

The concept of wholeness is so very great, so demanding of our uttermost powers of understanding, that most of us must be content to glimpse it, indirectly, so to speak, through art of some kind, and literary art as often as not. It is a benign concept, though many terrors are in the path of those who seek it. But because we recognize evil, and confront it as wisely as we may, we do not necessarily succumb to it. When we watch two men wrestling, they seem almost to be in a lovers' embrace, but we know that at last one will fall. Our hope is that Evil may fall at last. To conclude I shall quote the final passage from John Cowper Powys's *Autobiography*. In part, it is a reflection on death. 'It comes to pass, even while we are still in life, that when our soul loses itself in the long continuity of kindred lives, it does not lose itself in any power less gentle, less magical, less universal than itself, or less the enemy of cruelty; for what it finds is what it brings, and what it sees is what it is; and though the First Cause may be both good and evil, a Power has risen out of it against which all the evil in it and all the unthinkable atrocities it brings to pass are fighting a losing battle.'

But literature is the chronicle from the battlefield.

The Canada of
Myth and Reality

HE MUST BE *a rare Canadian indeed who does not feel himself moved, from time to time, in and out of season, to comment on some aspect of his country's fortunes, spiritual being, government, arts, sciences, economics, virtues and shortcomings, and any and every aspect of the national life. Such comment is a national sport even more popular than hockey. It is a different thing, however, to be asked to talk about one's own country in another land, to people who know little about it. This was my daunting experience when I was asked to talk about the myth and reality of Canada at a symposium promoted by the Association for Canadian Studies in the United States, the theme of which was Twentieth-Century Canadian Culture. There was only one thing to do—to speak truth in so far as it is given me to perceive truth—and this is what I said on April 5, 1977.*

WHAT QUALIFICATIONS HAVE I that excuse my temer-ity in appearing before you to talk about Canadian Myths and Realities? It sounds, doesn't it, as if I possessed some splendid certainty about which Canadian attitudes were the stuff of myth, and which were indisputable fact. But I have no such confidence; in my time I have seen realities dissolve at the first touch of serious investigation into myth, and I have seen myths given the validity of reality, and acted upon as if they were matters of accepted fact. So—who am I to draw distinctions?

Well, to begin with, I am a Canadian by birth, and, on my mother's side, by long descent. I have lived by far the greater part of my life in Canada, and I have some factual knowledge of it that I have gained first as a journalist and latterly as a university teacher; I have also another knowledge of Canada that I can only call a feeling in my bones, a congeries of intuitions and hunches belonging to my calling as an author. I am neither a politician nor an economist, and I cannot speak with any of the splendid authority that belongs to such people. But I am a Canadian right enough: I share all the Canadian perplexities and doubts: I approach them, however, with one eye cocked toward the concept of myth, which has been my study for many years, and the other eye clear, I hope, of that cataract growth of unwarrantable pride which is such a hindrance in any sort of national self-inspection.

What do I mean when I speak of myth? In national terms I mean the sort of attitude which most people take for granted, the belief that nobody questions because nobody troubles to put it in concrete terms. The myth of national character is familiar to us all: in your country it is summed up in the figure of Uncle Sam, a Down-East Yankee in the dress of 1830 or thereabouts, totally unlike most of your citizens in every way, though now and then, on the streets or in a photograph, one spies the reality on which the stereotype was founded. We all know John Bull, who is not at all like any Englishman we have ever met, and Marianne, that generous-hearted, big-breasted female who is such an incongruous symbol for modern France. But where is the Canadian stereotype? We had one once, a grinning fellow called Jack Canuck, who looked as if he were engaged in wheat-farming on a large scale, but we got rid of him because he simply didn't do. Of late years two stereotype figures have arisen from the pressures of our political situation; one is a wistful, large-eyed, pitiful girl in the peasant dress of the eighteenth century, and the other is a coarse-grained, large-footed, evil-visaged Scotch banker, to whom she is bound in a hateful marriage from which she seeks to escape. The mismated pair are, of course, Quebec, La Belle Province, and the other part of Canada. A queer song-and-dance team they are. But whatever reality they may have in Canada—and certainly they have some roots in popular belief, which is not to say roots in fact—they are not recognized outside Canada, and the essential point about national stereotypes is that they should have a wide acceptance among people of other nations.

Does this mean, then, that Canada has no national character, no myth by which it lives and from which it approaches the rest of mankind? No, it does not. It means only that Canada achieved adulthood comparatively recently, in an era of the world's history that has been immensely complicated by universal education, international social and political concern, and the sort of sophistication that relates to a highly developed technology. I do not mean that we are a young nation; we used to say that, but we are now aware that we are not really very young, and that in terms of some of the emerging nations of the Third World we are positively venerable.

Perhaps we have been a little late in coming to self-recognition. Sometimes when I think of the great world family of English-speaking peoples, I think of Canada as the Daughter Who Stayed at Home. I mean that in 1776 Columbia, a self-willed girl with a strong sense of her own independence, left her mother's house, after some high-pitched family rows, and set up a household of her own. At that time Canada elected to stay with Mother. It was not a simple decision, for Columbia offered us all the inducements that naughty girls have at their command; we have not forgotten the bags of gold (we suspected that they were of French origin) with which some of your very persuasive citizens—including that extremely persuasive, somewhat ambiguous character Benjamin Franklin—visited us, hoping that we might be bought. But, to continue this simplified version of history, we said: 'No, Mother needs us, and we shall always be true to Mother; so long as she needs a faithful daughter, we shall never desert her.' So what happened? Just what everybody with a knowledge of family behaviour might expect to happen: Columbia, the naughty daughter, prospered mightily and Mother (who always had a sharp eye for success) became very fond of her. And the Good Daughter Who Stayed at Home became, in the course of time, rather a bore. Many years have passed since that decision and that outcome: Mother has been having a rough time, and has taken up with all sorts of rowdy Continental companions. And the Good Daughter has begun, somewhat belatedly, to have very serious thoughts about her future. Where does it lie?

It does not require a very acute political sense to see that it lies with the North American continent, and there are those who say that the Good Daughter ought to have listened to Columbia two hundred years ago, and made a break with Home. Such attempts to unscramble historical omelets are a waste of time, and it is too late now for us to throw in our lot with you as ten more, very large, states. We have become too set in our ways, and in some important respects our ways are not your ways, nor are our thoughts your thoughts. Our ideas about education are not like yours, and although you have done very distinguished things in education on the top level, I think that on the middle level we have done better than you. In matters relating to the administration of justice we are accustomed to a system that it is fair to call more rigorous than yours, somewhat less open to political caprice. And particularly in political matters our system is markedly different from your own, apportioning power more evenly, and affording the means of getting rid of elected persons who do not please us with considerable dispatch. In many other respects we are manifestly your inferiors, and we borrow from you and copy from you without shame. In financial affairs our great defect is an extremity of caution; we seem to have been settled by a more penny-pinching class of person than you were, and we are, on the whole, resistant to feats of financial daring.

It is too late for us to change our spots now, and if some of our spots are manifestly blemishes, there are others that we consider rather becoming.

In one respect we are, if you will permit me to say so, more realistic than you. We have recognized that all nations of the first rank nowadays are socialist in their general political trend, and we act on that knowledge, sometimes ruefully, but with a philosophical determination. When you visit us, you may not immediately sense that you are in a socialist country. You see remnants of an old order—courts conducted with considerable ceremony and an antique form of dress; the majority of the populace according special treatment to persons who are representatives of the Crown; legislatures bound by ceremonial observance and a special kind of language. These things have an agreeable quaintness, and also a profoundly practical purpose in maintaining a proper decorum in the discharge of social and political affairs. But beneath all of this we are a people firmly set in the socialist pattern. We have bitten the socialist bullet, and it is a long time since we felt any perceptible toothache because of it.

One obvious way in which our socialism shows itself is in our government support for the arts and sciences. We have made it work, not always to everybody's satisfaction, but still with a kind of rough and perceptible justice. In so far as public encouragement *can* support art and science—and admittedly such support can only be very general and cannot be expected to produce wonders—we accept such a plan as part of the responsibility of the nation as a whole.

But where, you may ask, are the myths? Demonstrable differences are easily understood: what have you to say about those things which are more truly divisive, because they exist not in politics or law or banking or even in the arts, but in the less accessible realm of the spirit?

Our myths, or 'life-supporting illusions', as your great scholar of the mythic world Joseph Campbell calls them, are many, and I cannot explore them all. There is, for instance, our Myth of Innocence or Moral Superiority: deep in our hearts we Canadians cherish a notion—you see that I do not call it an idea, because an idea may be carefully formulated, whereas a notion is an elusive thing that takes form from every mind that embraces it—we cherish a notion that we are a simple folk, nourished on the simpler truths of Christianity, in whom certain rough and untutored instincts of nobility assert themselves. Now, of course you are rather in that line yourselves, so you will readily understand what I am talking about. But you will not understand it quite as a Canadian understands it, because of course such a Myth of Innocence is really a manifestation of pride, and it means Innocence in comparison with the flawed virtue of somebody else. And for us the somebody else is you.

When I was a boy, when history was still a compulsory subject for children, I learned some things that would surprise you. I have alluded already to one of them, concerning the war of 1776. You may be surprised to learn that for generations of Canadian children, you were the Bad Guys in that war, and you may think yourselves lucky to have won it, because if you had not, George Washington would have been hanged as a traitor. Of course as I grew older, and learned more history, I moderated this idea, but at my Canadian university nobody suggested that you were in the right. The Revolutionary War was a struggle between pig-headed Englishmen on both sides. England behaved badly, and you behaved badly, but there was one figure in that struggle who behaved with propriety and perhaps with nobility, and that was Canada.

Later on, in the War of 1812, you once again behaved in a manner deeply distressing to our feelings. Let me give it to you as it was given to me, when a child, and ready to accept whatever was said with sufficient authority. Set on by the French, in order to create a diversion on the North American continent and to divert British troops from the European struggle, you attempted to invade Canada. Perhaps you did not try very hard: we, with inferior numbers, drove you back home again. Of course the Sword of the Lord was on our side. I do not suppose that the Battle of Stoney Creek bulks very large in your national consciousness, but it is tremendous in mine, because much of it was fought on the farm of one of my forebears, and in that battle we wiped your noses rather roughly.

Why were we able to do it? Reason suggests that your forces had been misinformed; you thought we would welcome you as liberators; it is quite a common error of invading armies. When the farm boys on your side saw the farm boys on our side as mad as wet hens and firing hot lead out of farm-house windows, they very sensibly decided that it was time to go home and reconsider the whole thing.

It was not a very terrible war, but the people who died in it were just as dead as any other soldiers who were trying to do what they were told, and we are still proud of them. I greatly admire the United States, but I am a creature of irrational passions just like everybody else, and when I visit the battle-ground of Queenston Heights, where the names of some of my ancestors appear on the monument, both as foot-soldiers and as officers, I am extremely glad we licked you, and if the grass grows green there, it is not just the Canadian blood, but the Yankee blood, that gives it a special coppery lustre. Our Myth of Innocence, of having behaved well under stress, haunts those battlegrounds. And, alas, where Innocence flourishes, her shadow, Moral Superiority, is to be found as well.

Please do not misunderstand me; I have not come to Washington to fight the War of 1812 over again, but I cannot talk of our Myth of Innocence without speaking about it. I was also taught in school that in our dealings with the Indians we were greatly superior to you, because you cheated them and killed them and were thoroughly miserable to them, whereas we explained to them about the Great Mother beyond the sea, who loved them so much that she had prepared lovely reservations for them; the Indians understood perfectly, and sent the Great Mother presents of war-bonnets and tomahawks (which, so far as I know, she never wore in public). It is only in comparatively recent times that the Indians have suggested that perhaps our Myth of Innocence needs a few footnotes, written by themselves.

Perhaps you are ready to say that my Myth of Innocence is nothing but a disagreeable self-righteousness, and certainly that plays its part in the myth, though I do not think it is the whole thing. But self-righteousness is part of the blood and bone of this continent, and I think it is somewhat stronger in Canada than it is among you. Self-righteousness is bound to be a characteristic of colonizing peoples; a grabber always wants moral backing when he grabs. If the grabber is an aristocrat in feeling, he justifies his grabbing on the simple ground that he is the stronger and therefore the superior, and that what he can seize he will hold. You had some aristocrats among your forefathers. Very few of the early settlers, or the later ones, of Canada were of aristocratic antecedents. They were humble people, who came to a new land because there was nothing for them in the old land, and it is a bitter Canadian saying that, of those who came, the only ones who stayed were those who did not have the return fare.

Humble people: how we exalt them in our history books and in our popular literature! And rightly so, for to their bravery and endurance we owe much of what we now are.

They are, unquestionably, the salt of the earth. But as my own ancestry was indisputably humble, I may be permitted to say that a small quantity of salt is enough; it is the manifest duty of humble people to stop being humble just as fast as they can, because the shadow of their humility is a know-nothing, cantankerous self-righteousness. The very moment that humble people realize that they are humble and that humility is a very fine thing, their goose is cooked. In Canada we have had more than enough of such vaunting humility, and the neglect of intellectual and spiritual aspiration that it fosters. I do not suggest that the alternative is the grasping, self-serving spirit that is the shadow of aristocracy, but surely we can find a model for Modern Man that avoids both these extremes. We must rid ourselves of the Myth of Innocence on both sides of our border, for it is a potent source of mischief and a breeding-ground for many dangerous sorts of stupidity. Innocence preserved too long sours into ignorance.

What other myths have we? I could talk of our Myth of Frugality, which is another pioneer inheritance, and like our Myth of Innocence degenerates rather too easily, and becomes mere pettiness and, in the world of the spirit, a mean-mindedness.

But I shall not linger over our lesser myths, because there is one, very apparent in our national life now, and a mighty mischief-maker, on which I wish to spend some time. It is our Myth of Difference.

We are more like you than we are like any other nation on earth. Yet how quick we are to contradict an Englishman, let us say, who calls one of us an American. And when he says, as he often does, What's the difference? we are puzzled to give a short answer. If you ask a Swiss how he differs from a Frenchman, or an Italian, or a German, he can tell you at once, and probably he will say that, long years ago, he fought for his difference. I have spoken of the War of 1812, in which we fought for our difference; Canadians have fought in many wars (we once mustered a regiment to go to Italy to defend the Papal States) but we have only fought on that one occasion to preserve our own land and our own difference. In the light of what was going on in the world at the time, it was not a fight that bulks very large in the chronicles. But there is more than one kind of fighting, and anybody who reads the newspapers with his eyes open knows that the great battles of our time are the psychological battles, though these are often disguised as ideological battles. You made a great advance in your nationhood when you fought an ideological battle—for that was what it was, though it was fought with shot and shell—at the time of your Civil War. We are fighting our Civil War right now, and we are fighting it on what appear to be ideological grounds. Below that level, however, it is a psychological war, and the contestants are not only the Province of Quebec against the remainder of Canada,but the provinces against the Dominion government, the rich areas against the poor areas, and an unformed New Canada against an Old Canada that has served its turn. We are fighting the psychological war without revolution, though we may have to come to terms with some devolution, and the fullest stress of the psychological war has still to make itself known among us.

It is a war of immeasurable importance to us, and we fight it very much alone, because we cannot expect other nations to understand it deeply, nor could we tolerate any interference from them. We do not understand it wholly ourselves, and sometimes it seems that several wars are being fought. Those who can see only the wrangle with Quebec do not give full importance to the struggle that is going on between the industrial East and the newly rich West. And there are great numbers of us who think that the war is with you. You are supposed to have seized effective control of our primary resources and our industry. The fact that, if this is so, it happened because we had not wit enough or pride enough to keep what was our own only makes your wickedness more dreadful. There are also people who think that you have smothered our intellectual development and robbed us of our identity. Again, if this is so—and I beg you to note that I am not saying that it is so—it must have been because you were smarter than we were, which of course is intolerable. These deeply offended people want our identity back, and they often seem to think that it can be returned by you if only we abuse you loudly enough.

To my mind, all these struggles are part of a great struggle, comparable in its rigours to your Civil War, but fought very differently, inflicting different wounds, creating

casualties of a different order, and leaving scars no less terrible. But the outcome will be—must be—a different Canada.

Many Canadians expect that it will be a Canada with
what they call 'a recognizable identity'. We have, you see, been
undergoing what is fashionably called an Identity Crisis. It is
supposed that we do not know who we are, and that we wallow
in an intolerable morass of self-doubt. This belief is attaining to
the stature of a myth. It does not seem to occur to the people
who talk most about it that only a minority of people, not to
speak of peoples, have complete certainty about who they are
and where they are going. Earlier I spoke of the national
figures who serve as a cartoonist's shorthand for many
nations—Uncle Sam, Marianne, John Bull, and the like; it
sometimes seems that our Identity Crisis people want to secure
one of those figures for us. They are the kind of people who
attach immense importance to external things—to national
costumes, folk-arts (those dreary enthusiasms of the aesthetically stunted), national shrines, and the like. But surely everybody knows that such things are manifestations of a national
spirit, rather than the origins of it.

People who look deeper into our national predicament
desire more durable evidences of identity. They seek it in the
arts. Science is of no help because scientists, benign or malignant, refuse to play the national game. Music is a lost cause,
because the time for national schools of music seems to have
passed; music is of international worth or it is nothing, and
some of our contemporary music has won gratifying acceptance in the larger musical world. Painting is a different matter, and certainly some of the painting done in Canada in the
present century has strong national inspiration and individuality. But it is in poetry and fiction that the questers repose their
greatest hopes. A Canadian literature, recognizable as such at
home and abroad, is what they want. But the creation of a
national literature is almost as slow as the building of a coral
atoll; toil as we may, the recognizable island will not rise above
the waves in a very great hurry. But we are working at it, and
we have made rather more progress than some of our most
anxious Canadian watchers seem to understand.

Here I walk on dangerous ground, for I am myself a
Canadian writer, and my work has been treated with friendli-

ness and generosity outside my own country, and with special generous friendliness by your country. I have always had a friendly reception from a body of readers in Canada, but upon the whole the label of 'satirist' has been attached to me, and countries that are not sure of their own identity are understandably suspicious of satirists. I have never thought of myself as a satirist: I do not sit down to my work sniggering with malice and muttering, 'Here goes with the acid!' But I have certainly been strongly aware of the power of myth in Canadian thinking, and I do not share or admire many of our most popular myths; there are, however, other mythical elements in Canadian life and the Canadian ambience which I think deserve greater attention than they get, and I have tried to bring them into prominence. This is not what satirists do, and the recognition of what I am really attempting has been swifter and more sympathetic abroad than at home, and I am deeply grateful for understanding from any quarter.

One of the tasks of the Canadian writer is to show Canada to itself. He is not obliged to do this, but it is one of his options. Canadians—perhaps I should say the critical and academic world of Canada—are anxious for this kind of revelation, and so there is a strong temptation to fake it. Very few people seem to be aware how strong the pull of public opinion and public expectation is on an artist of any sort, and when he tries to give his public what it wants he is not perhaps a conscious faker, but what he produces is certainly a fake. The artist who binds himself to what might be called the national service can only do worthy and effective work if he is wholly true to himself: if his allegiance is to some form of public expectation, he is not serving his country as an artist should. An extreme example of this sort of dilemma is to be seen today in Russia, where public expectation and what the artist is driven to do by his true self are often widely at odds, and where the artist may suffer grievously if he does not toe the line.

To show Canada to itself—a serious and heavy task, and it cannot be undertaken by anyone whose determination is to wipe out the past. The odd thing is that so many Canadians who are eager to bring forth a new spirit seem to think either that we have no past, or that it is unworthy of consideration. I do not speak of an historical past in terms of lands seized and conquered, battles fought, and political crises endured, because nobody can deny the existence of such things: I mean a cultural past. Canada has a cultural past, and in my opinion it is a curious and interesting one, in which we were like the younger member of a large family who appears incongruously and somewhat comically in the cut-down garments of his elders. The young Canada during the whole of the nineteenth century wore a strange rig-out that we might imagine as a pair of pants cut down from Uncle Sam's very long legs, and the Union Jack waistcoat of John Bull, arranged with safety-pins to fit a figure that lacked the John Bull paunch. Very often, instead of Uncle Sam's gaudy pants, a Scottish kilt, stained with the blood of age-old grievance and betrayal, shrouded the lower part of the body. And oh! the hats! A shabby tricorne in Quebec; the battered chimney-pot of the Irishman in Ontario; the forbidding black puritan stove-lid of the Mennonite in the West. We had hats for all seasons. It was a scarecrow outfit, beyond any doubt, but it was surprisingly warm, and when worn with an air it was by no means unattractive. Now that we are in a position to afford a new cultural suit I don't think that we should pretend that we never wore cultural cast-offs when they were all we had. But we need not make our new garments fashionable versions of the old.

I remember these cultural cast-offs with clarity and with affection, because when first I went to school every child was coursed through a variety of 'readers' whose purpose was to extend his vocabulary and grammar and sense of rhetoric, and also to instruct him in what the world expected of him. Longfellow's 'Psalm of Life' told us about footsteps on the sands of time, and Ben Jonson told us that

> *It is not growing like a tree*
> *In bulk, doth make men better be.*

Benjamin Franklin, whose *Reader's Digest* morality disgusted me even as a child, warned us not to pay too much for our whistle (as if you could pay too much for a really enchanting whistle), and Sir Henry Newbolt adjured us to 'play up, play up, and play the game', though as the game was cricket we were not very clear about how it was to be done. We read about the heroism of Grace Darling in saving shipwrecked mariners off the coast of Scotland, and we read about Brave John Maynard, who perished with his ship on Lake Michigan in order to save its passengers. People say now that we were badly used because none of the heroes, and moral gurus, were Canadians, but I can tell you truthfully that no such thought ever entered the heads of the children with whom I went to school. To us a hero was a hero and a guru was a guru and we felt no overmastering desire to know any of them personally.

My parents were great consumers of periodicals, and printed matter crowded into our house from England and the United States every month. They even took in two magazines for me, which gave me a confused notion of international boyhood. One was *The Youth's Companion*, originating in Boston, and it abounded in tales of boys with splendid characters who could not lie or steal, spoke in elegant periods, and earned their own pocket-money by methods of unimpeachable honesty. The other, called *Chums,* came from England and it was about boys whose sole aim in life was to reduce their schools to a state of anarchy, and their masters to sobbing idiocy. Many of these English boys were conjurors, hypnotists, and somnambulists; when I came later to study English political history I understood exactly who its principal characters were, and how they had been educated. But my schooling, and my companions, did not belong in either of these categories. I was reconciled to the fact that life in Canada was rather a quiet experience.

As I grew older, like many young Canadians, I did not wholly accept this quietude, and I sometimes fretted against the ill-fitting old clothes that—in a cultural sense—we all seemed to be wearing. I was troubled by a question that one of our present Canadian cultural leaders, Professor Northrop Frye, has reduced to the query: 'Where is here?' In modern terms, I wondered, why isn't Canada getting a piece of the action? And like thousands of young Canadians, when the time came I tried to solve the problem by leaving Canada and going to where the action seemed to be. And like thousands of young Canadians, circumstances and inclination led me back to Canada, hopeful that some of the action might be generated there.

That is what is happening now. The younger Canadians are vastly more impatient than was my own generation, but in the world of cultural growth you cannot make things happen merely by wishing to do so. A Canadian poet of my grandmother's generation summed it up in one of those lines of leaden obviousness and undoubted truth, when he said

The growth of what is excellent is slow.

Cabbages can be grown quite quickly; an oak takes longer, and I do not think my country should be contented with a cabbage culture.

Nor will a cabbage culture suffice for us, however many persuasive political and literary people of the truck-garden and green-grocer persuasion may appear among us. We are, in our innermost hearts, too good a people to settle for cabbages. But at present the uproar is for a Canadian identity. What is it, and where is it to be sought?

We have many people who like the question so much that they do not seem to trouble very much about the answer. But there is an answer. I have known it, and many other Canadians have known it, for a long time. But it is not an answer that I can give you in blunt language; like so many of the important answers, it must be approached by indirection.

For me, for many years, the answer has best been formulated in a Canadian poem by one of our finest poets, who has already spoken to you in one of these meetings, Douglas LePan. It is in a poem, published in 1948, called 'Coureurs de bois'. It speaks of only one Canadian, but as a true poem should, it speaks also for many thousands. Here it is:

> Thinking of you, I think of the *coureurs de bois*,
> Swarthy men grown almost to savage size
> Who put their brown wrists through the arras of the woods
> And were lost—sometimes for months. Word would come back:
> One had been seen at Crève-coeur, deserted and starving,
> One at Sault Sainte Marie shouldering the rapids.
> Giant-like, their labours stalked in the streets of Quebec
> Though they themselves had dwindled in distance: names only;
> Rumours; quicksilvery spies into nature's secrets;